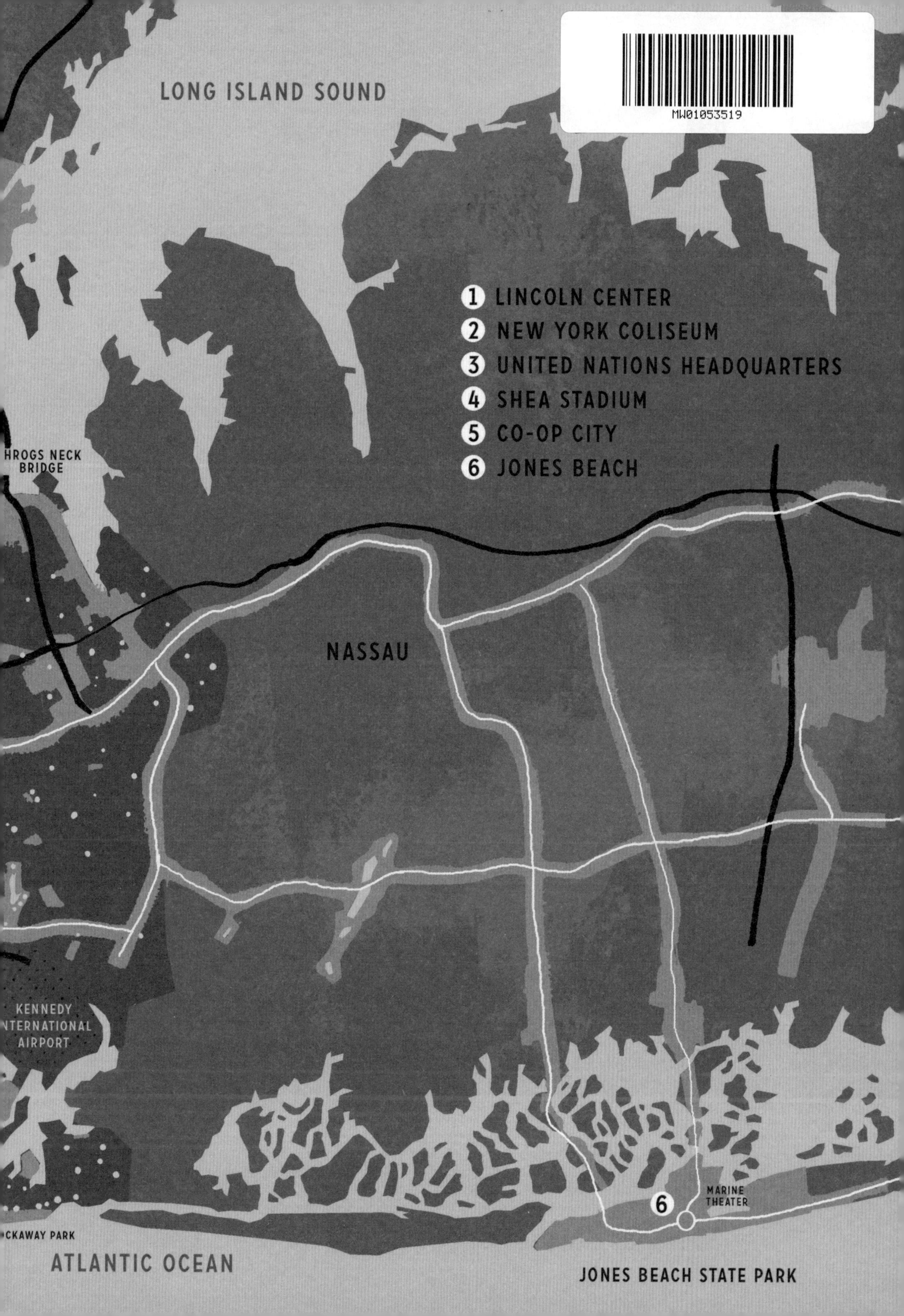
LONG ISLAND SOUND
1 LINCOLN CENTER
2 NEW YORK COLISEUM
3 UNITED NATIONS HEADQUARTERS
4 SHEA STADIUM
5 CO-OP CITY
6 JONES BEACH
HROGS NECK BRIDGE
NASSAU
KENNEDY
NTERNATIONAL
AIRPORT
6
MARINE THEATER
CKAWAY PARK
ATLANTIC OCEAN
JONES BEACH STATE PARK

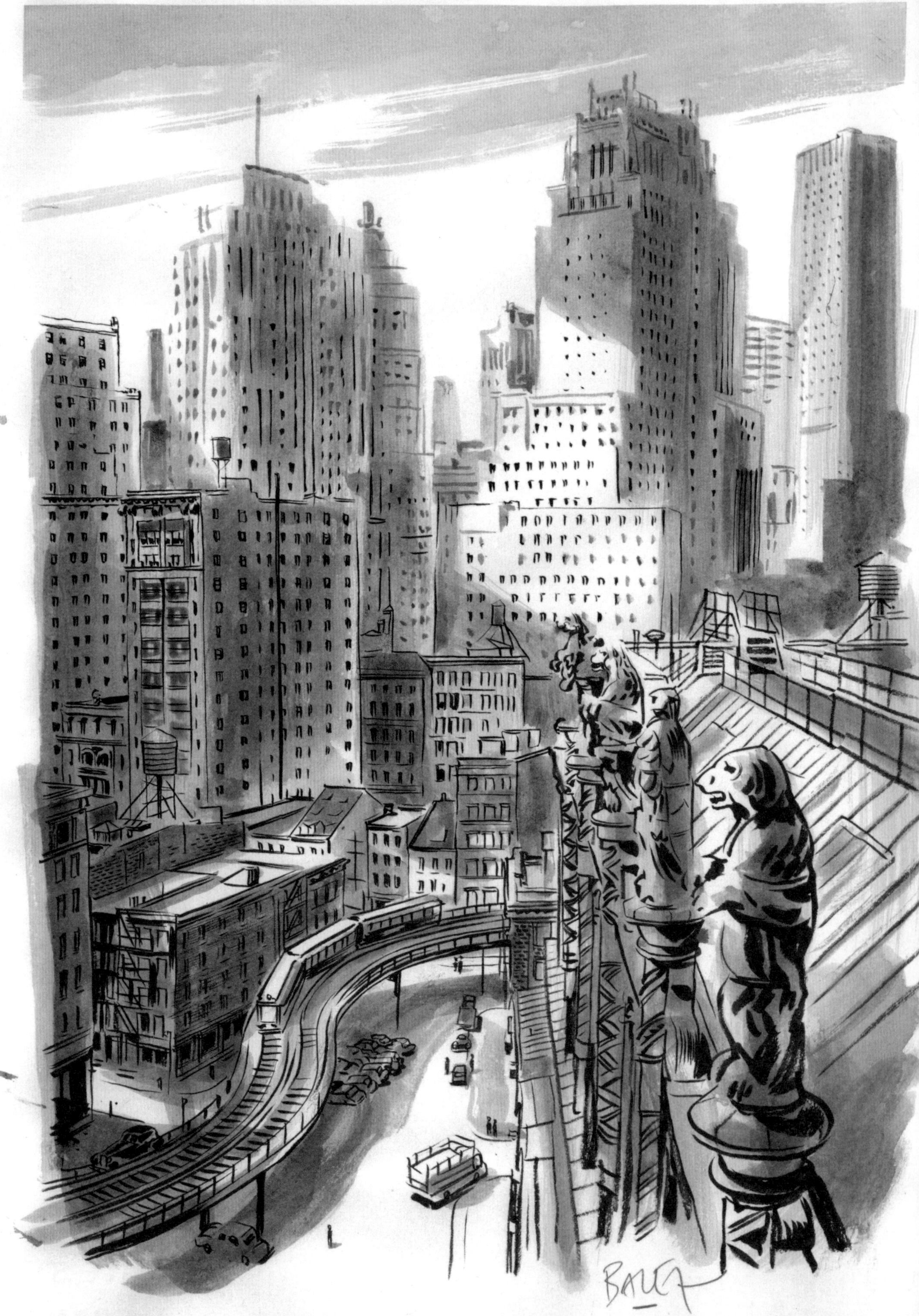
BALET

HAVE NO FEAR OF CHANGE AS SUCH AND, ON THE OTHER HAND,
NO LIKING FOR IT MERELY FOR ITS OWN SAKE.
**ROBERT MOSES**

CITIES HAVE THE CAPABILITY OF PROVIDING SOMETHING FOR EVERYBODY, ONLY BECAUSE,
AND ONLY WHEN, THEY ARE CREATED BY EVERYBODY.
**JANE JACOBS**

*FOR FLORENCE*
**PIERRE**

*FOR MY PARENTS AND ISIDORA, THE PLANNER OF MY LIFE*
**OLIVIER**

This is a first edition published in 2014 by Nobrow Ltd. 62 Great Eastern Street,
London, EC2A 3QR.

Original Title: Robert Moses, Le Maître Cache de New York
Authors: P. Christin, O. Balez

Published in the US by Nobrow (US) Inc.

Printed in Poland on FSC assured paper.
ISBN: 978-1-907704-96-3

Order from www.nobrow.net

PIERRE CHRISTIN OLIVIER BALEZ

# ROBERT MOSES

## MASTER BUILDER OF NEW YORK CITY

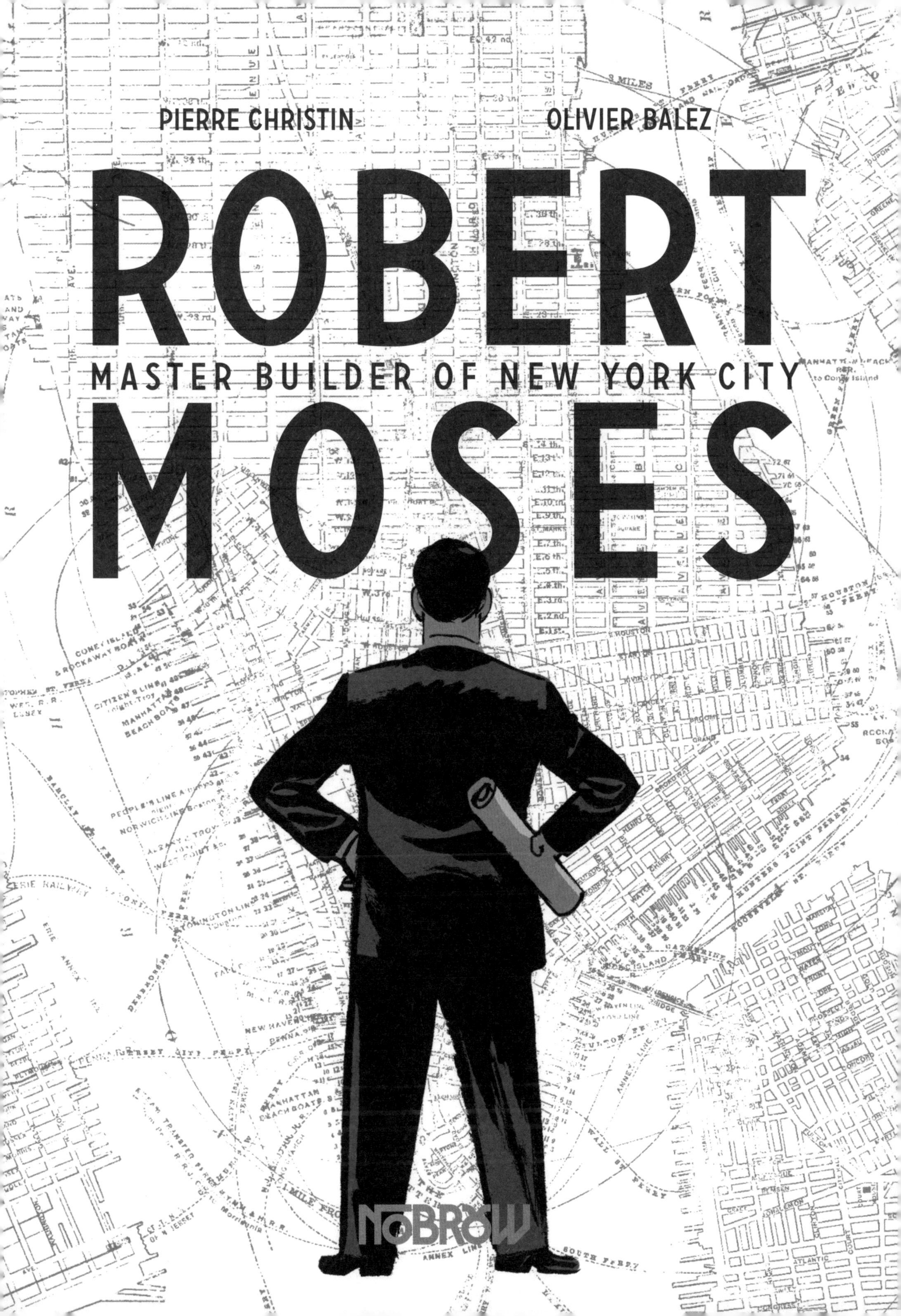

NOBROW

# CHAPTER 1

## The childhood of a leader

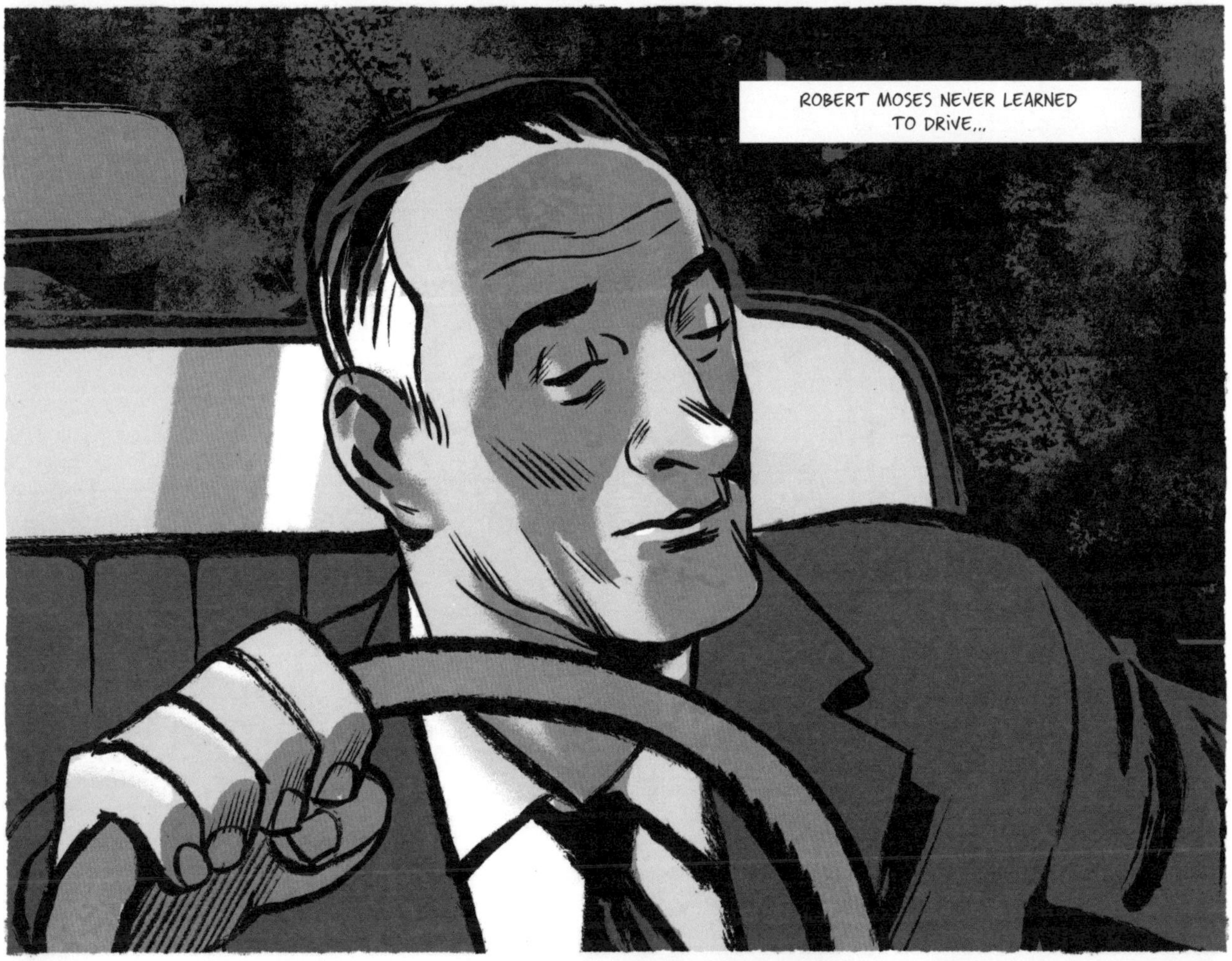
ROBERT MOSES NEVER LEARNED TO DRIVE...

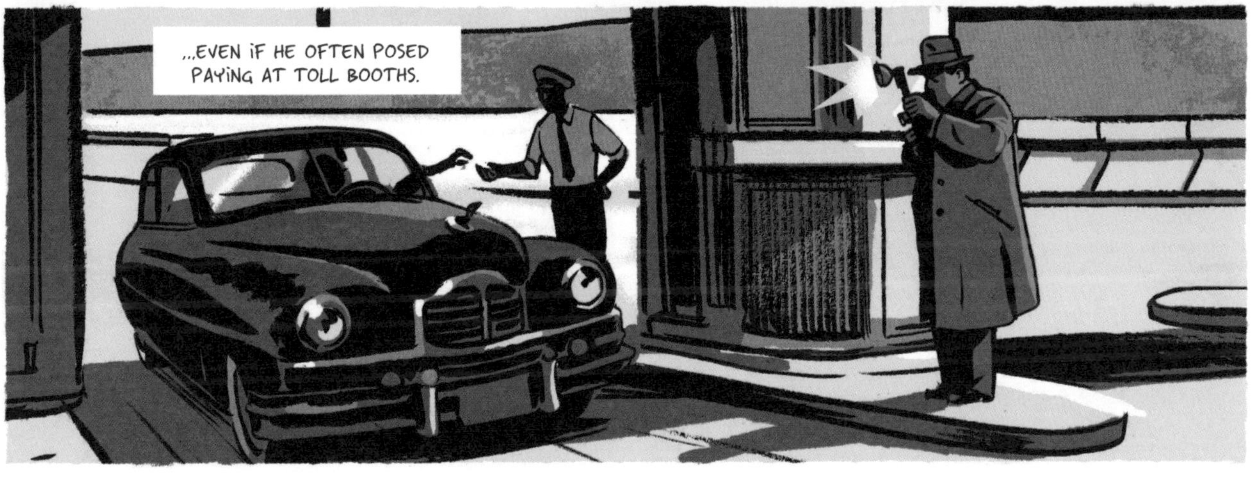
...EVEN IF HE OFTEN POSED PAYING AT TOLL BOOTHS.

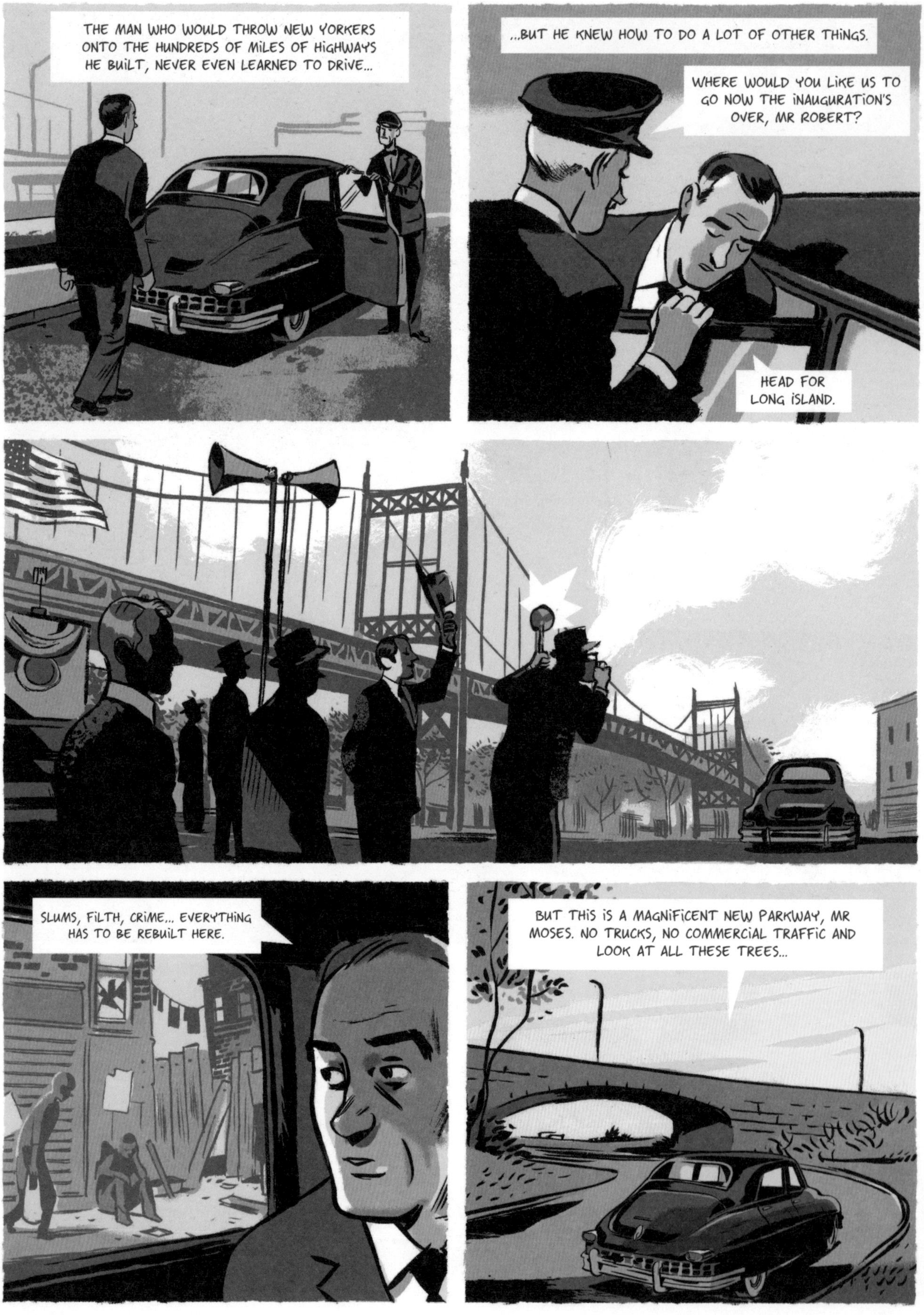
THE MAN WHO WOULD THROW NEW YORKERS ONTO THE HUNDREDS OF MILES OF HIGHWAYS HE BUILT, NEVER EVEN LEARNED TO DRIVE...
...BUT HE KNEW HOW TO DO A LOT OF OTHER THINGS.
WHERE WOULD YOU LIKE US TO GO NOW THE INAUGURATION'S OVER, MR ROBERT?
HEAD FOR LONG ISLAND.
SLUMS, FILTH, CRIME... EVERYTHING HAS TO BE REBUILT HERE.
BUT THIS IS A MAGNIFICENT NEW PARKWAY, MR MOSES. NO TRUCKS, NO COMMERCIAL TRAFFIC AND LOOK AT ALL THESE TREES...

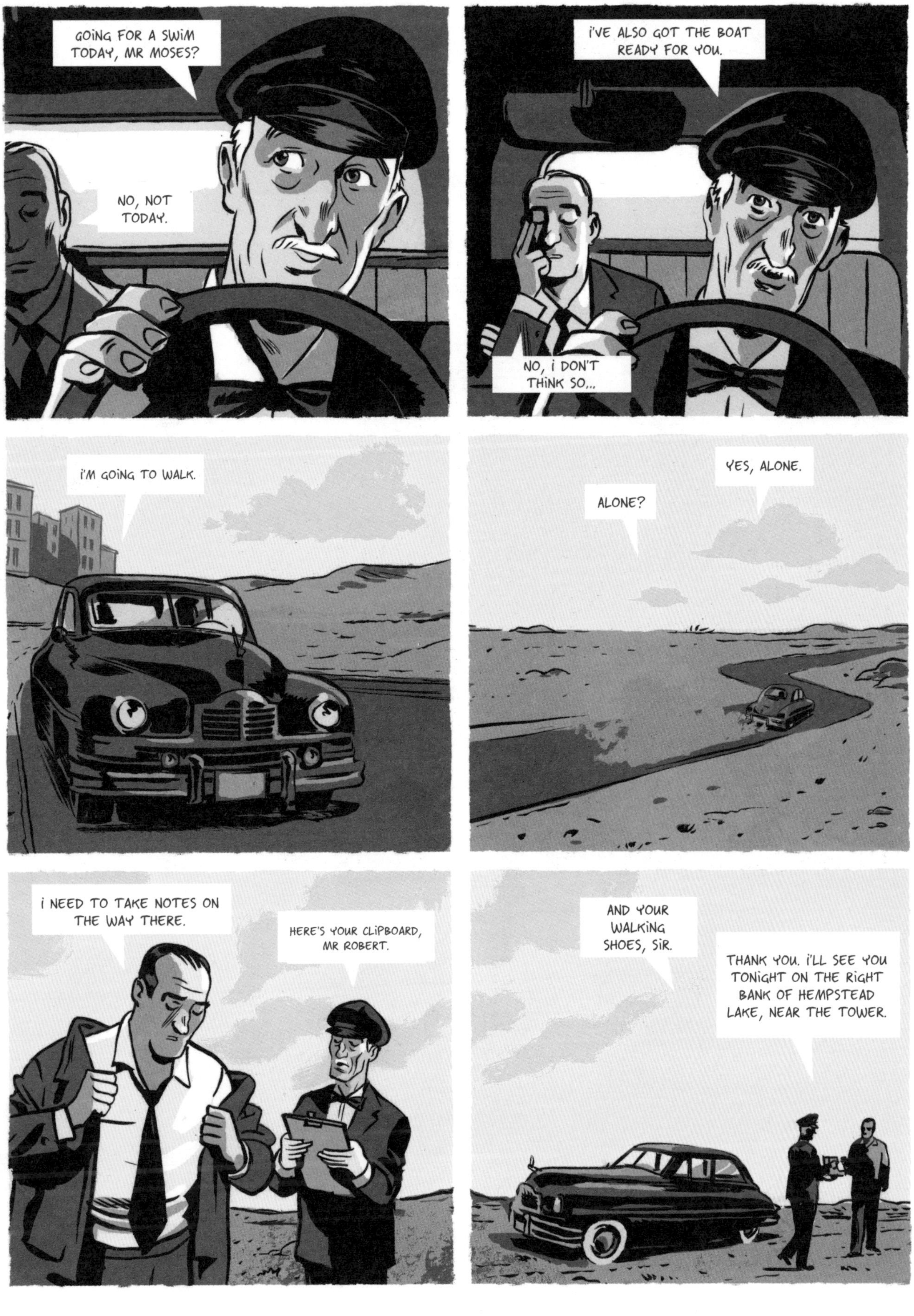
GOING FOR A SWIM TODAY, MR MOSES?
NO, NOT TODAY.
I'VE ALSO GOT THE BOAT READY FOR YOU.
NO, I DON'T THINK SO...
I'M GOING TO WALK.
ALONE?
YES, ALONE.
I NEED TO TAKE NOTES ON THE WAY THERE.
HERE'S YOUR CLIPBOARD, MR ROBERT.
AND YOUR WALKING SHOES, SIR.
THANK YOU. I'LL SEE YOU TONIGHT ON THE RIGHT BANK OF HEMPSTEAD LAKE, NEAR THE TOWER.

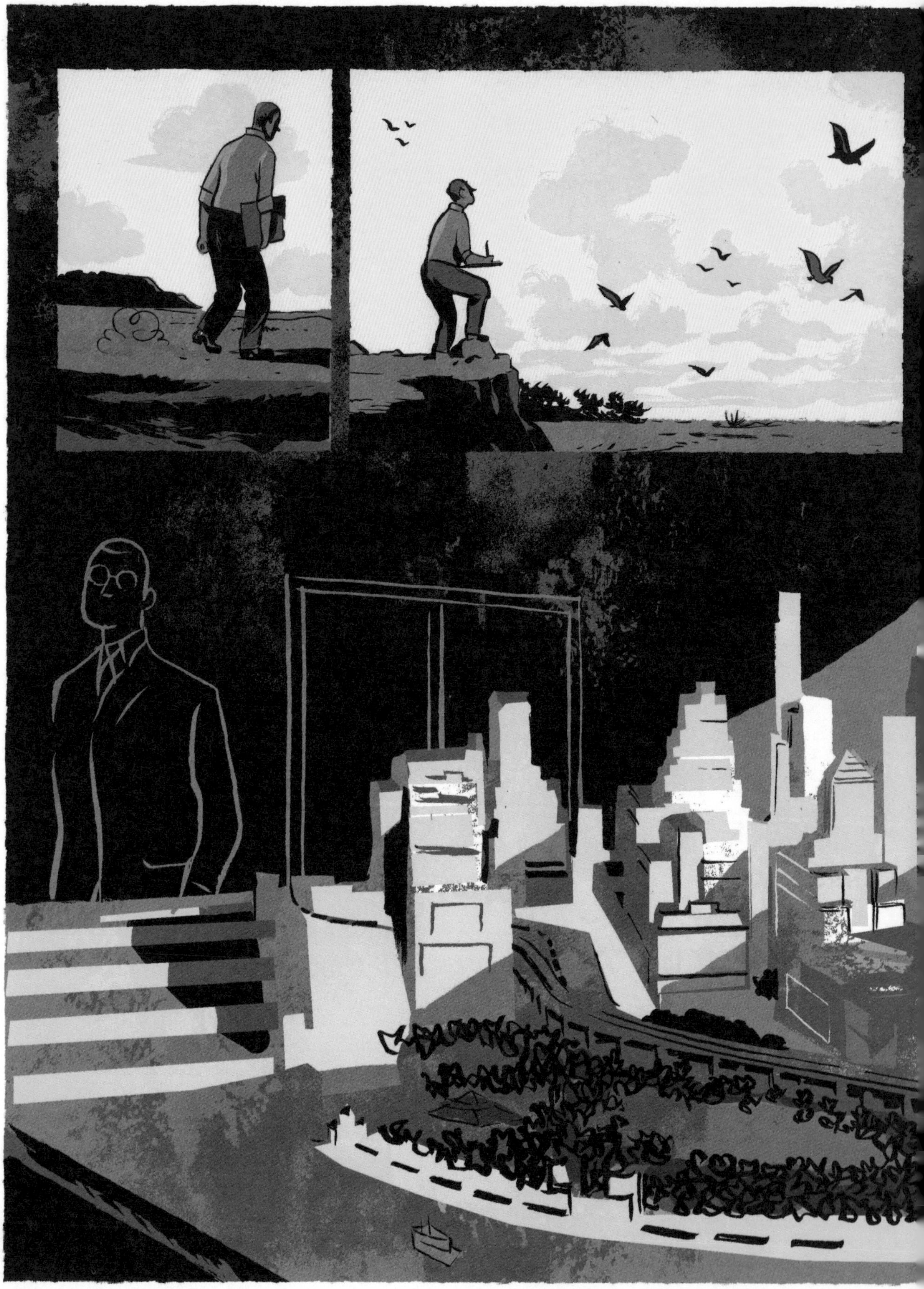

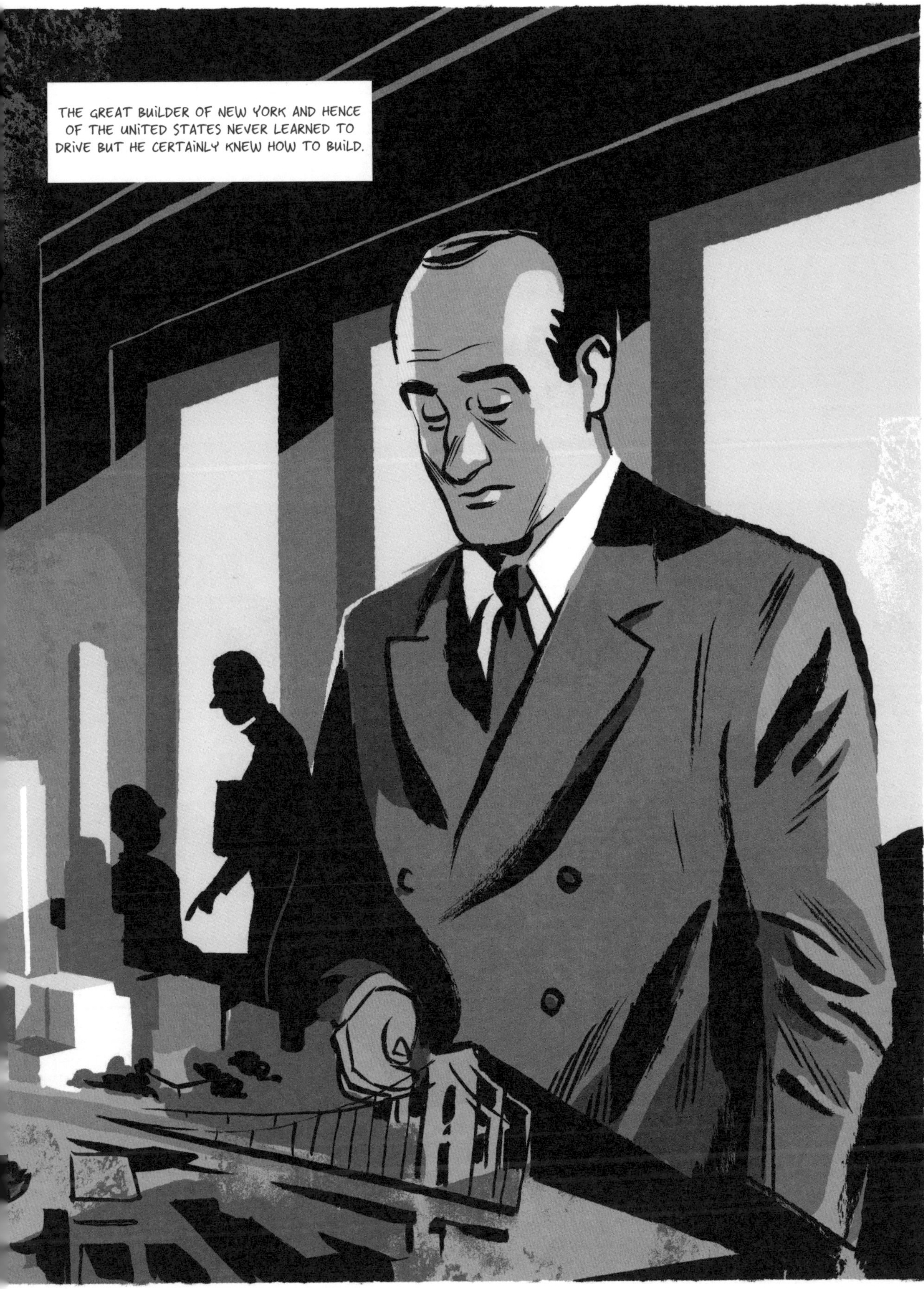
THE GREAT BUILDER OF NEW YORK AND HENCE OF THE UNITED STATES NEVER LEARNED TO DRIVE BUT HE CERTAINLY KNEW HOW TO BUILD.

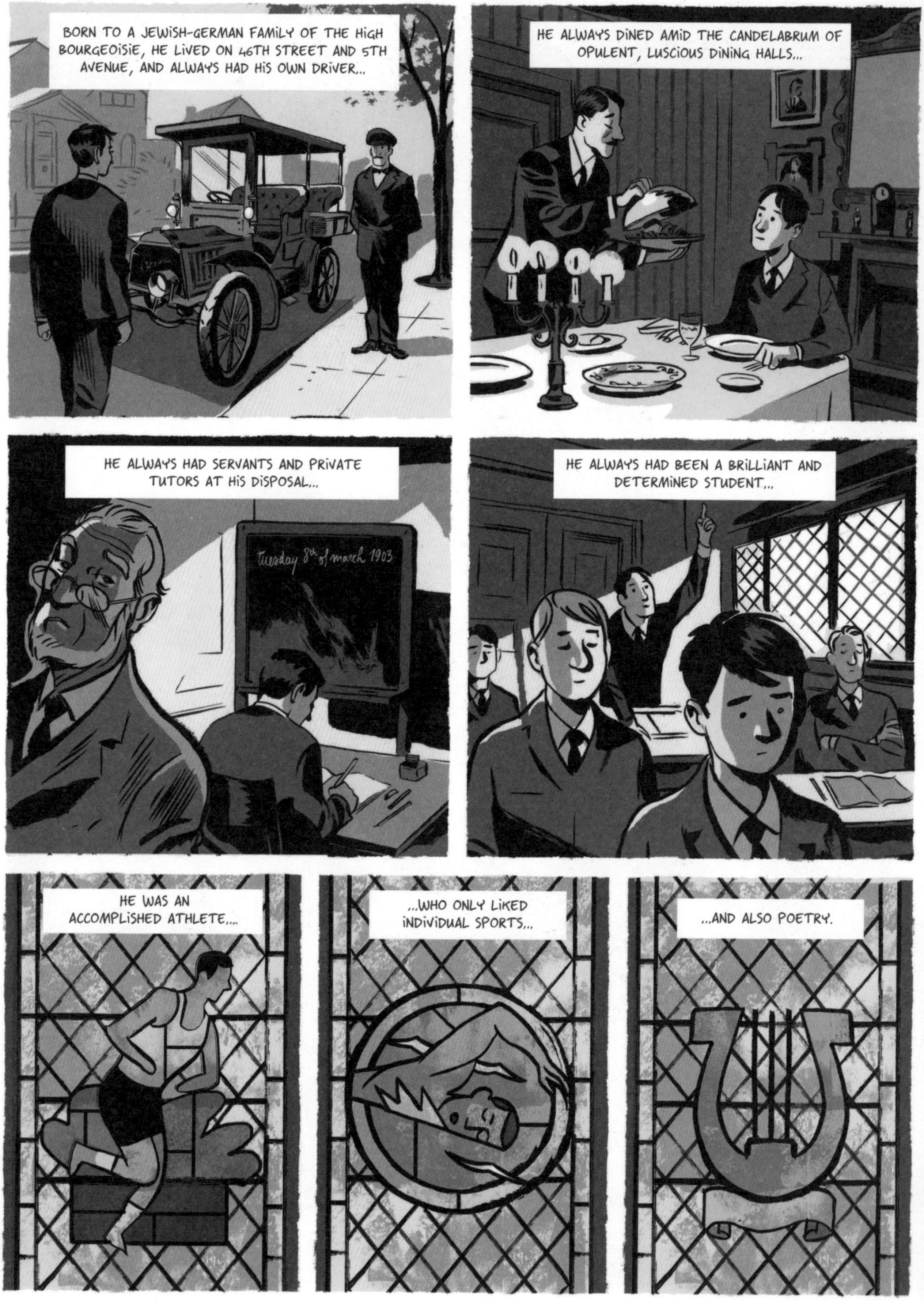

BORN TO A JEWISH-GERMAN FAMILY OF THE HIGH BOURGEOISIE, HE LIVED ON 46TH STREET AND 5TH AVENUE, AND ALWAYS HAD HIS OWN DRIVER...
HE ALWAYS DINED AMID THE CANDELABRUM OF OPULENT, LUSCIOUS DINING HALLS...
HE ALWAYS HAD SERVANTS AND PRIVATE TUTORS AT HIS DISPOSAL...
Tuesday 8th of march 1903
HE ALWAYS HAD BEEN A BRILLIANT AND DETERMINED STUDENT...
HE WAS AN ACCOMPLISHED ATHLETE,...
...WHO ONLY LIKED INDIVIDUAL SPORTS,...
...AND ALSO POETRY.

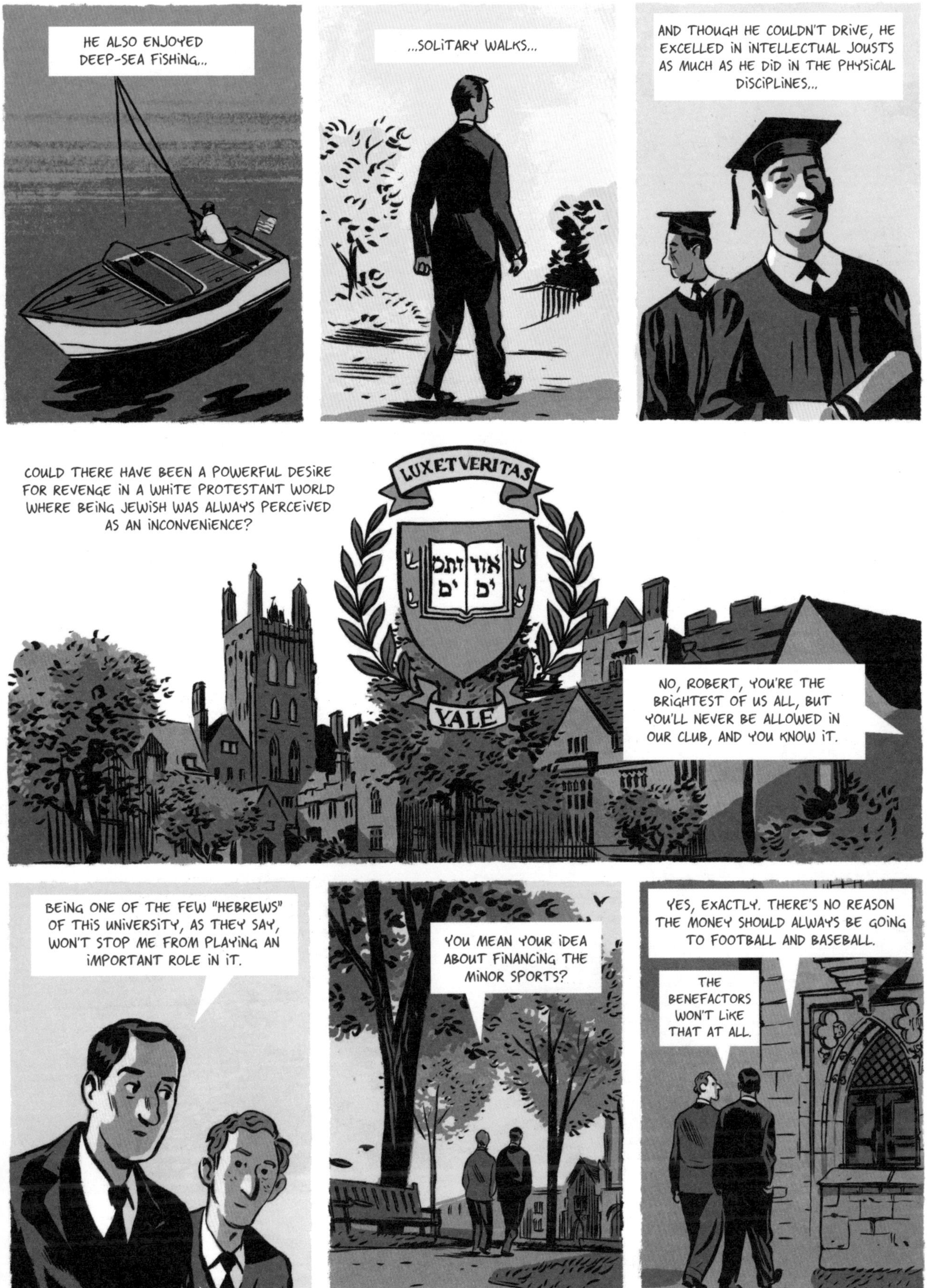
HE ALSO ENJOYED DEEP-SEA FISHING...
...SOLITARY WALKS...
AND THOUGH HE COULDN'T DRIVE, HE EXCELLED IN INTELLECTUAL JOUSTS AS MUCH AS HE DID IN THE PHYSICAL DISCIPLINES...
COULD THERE HAVE BEEN A POWERFUL DESIRE FOR REVENGE IN A WHITE PROTESTANT WORLD WHERE BEING JEWISH WAS ALWAYS PERCEIVED AS AN INCONVENIENCE?
LUXETVERITAS
YALE
NO, ROBERT, YOU'RE THE BRIGHTEST OF US ALL, BUT YOU'LL NEVER BE ALLOWED IN OUR CLUB, AND YOU KNOW IT.
BEING ONE OF THE FEW "HEBREWS" OF THIS UNIVERSITY, AS THEY SAY, WON'T STOP ME FROM PLAYING AN IMPORTANT ROLE IN IT.
YOU MEAN YOUR IDEA ABOUT FINANCING THE MINOR SPORTS?
YES, EXACTLY. THERE'S NO REASON THE MONEY SHOULD ALWAYS BE GOING TO FOOTBALL AND BASEBALL.
THE BENEFACTORS WON'T LIKE THAT AT ALL.

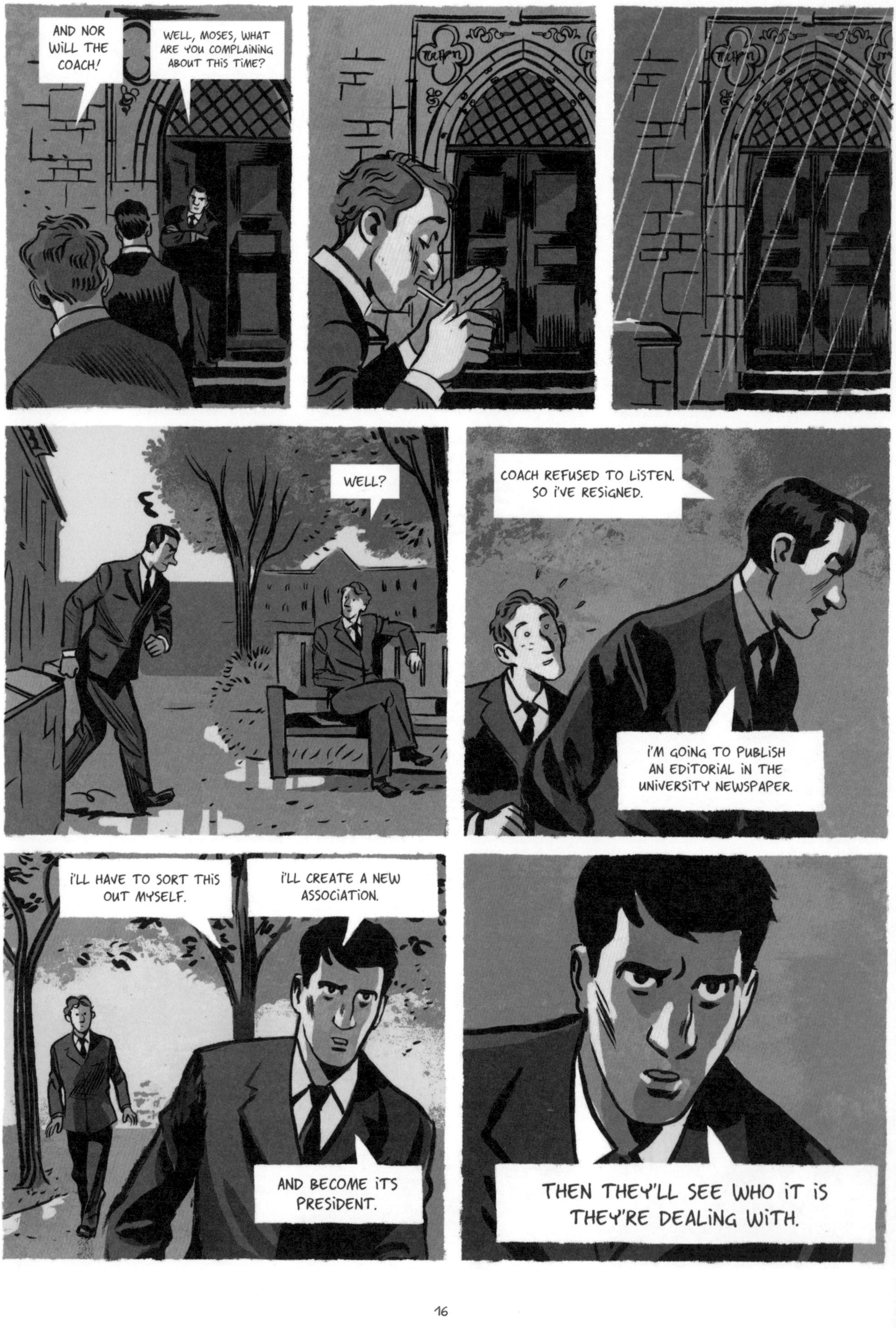
AND NOR WiLL THE COACH!
WELL, MOSES, WHAT ARE YOU COMPLAiNiNG ABOUT THiS TiME?
WELL?
COACH REFUSED TO LiSTEN. SO i'VE RESiGNED.
i'M GOiNG TO PUBLiSH AN EDiTORiAL iN THE UNiVERSiTY NEWSPAPER.
i'LL HAVE TO SORT THiS OUT MYSELF.
i'LL CREATE A NEW ASSOCiATiON.
AND BECOME iTS PRESiDENT.
THEN THEY'LL SEE WHO iT iS THEY'RE DEALiNG WiTH.

AFTER GRADUATING FROM YALE, MOSES GOES TO OXFORD WHERE HE SHINES JUST AS BRIGHTLY...

WHETHER AS THE CAPTAIN OF THE WATER POLO TEAM...

...OR SOCIALIZING WITH YOUNG ARISTOCRATS DESTINED TO BECOME GREAT SUBJECTS OF THE CROWN...

IT'S HERE THAT HE DECIDES TO WRITE HIS THESIS ON HIGH-LEVEL BRITISH ADMINISTRATION...

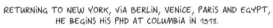

RETURNING TO NEW YORK, VIA BERLIN, VENICE, PARIS AND EGYPT, HE BEGINS HIS PHD AT COLUMBIA IN 1913.

NOW A YOUNG REFORMIST, BOTH IDEALISTIC AND ELITIST, HE BECOMES A STAUNCH CRITIC OF "ROBBER BARONS", SPECULATORS, INCOMPETENT BUREAUCRATS AND CORRUPT POLITICIANS.

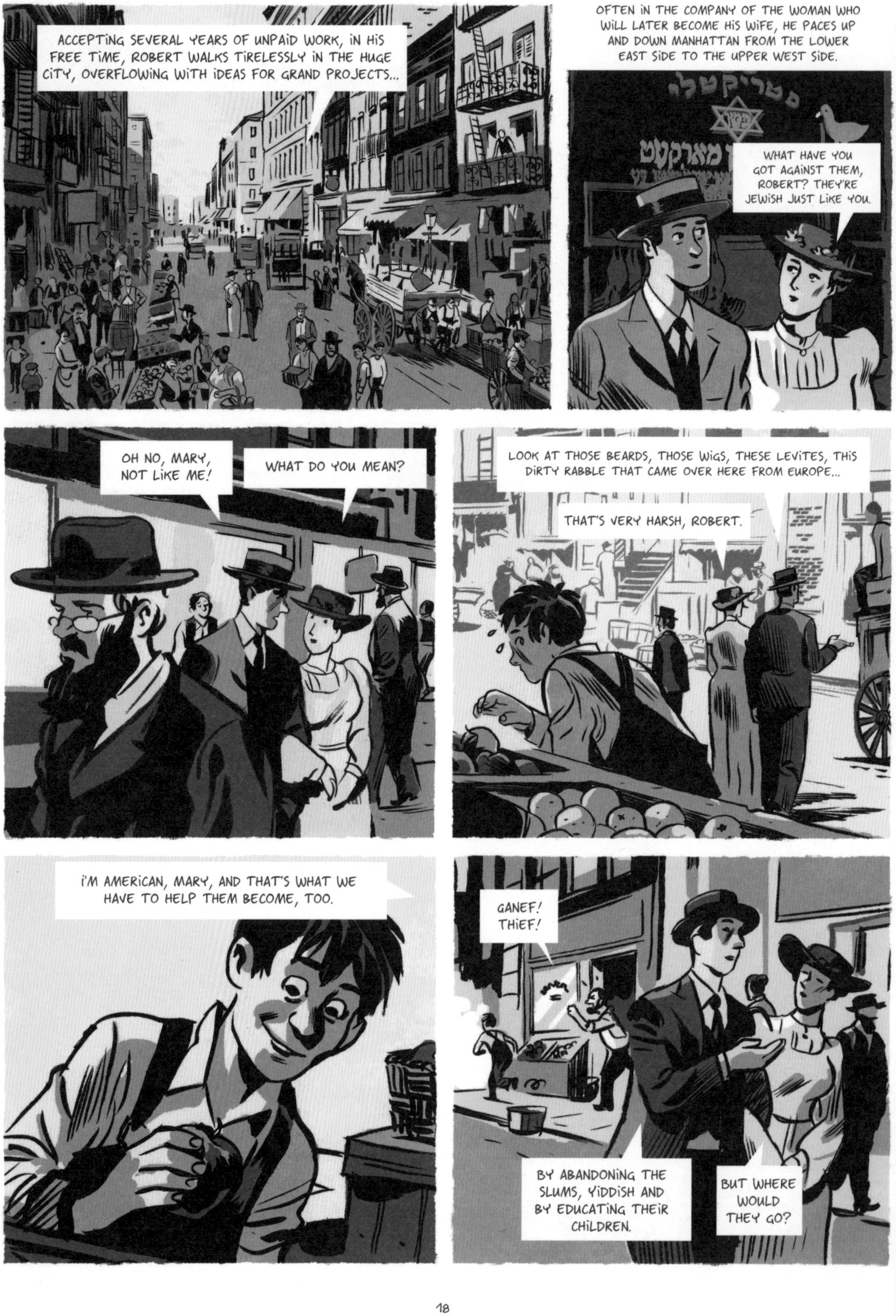
ACCEPTING SEVERAL YEARS OF UNPAID WORK, IN HIS FREE TIME, ROBERT WALKS TIRELESSLY IN THE HUGE CITY, OVERFLOWING WITH IDEAS FOR GRAND PROJECTS...
OFTEN IN THE COMPANY OF THE WOMAN WHO WILL LATER BECOME HIS WIFE, HE PACES UP AND DOWN MANHATTAN FROM THE LOWER EAST SIDE TO THE UPPER WEST SIDE.
WHAT HAVE YOU GOT AGAINST THEM, ROBERT? THEY'RE JEWISH JUST LIKE YOU.
OH NO, MARY, NOT LIKE ME!
WHAT DO YOU MEAN?
LOOK AT THOSE BEARDS, THOSE WIGS, THESE LEVITES, THIS DIRTY RABBLE THAT CAME OVER HERE FROM EUROPE...
THAT'S VERY HARSH, ROBERT.
I'M AMERICAN, MARY, AND THAT'S WHAT WE HAVE TO HELP THEM BECOME, TOO.
GANEF! THIEF!
BY ABANDONING THE SLUMS, YIDDISH AND BY EDUCATING THEIR CHILDREN.
BUT WHERE WOULD THEY GO?

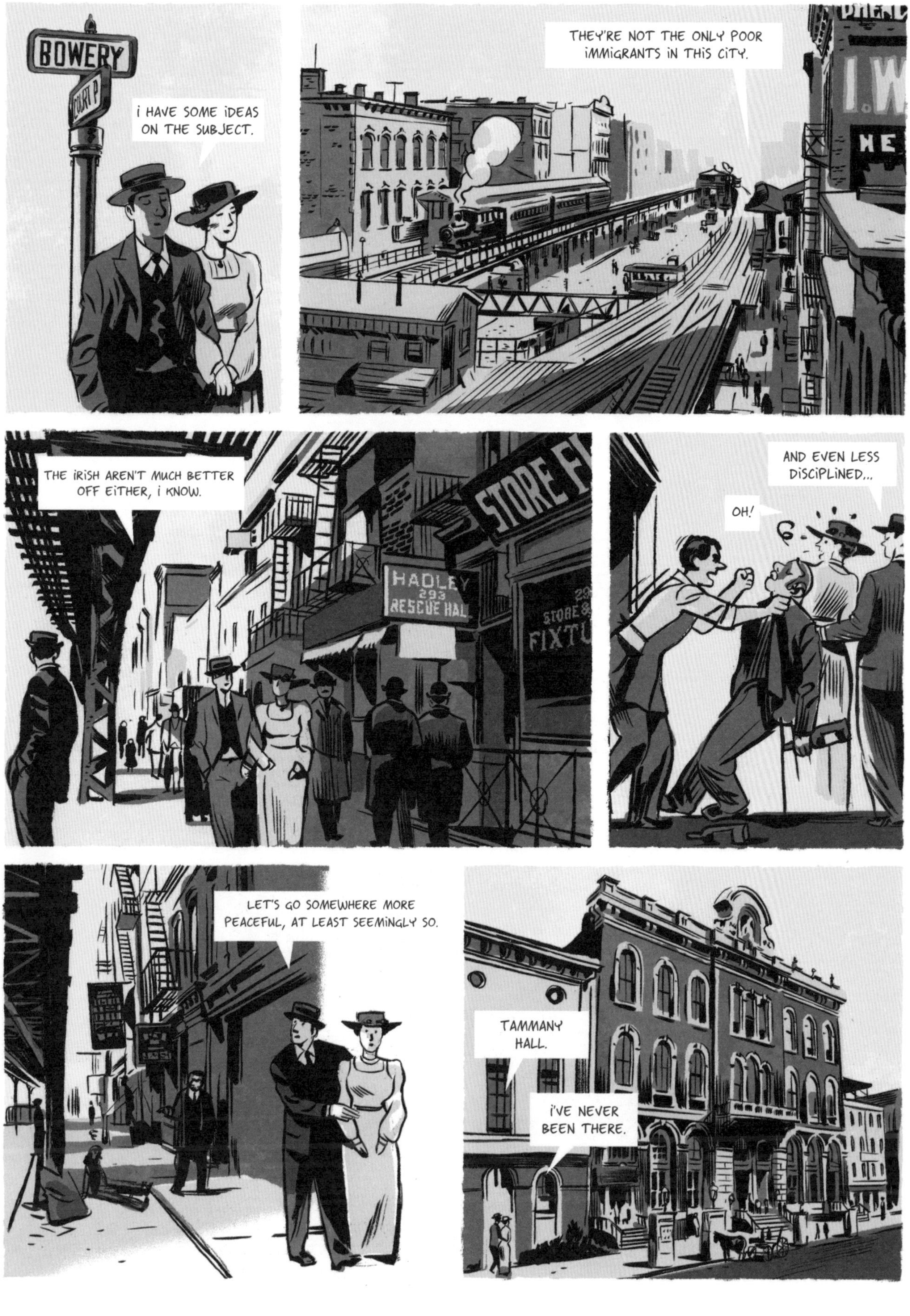
BOWERY
COURT P
I HAVE SOME IDEAS ON THE SUBJECT.
THEY'RE NOT THE ONLY POOR IMMIGRANTS IN THIS CITY.
I.W
NE
THE IRISH AREN'T MUCH BETTER OFF EITHER, I KNOW.
STORE F
HADLEY 293 RESCUE HALL
STORE &
FIXTU
AND EVEN LESS DISCIPLINED...
OH!
LET'S GO SOMEWHERE MORE PEACEFUL, AT LEAST SEEMINGLY SO.
TAMMANY HALL.
I'VE NEVER BEEN THERE.

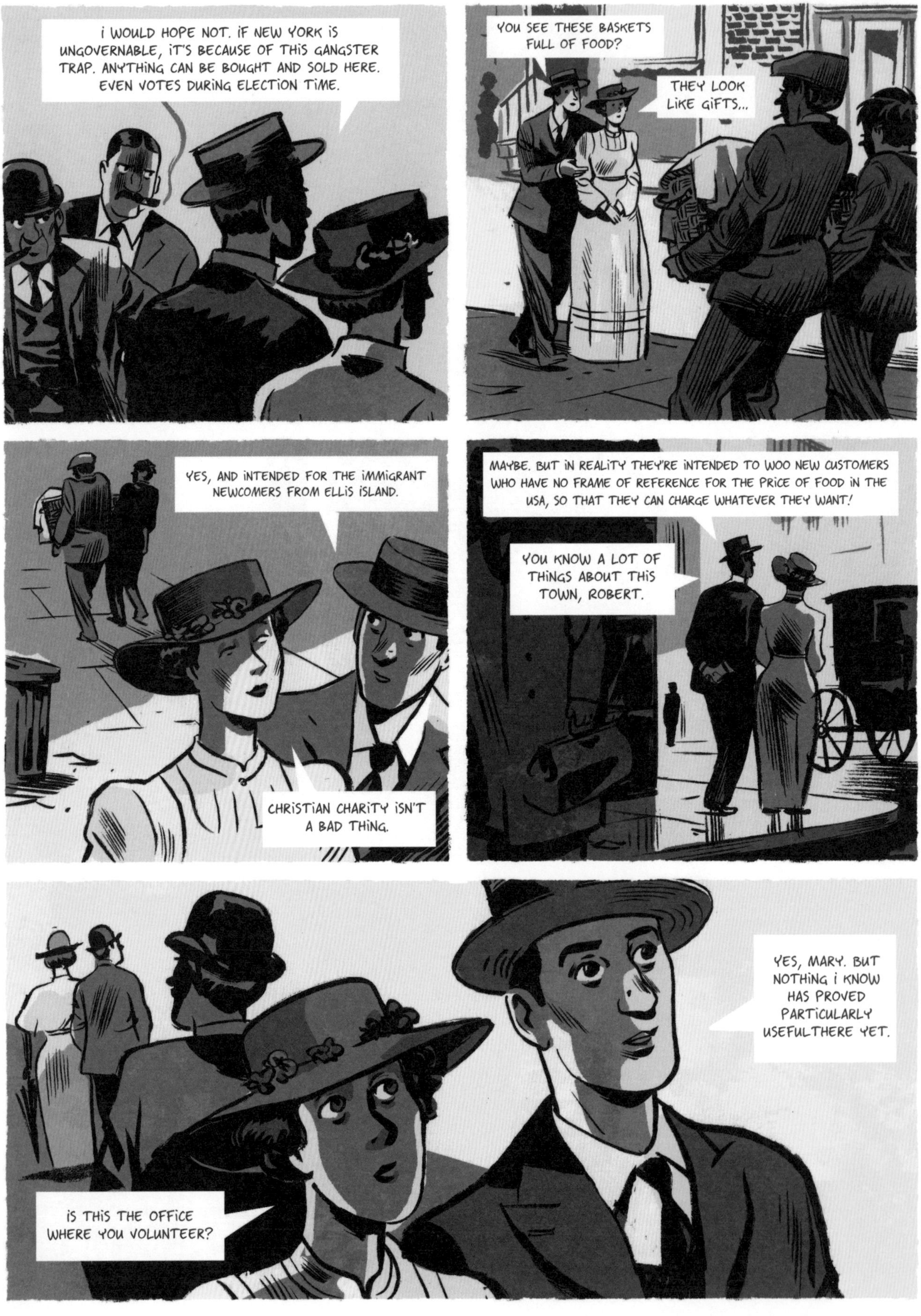
I WOULD HOPE NOT. IF NEW YORK IS UNGOVERNABLE, IT'S BECAUSE OF THIS GANGSTER TRAP. ANYTHING CAN BE BOUGHT AND SOLD HERE. EVEN VOTES DURING ELECTION TIME.
YOU SEE THESE BASKETS FULL OF FOOD?
THEY LOOK LIKE GIFTS...
YES, AND INTENDED FOR THE IMMIGRANT NEWCOMERS FROM ELLIS ISLAND.
CHRISTIAN CHARITY ISN'T A BAD THING.
MAYBE. BUT IN REALITY THEY'RE INTENDED TO WOO NEW CUSTOMERS WHO HAVE NO FRAME OF REFERENCE FOR THE PRICE OF FOOD IN THE USA, SO THAT THEY CAN CHARGE WHATEVER THEY WANT!
YOU KNOW A LOT OF THINGS ABOUT THIS TOWN, ROBERT.
YES, MARY. BUT NOTHING I KNOW HAS PROVED PARTICULARLY USEFULTHERE YET.
IS THIS THE OFFICE WHERE YOU VOLUNTEER?

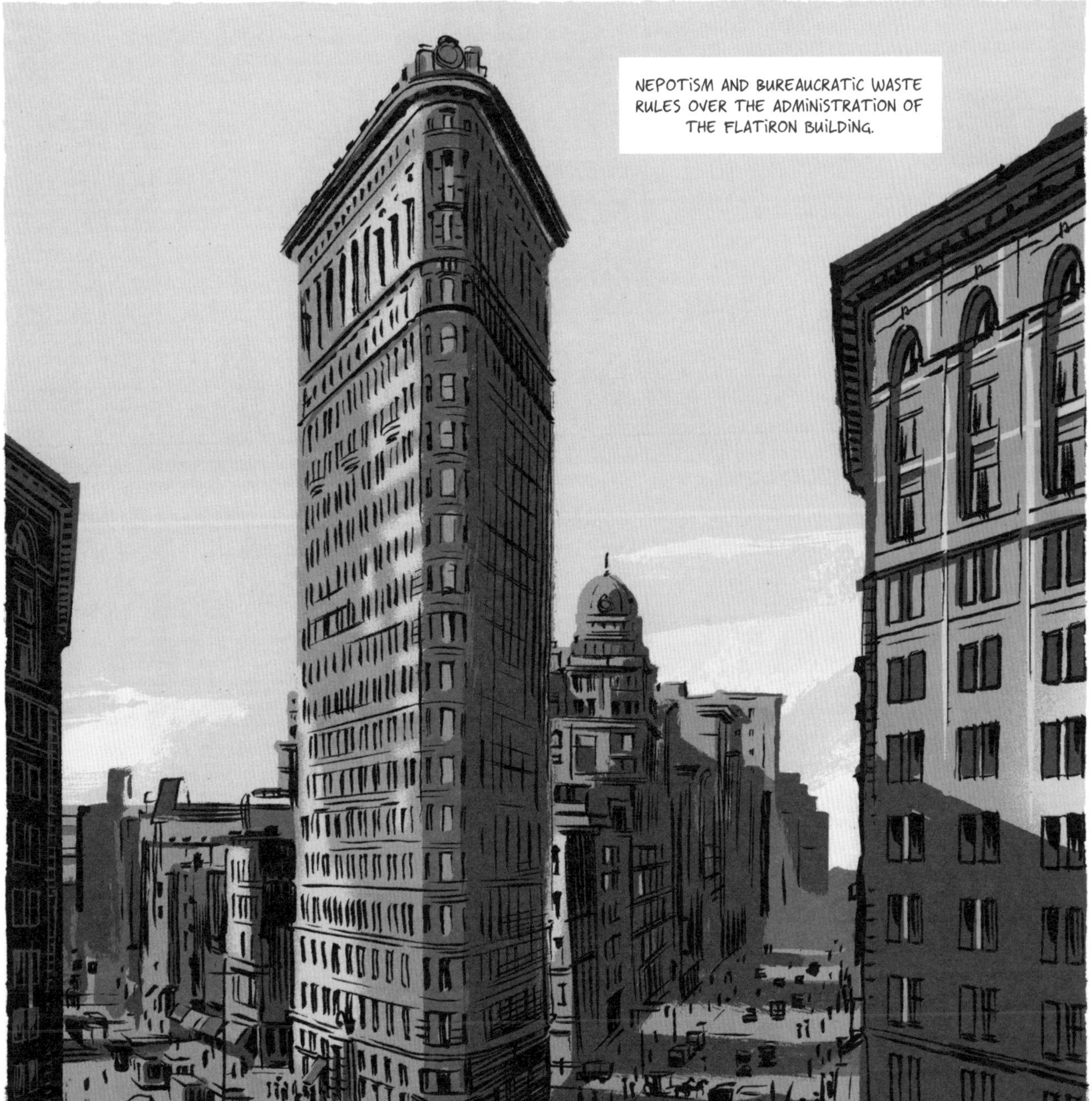
NEPOTISM AND BUREAUCRATIC WASTE RULES OVER THE ADMINISTRATION OF THE FLATIRON BUILDING.

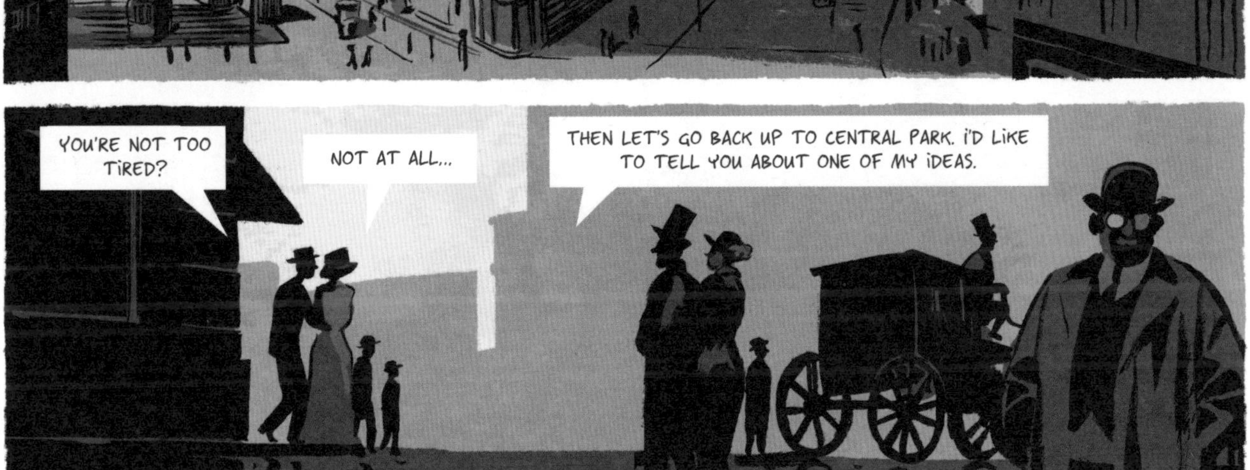
YOU'RE NOT TOO TIRED?
NOT AT ALL...
THEN LET'S GO BACK UP TO CENTRAL PARK. I'D LIKE TO TELL YOU ABOUT ONE OF MY IDEAS.

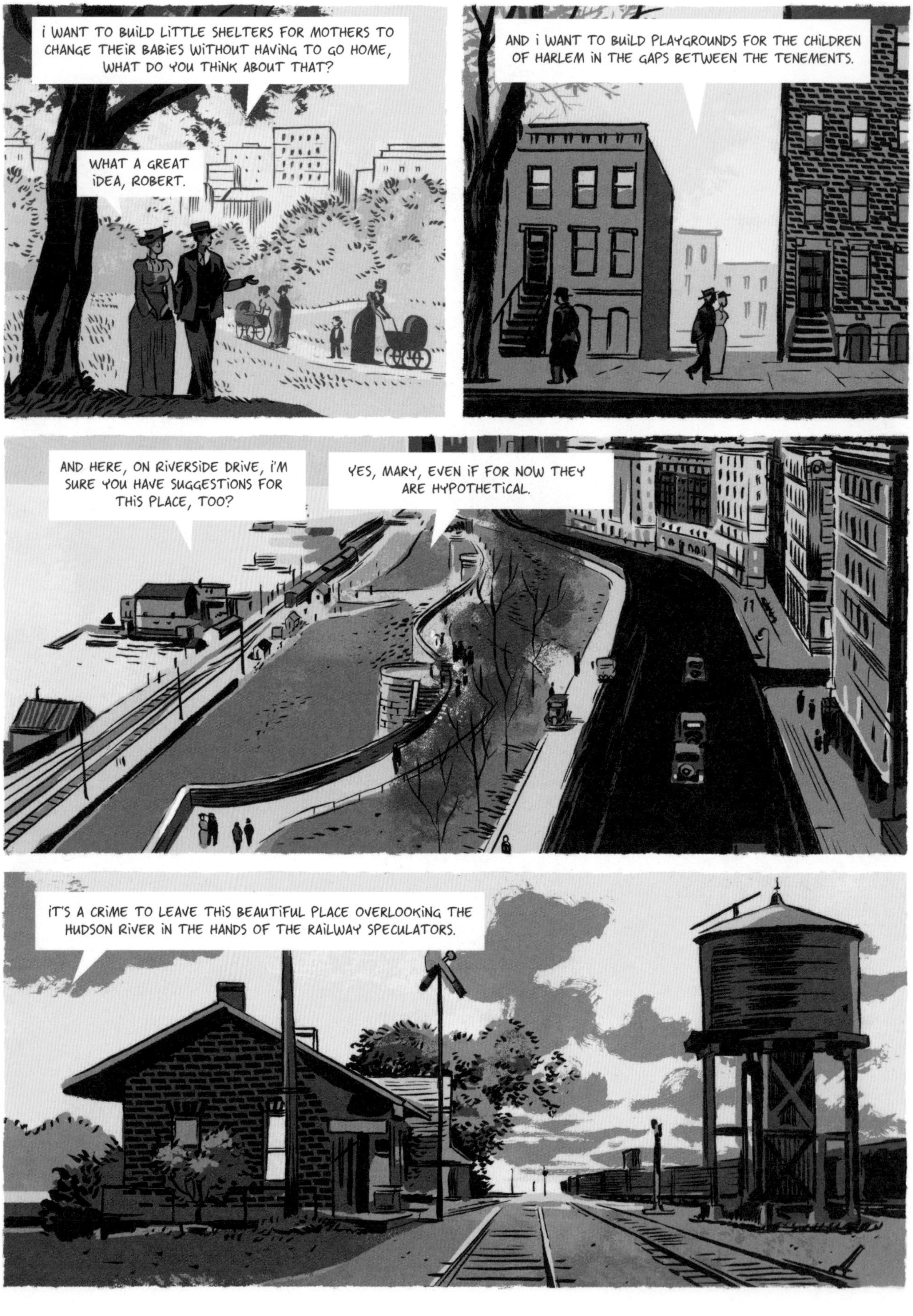
I WANT TO BUILD LITTLE SHELTERS FOR MOTHERS TO CHANGE THEIR BABIES WITHOUT HAVING TO GO HOME, WHAT DO YOU THINK ABOUT THAT?
WHAT A GREAT IDEA, ROBERT.
AND I WANT TO BUILD PLAYGROUNDS FOR THE CHILDREN OF HARLEM IN THE GAPS BETWEEN THE TENEMENTS.
AND HERE, ON RIVERSIDE DRIVE, I'M SURE YOU HAVE SUGGESTIONS FOR THIS PLACE, TOO?
YES, MARY, EVEN IF FOR NOW THEY ARE HYPOTHETICAL.
IT'S A CRIME TO LEAVE THIS BEAUTIFUL PLACE OVERLOOKING THE HUDSON RIVER IN THE HANDS OF THE RAILWAY SPECULATORS.

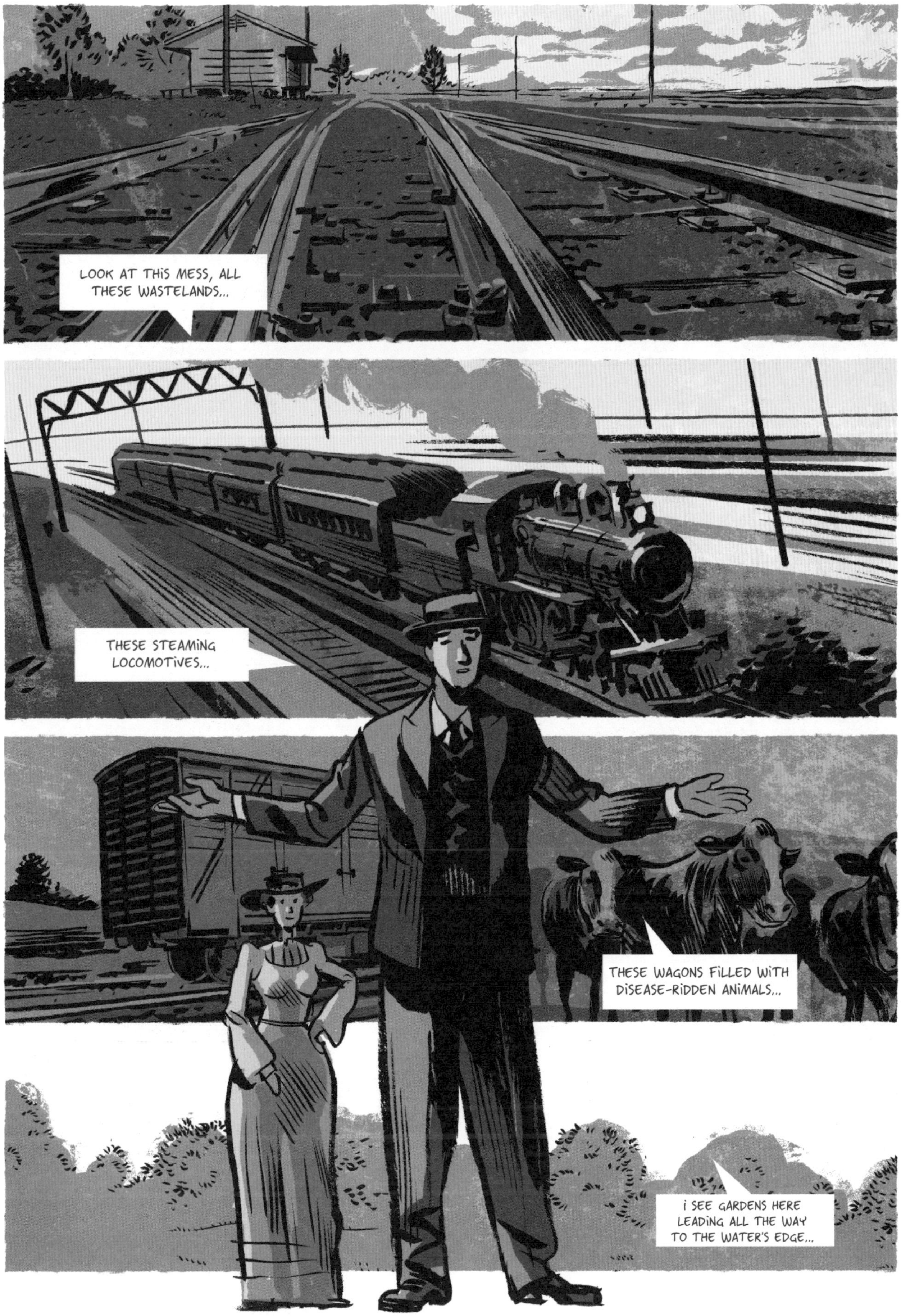
LOOK AT THiS MESS, ALL THESE WASTELANDS...
THESE STEAMiNG LOCOMOTiVES...
THESE WAGONS FiLLED WiTH DiSEASE-RiDDEN ANiMALS...
i SEE GARDENS HERE LEADiNG ALL THE WAY TO THE WATER'S EDGE...

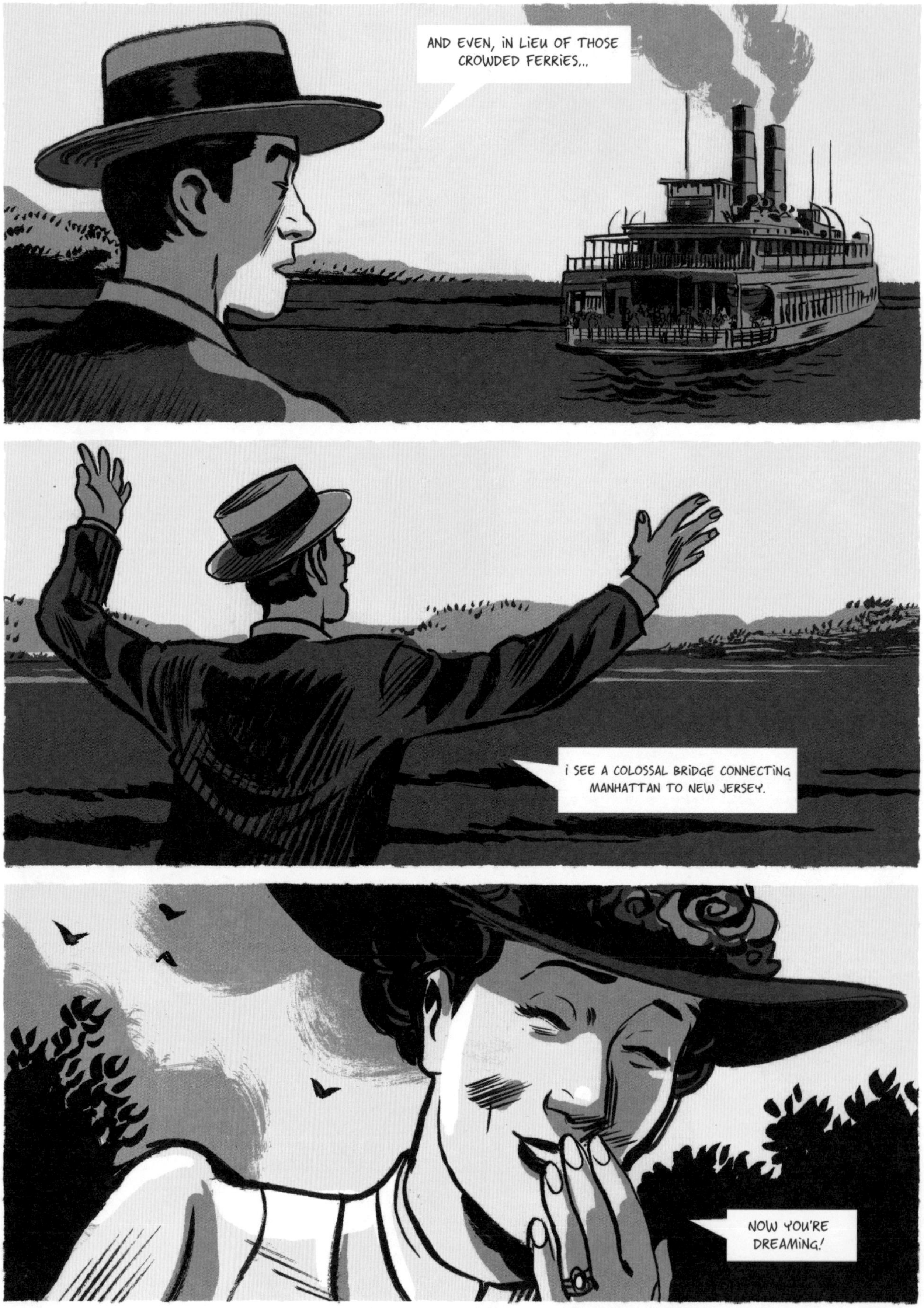
AND EVEN, IN LIEU OF THOSE CROWDED FERRIES...
I SEE A COLOSSAL BRIDGE CONNECTING MANHATTAN TO NEW JERSEY.
NOW YOU'RE DREAMING!

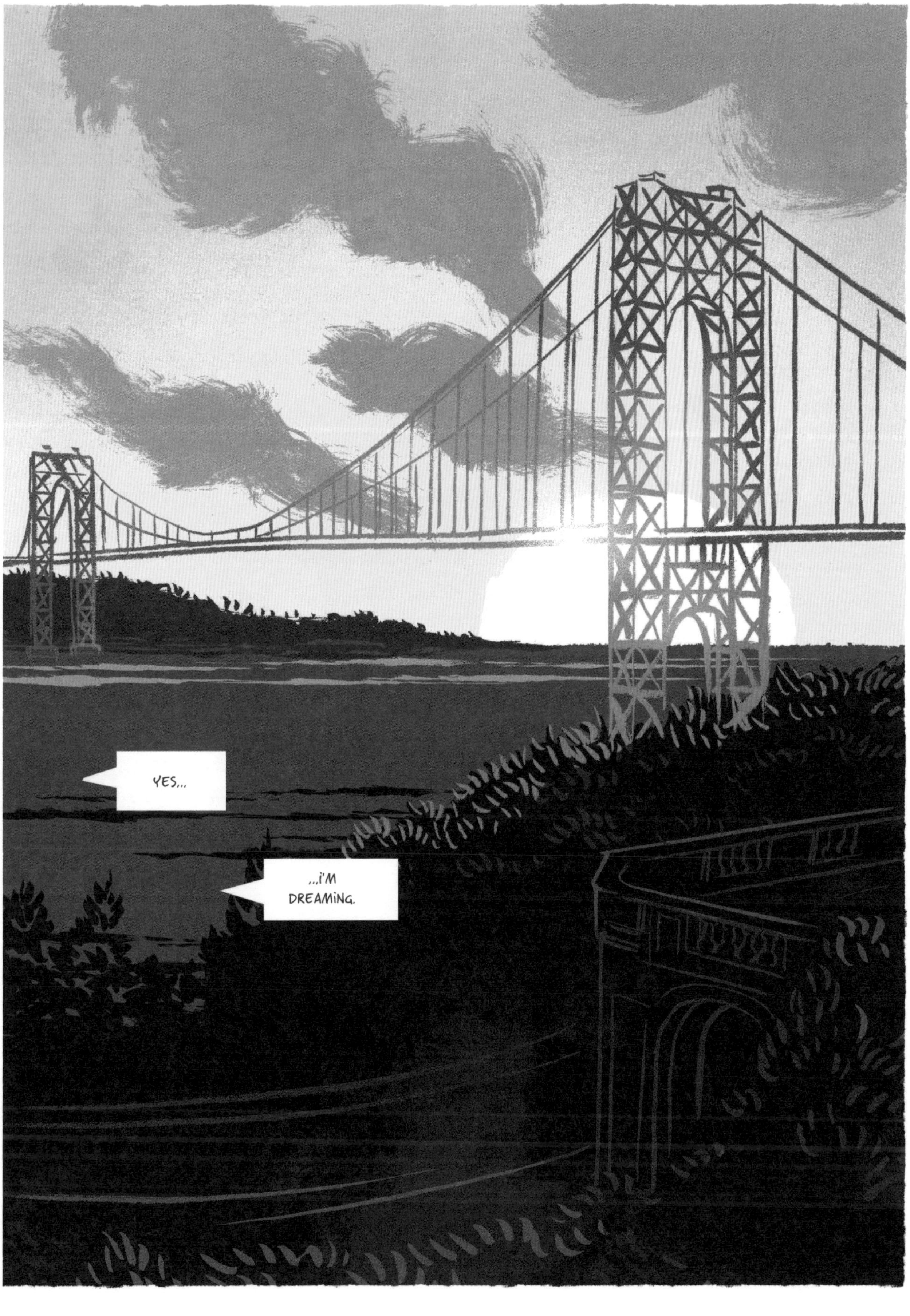
YES...
...I'M DREAMING.

BUT THE REALITY IS LESS BRIGHT. THE PLAN THAT ROBERT MOSES IS WORKING ON FOR RADICAL ADMINISTRATIVE REFORM IS SABOTAGED BY THE VERY PEOPLE WHO SUPPORTED IT.

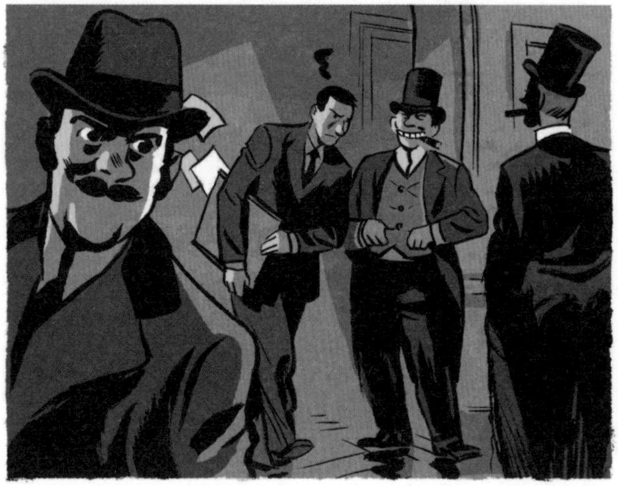

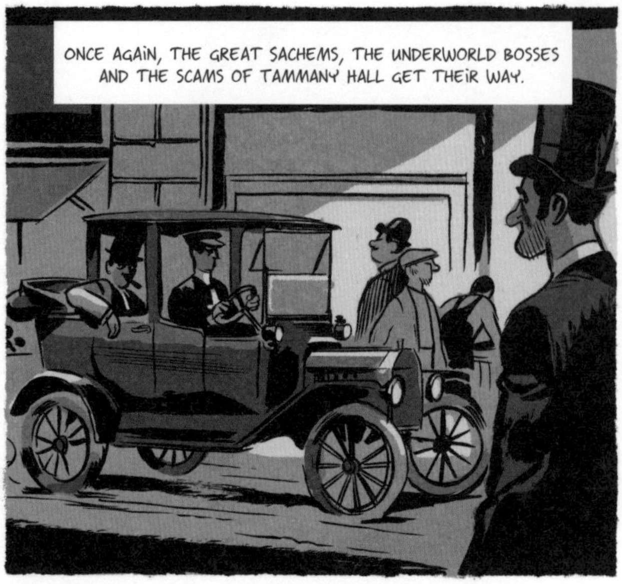
ONCE AGAIN, THE GREAT SACHEMS, THE UNDERWORLD BOSSES AND THE SCAMS OF TAMMANY HALL GET THEIR WAY.

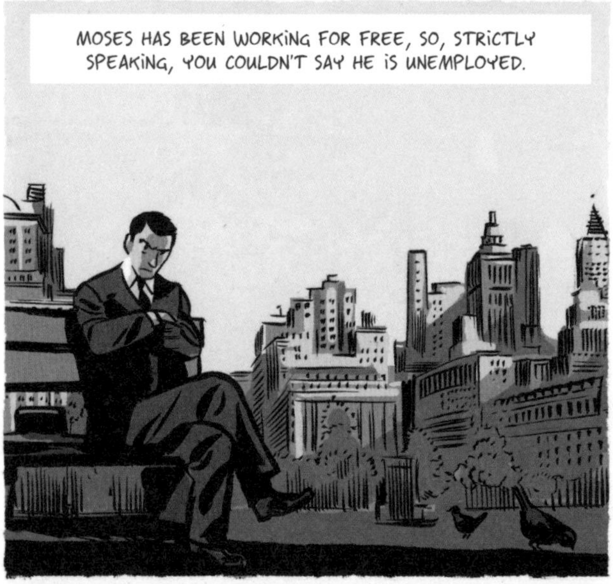
MOSES HAS BEEN WORKING FOR FREE, SO, STRICTLY SPEAKING, YOU COULDN'T SAY HE IS UNEMPLOYED.

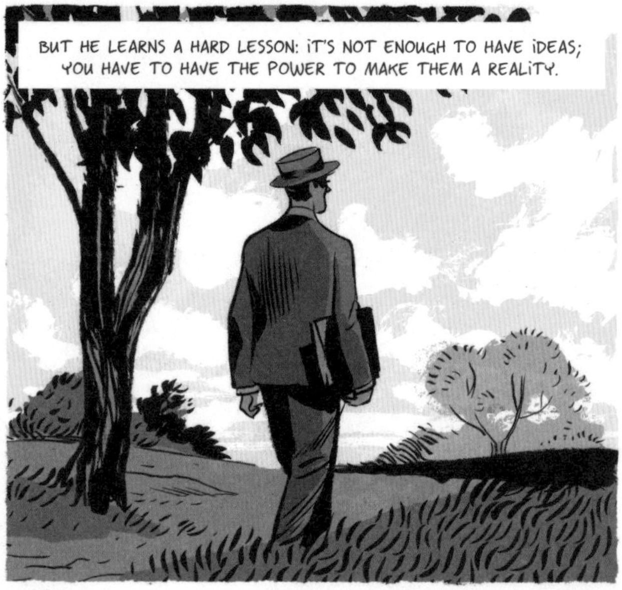
BUT HE LEARNS A HARD LESSON: IT'S NOT ENOUGH TO HAVE IDEAS; YOU HAVE TO HAVE THE POWER TO MAKE THEM A REALITY.

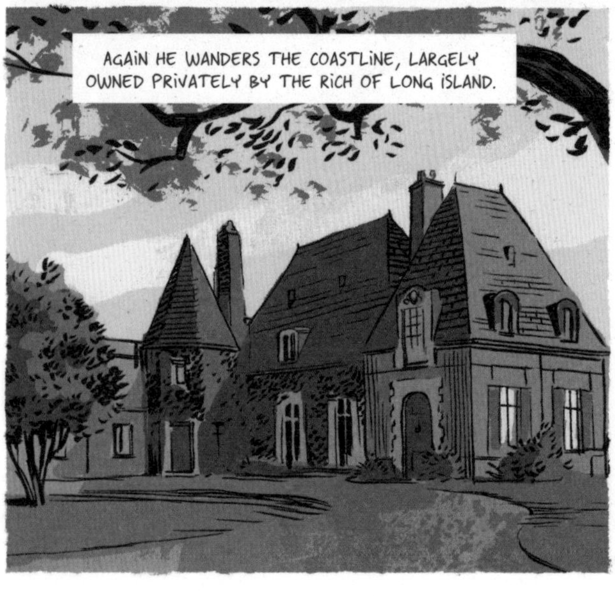
AGAIN HE WANDERS THE COASTLINE, LARGELY OWNED PRIVATELY BY THE RICH OF LONG ISLAND.

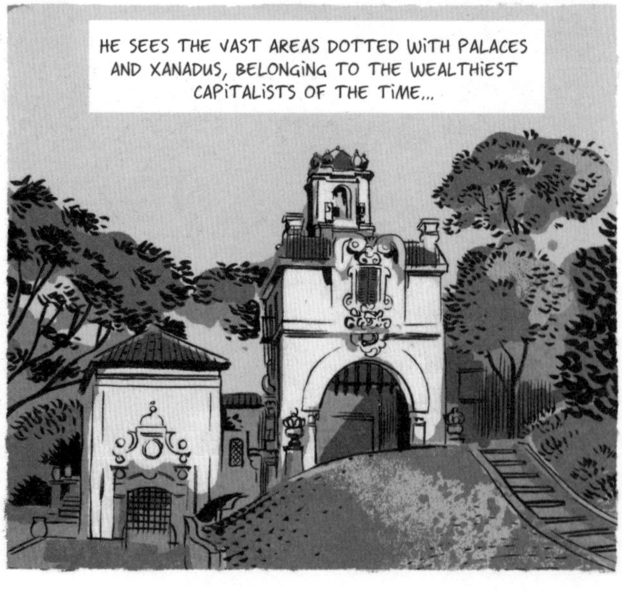
HE SEES THE VAST AREAS DOTTED WITH PALACES AND XANADUS, BELONGING TO THE WEALTHIEST CAPITALISTS OF THE TIME...

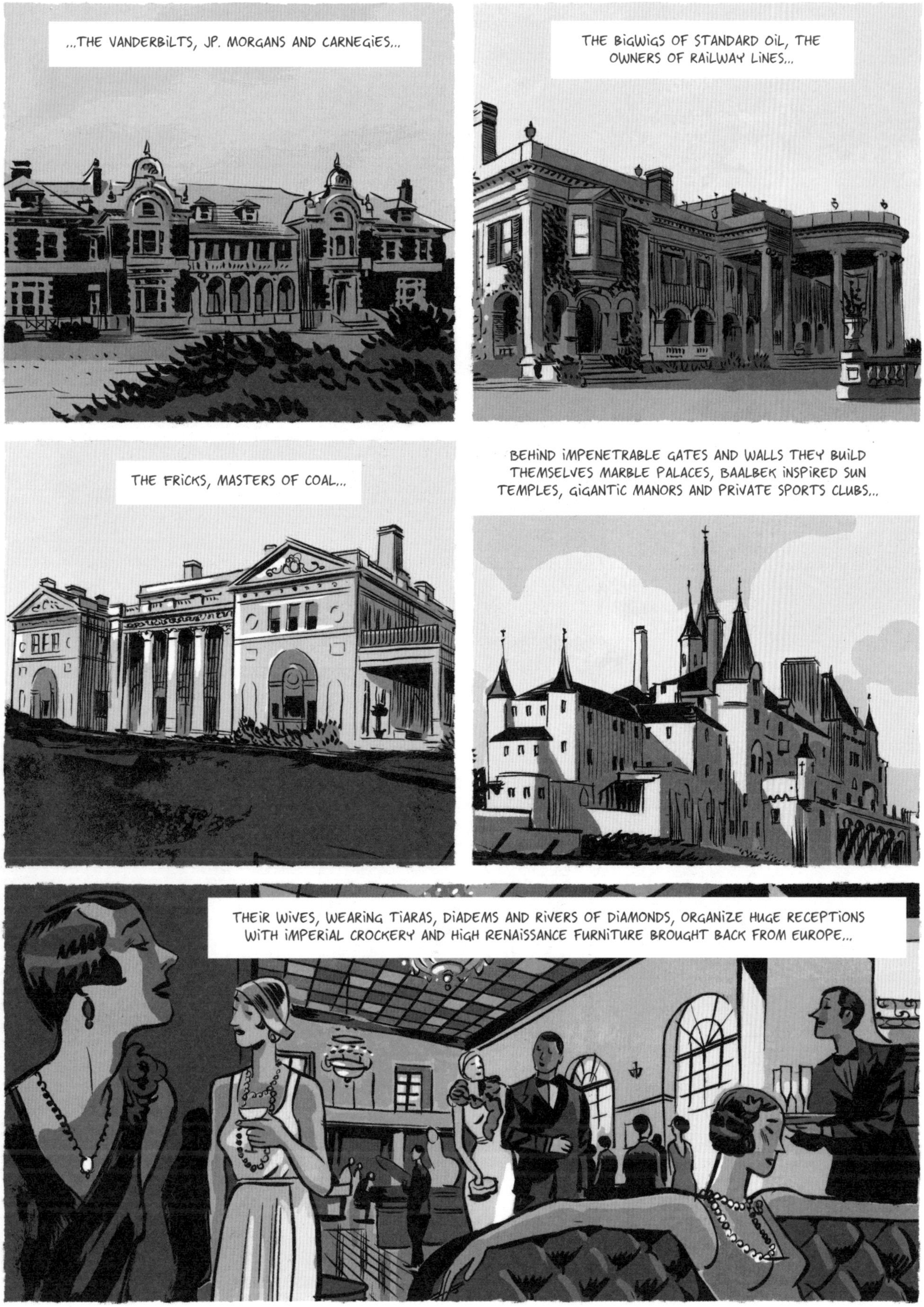
...THE VANDERBILTS, JP. MORGANS AND CARNEGIES...
THE BIGWIGS OF STANDARD OIL, THE OWNERS OF RAILWAY LINES...
THE FRICKS, MASTERS OF COAL...
BEHIND IMPENETRABLE GATES AND WALLS THEY BUILD THEMSELVES MARBLE PALACES, BAALBEK INSPIRED SUN TEMPLES, GIGANTIC MANORS AND PRIVATE SPORTS CLUBS...
THEIR WIVES, WEARING TIARAS, DIADEMS AND RIVERS OF DIAMONDS, ORGANIZE HUGE RECEPTIONS WITH IMPERIAL CROCKERY AND HIGH RENAISSANCE FURNITURE BROUGHT BACK FROM EUROPE...

ALCOHOL FLOWS FREELY, DESPITE PROHIBITION, AT PARTIES THAT RESEMBLE THOSE OF THE MYSTERIOUS GATSBY...

THEY SAY RAILWAY TYCOONS HAVE AMASSED LAND EQUAL IN SIZE TO THE STATE OF TEXAS...

MOSES STILL DREAMS OF PLACES ACCESSIBLE TO THE PEOPLE OF NEW YORK WHO MUST CONTENT THEMSELVES WITH SHABBY BEACHES THAT TAKE HOURS TO REACH ON ROADS MADE DELIBERATELY UNSERVICEABLE...

IN 1918, AFTER THE FIRST WORLD WAR, WHICH HE DIDN'T FIGHT IN, A MEETING TAKES PLACE THAT WILL BE DECISIVE BOTH FOR HIM AND FOR WHAT IS TO COME.

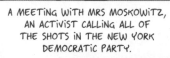

A MEETING WITH MRS MOSKOWITZ, AN ACTIVIST CALLING ALL OF THE SHOTS IN THE NEW YORK DEMOCRATIC PARTY.

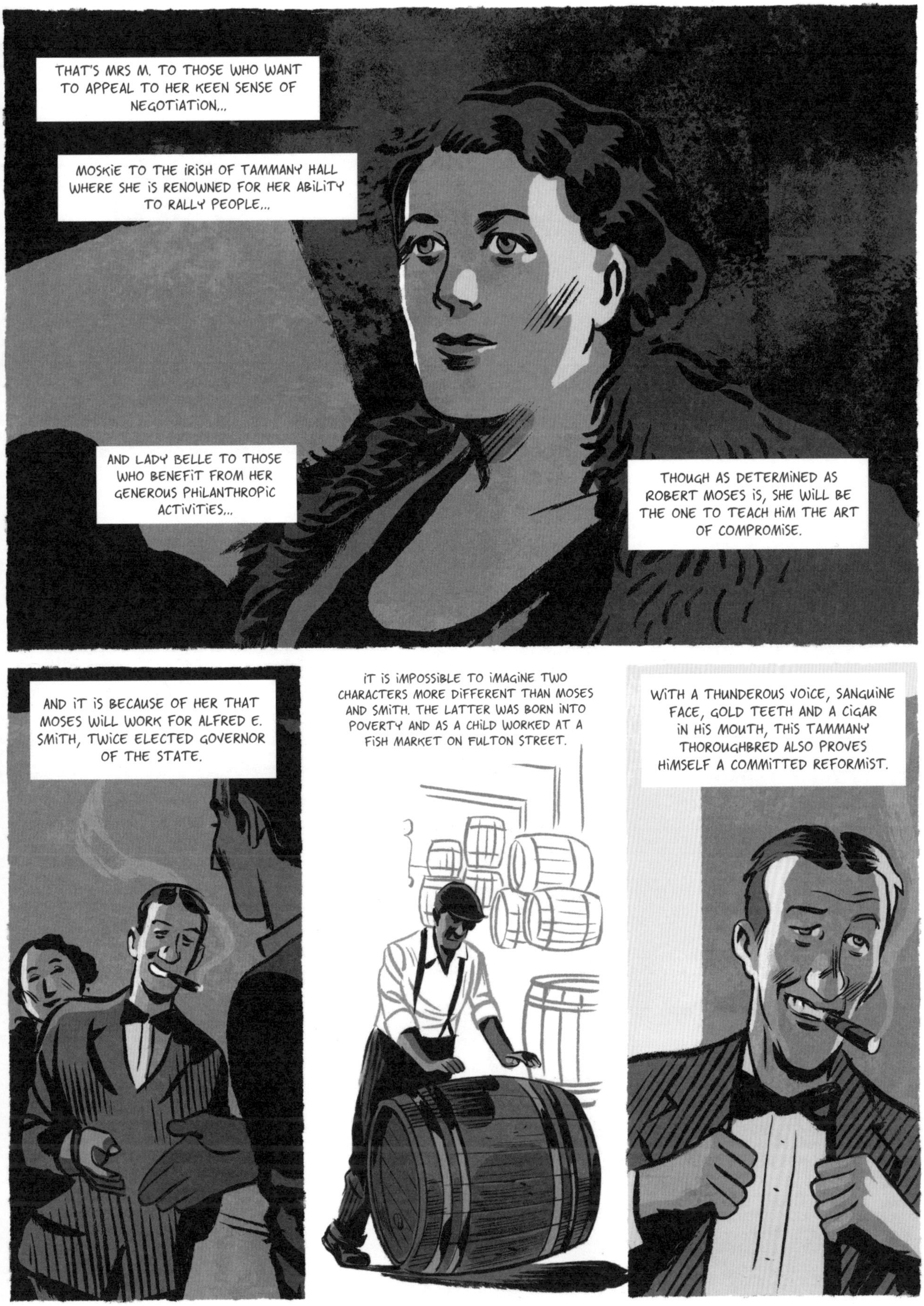
THAT'S MRS M. TO THOSE WHO WANT TO APPEAL TO HER KEEN SENSE OF NEGOTIATION...
MOSKIE TO THE IRISH OF TAMMANY HALL WHERE SHE IS RENOWNED FOR HER ABILITY TO RALLY PEOPLE...
AND LADY BELLE TO THOSE WHO BENEFIT FROM HER GENEROUS PHILANTHROPIC ACTIVITIES...
THOUGH AS DETERMINED AS ROBERT MOSES IS, SHE WILL BE THE ONE TO TEACH HIM THE ART OF COMPROMISE.
AND IT IS BECAUSE OF HER THAT MOSES WILL WORK FOR ALFRED E. SMITH, TWICE ELECTED GOVERNOR OF THE STATE.
IT IS IMPOSSIBLE TO IMAGINE TWO CHARACTERS MORE DIFFERENT THAN MOSES AND SMITH. THE LATTER WAS BORN INTO POVERTY AND AS A CHILD WORKED AT A FISH MARKET ON FULTON STREET.
WITH A THUNDEROUS VOICE, SANGUINE FACE, GOLD TEETH AND A CIGAR IN HIS MOUTH, THIS TAMMANY THOROUGHBRED ALSO PROVES HIMSELF A COMMITTED REFORMIST.

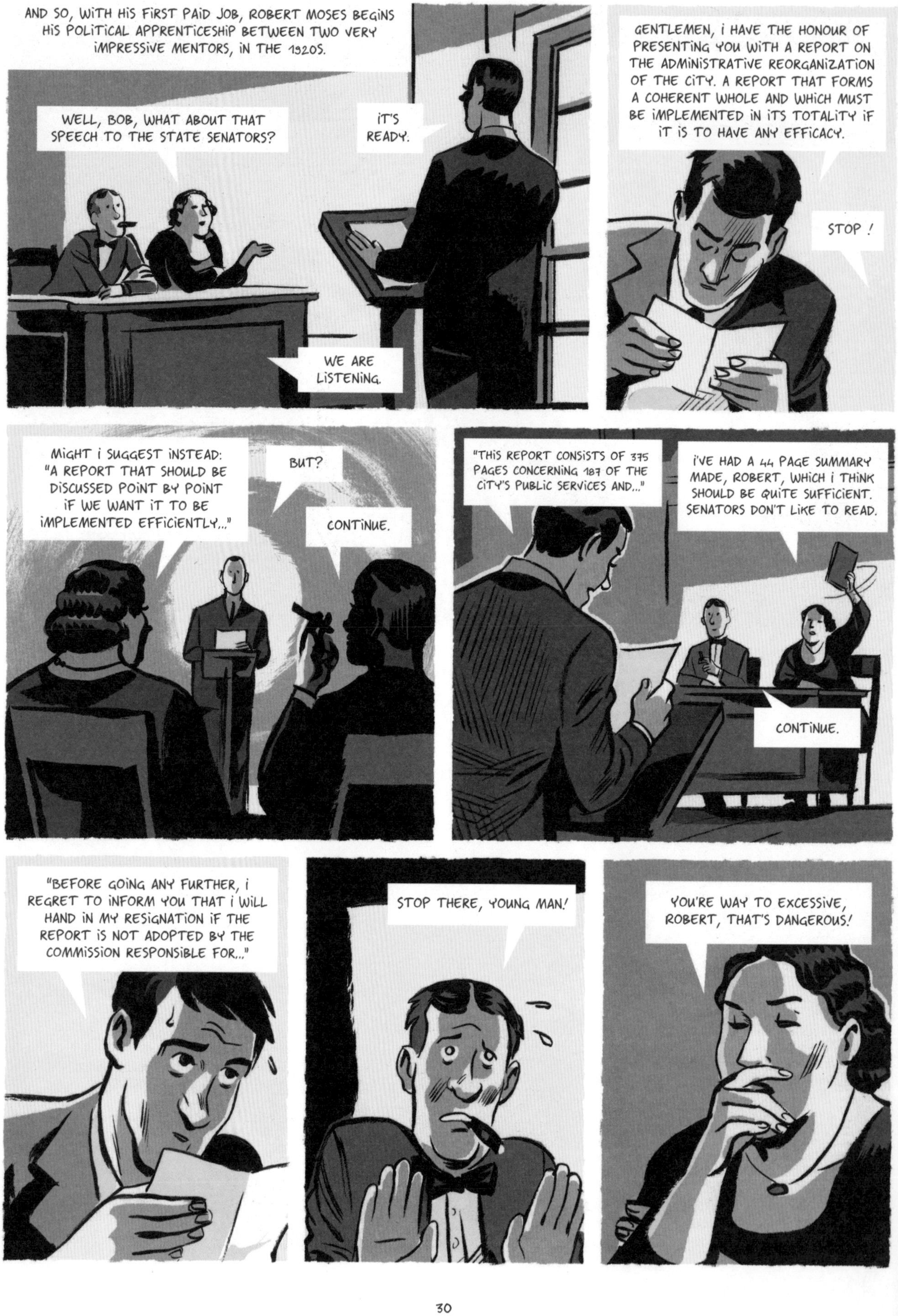
AND SO, WITH HIS FIRST PAID JOB, ROBERT MOSES BEGINS HIS POLITICAL APPRENTICESHIP BETWEEN TWO VERY IMPRESSIVE MENTORS, IN THE 1920S.
WELL, BOB, WHAT ABOUT THAT SPEECH TO THE STATE SENATORS?
IT'S READY.
WE ARE LISTENING.
GENTLEMEN, I HAVE THE HONOUR OF PRESENTING YOU WITH A REPORT ON THE ADMINISTRATIVE REORGANIZATION OF THE CITY. A REPORT THAT FORMS A COHERENT WHOLE AND WHICH MUST BE IMPLEMENTED IN ITS TOTALITY IF IT IS TO HAVE ANY EFFICACY.
STOP !
MIGHT I SUGGEST INSTEAD: "A REPORT THAT SHOULD BE DISCUSSED POINT BY POINT IF WE WANT IT TO BE IMPLEMENTED EFFICIENTLY..."
BUT?
CONTINUE.
"THIS REPORT CONSISTS OF 375 PAGES CONCERNING 187 OF THE CITY'S PUBLIC SERVICES AND..."
I'VE HAD A 44 PAGE SUMMARY MADE, ROBERT, WHICH I THINK SHOULD BE QUITE SUFFICIENT. SENATORS DON'T LIKE TO READ.
CONTINUE.
"BEFORE GOING ANY FURTHER, I REGRET TO INFORM YOU THAT I WILL HAND IN MY RESIGNATION IF THE REPORT IS NOT ADOPTED BY THE COMMISSION RESPONSIBLE FOR..."
STOP THERE, YOUNG MAN!
YOU'RE WAY TO EXCESSIVE, ROBERT, THAT'S DANGEROUS!

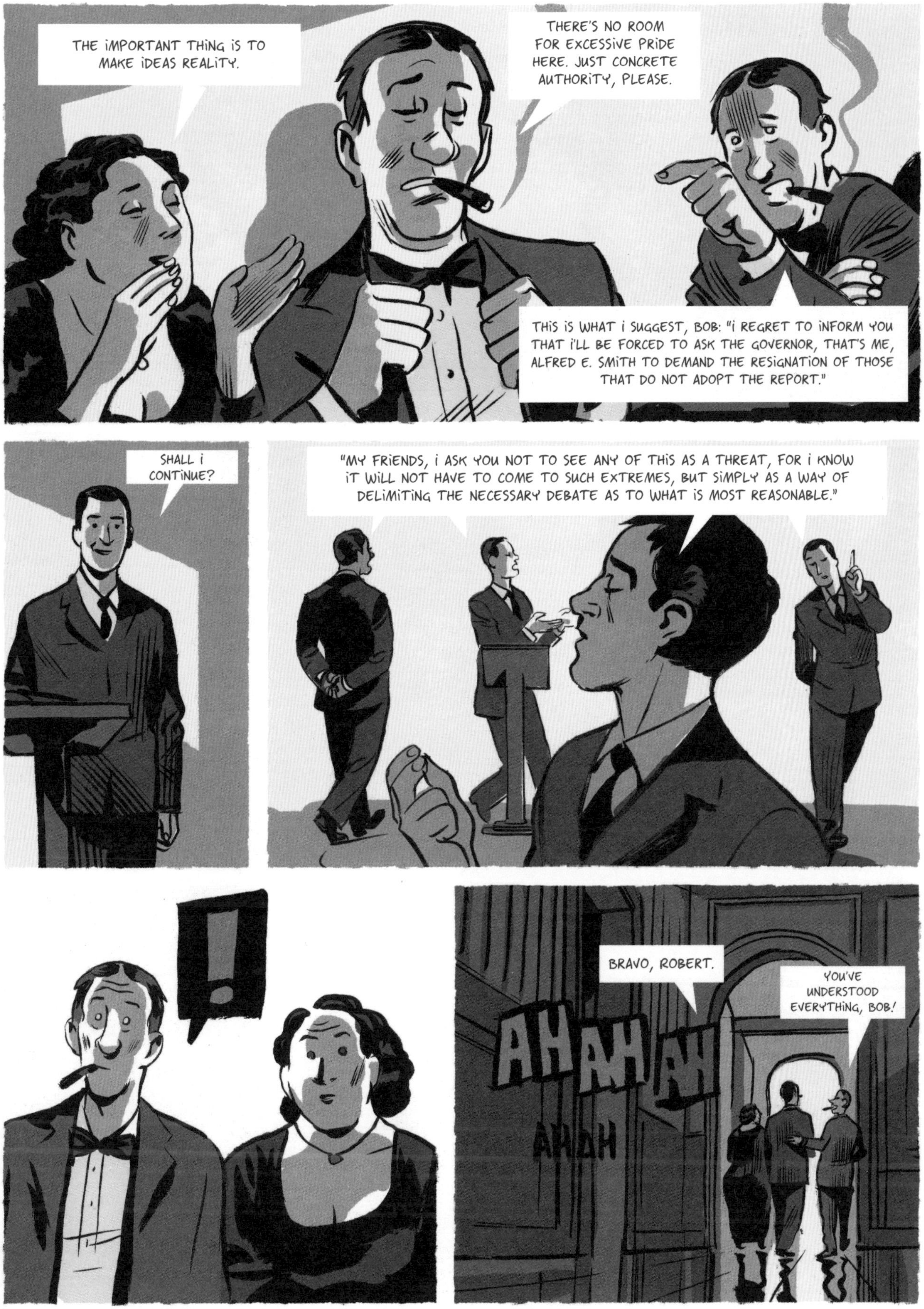
THE iMPORTANT THiNG iS TO MAKE iDEAS REALiTY.
THERE'S NO ROOM FOR EXCESSIVE PRIDE HERE. JUST CONCRETE AUTHORiTY, PLEASE.
THiS iS WHAT i SUGGEST, BOB: "i REGRET TO iNFORM YOU THAT i'LL BE FORCED TO ASK THE GOVERNOR, THAT'S ME, ALFRED E. SMiTH TO DEMAND THE RESiGNATiON OF THOSE THAT DO NOT ADOPT THE REPORT."
SHALL i CONTiNUE?
"MY FRiENDS, i ASK YOU NOT TO SEE ANY OF THiS AS A THREAT, FOR i KNOW iT WiLL NOT HAVE TO COME TO SUCH EXTREMES, BUT SiMPLY AS A WAY OF DELiMiTiNG THE NECESSARY DEBATE AS TO WHAT iS MOST REASONABLE."
!
BRAVO, ROBERT.
YOU'VE UNDERSTOOD EVERYTHiNG, BOB!
AH AH AH
AHAH

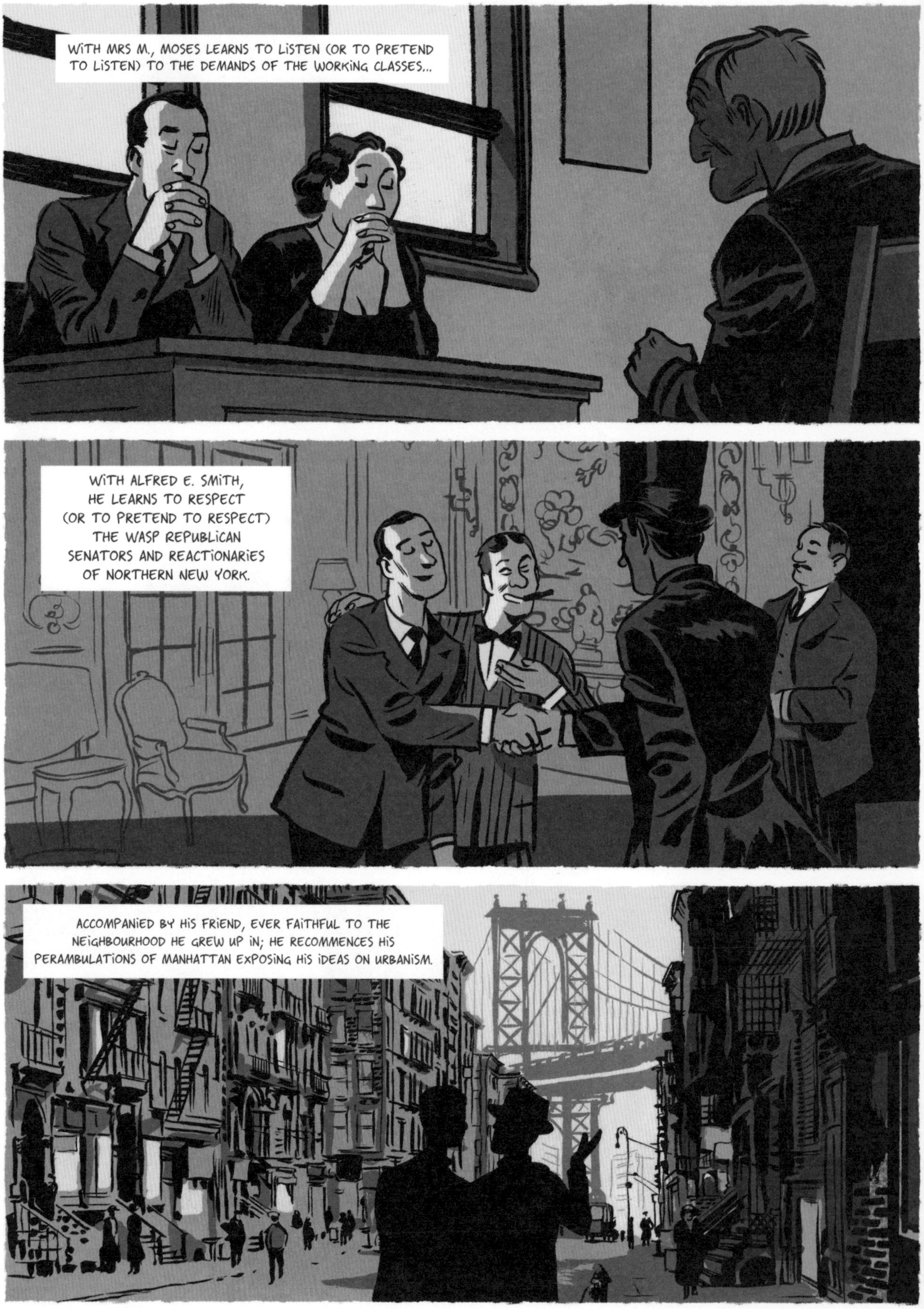
WITH MRS M., MOSES LEARNS TO LISTEN (OR TO PRETEND TO LISTEN) TO THE DEMANDS OF THE WORKING CLASSES...
WITH ALFRED E. SMITH, HE LEARNS TO RESPECT (OR TO PRETEND TO RESPECT) THE WASP REPUBLICAN SENATORS AND REACTIONARIES OF NORTHERN NEW YORK.
ACCOMPANIED BY HIS FRIEND, EVER FAITHFUL TO THE NEIGHBOURHOOD HE GREW UP IN; HE RECOMMENCES HIS PERAMBULATIONS OF MANHATTAN EXPOSING HIS IDEAS ON URBANISM.

# CHAPTER 2

## The rise of a builder

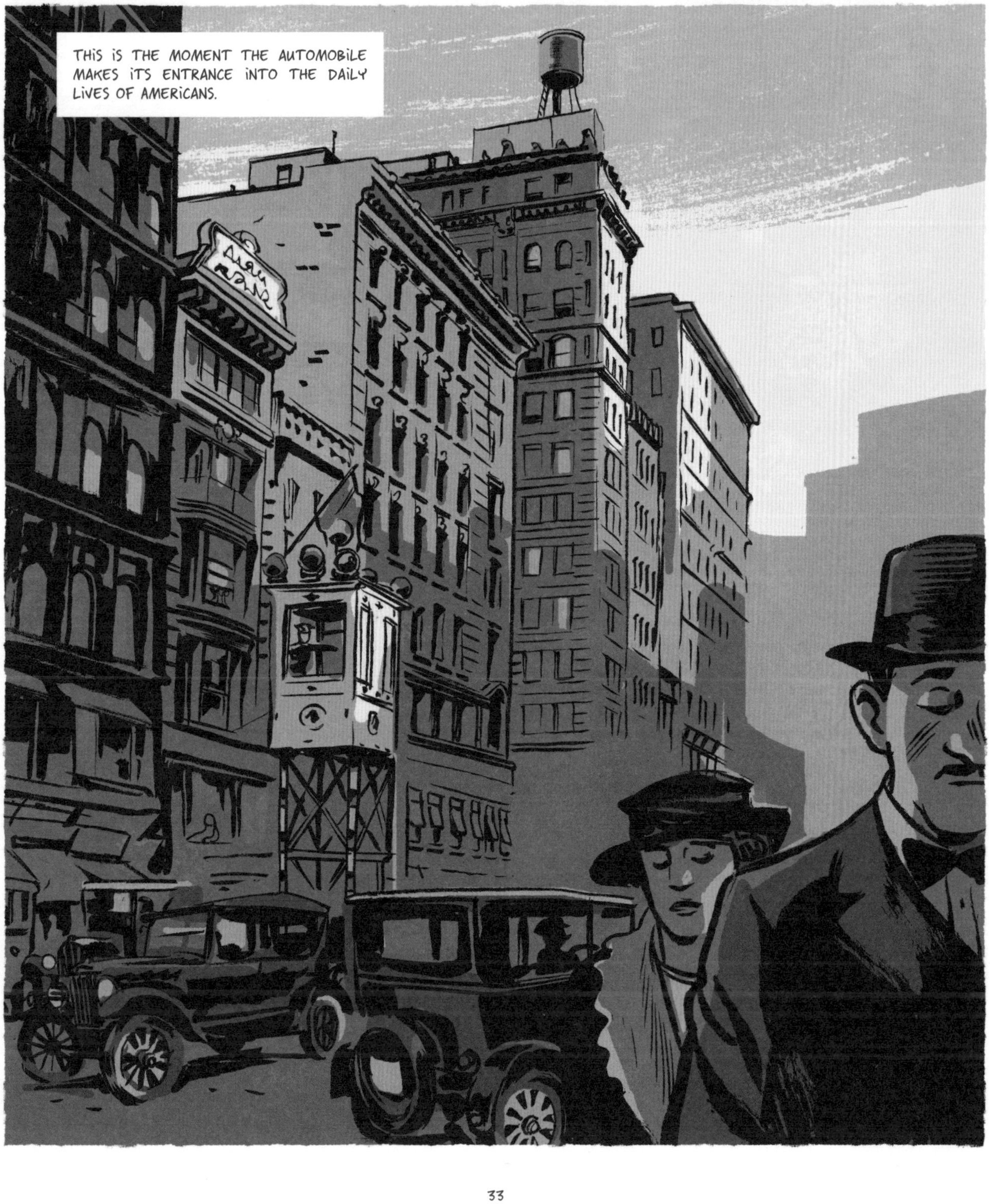
THIS IS THE MOMENT THE AUTOMOBILE MAKES ITS ENTRANCE INTO THE DAILY LIVES OF AMERICANS.

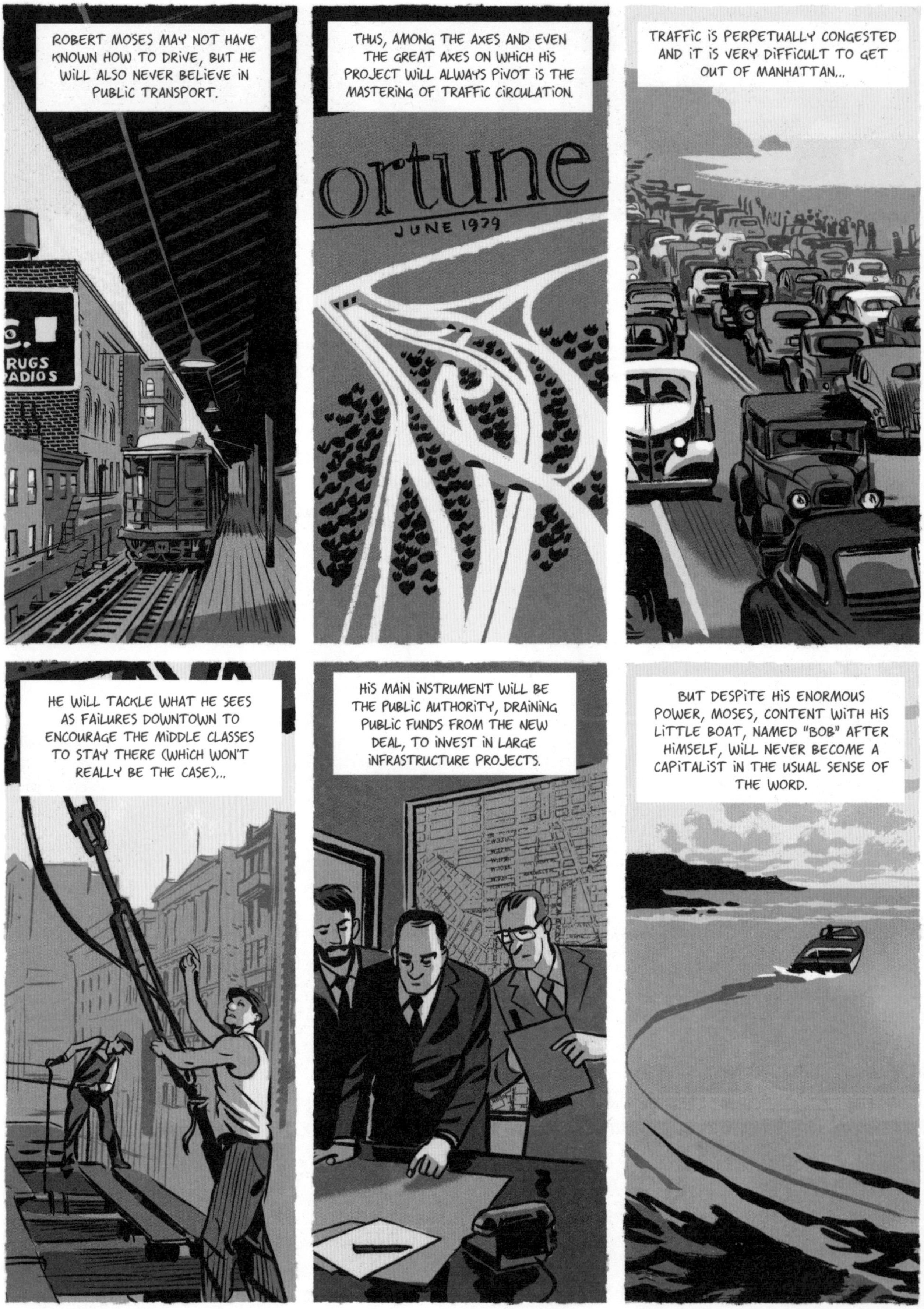
ROBERT MOSES MAY NOT HAVE KNOWN HOW TO DRIVE, BUT HE WILL ALSO NEVER BELIEVE IN PUBLIC TRANSPORT.
THUS, AMONG THE AXES AND EVEN THE GREAT AXES ON WHICH HIS PROJECT WILL ALWAYS PIVOT IS THE MASTERING OF TRAFFIC CIRCULATION.
ortune
JUNE 1929
TRAFFIC IS PERPETUALLY CONGESTED AND IT IS VERY DIFFICULT TO GET OUT OF MANHATTAN...
HE WILL TACKLE WHAT HE SEES AS FAILURES DOWNTOWN TO ENCOURAGE THE MIDDLE CLASSES TO STAY THERE (WHICH WON'T REALLY BE THE CASE)...
HIS MAIN INSTRUMENT WILL BE THE PUBLIC AUTHORITY, DRAINING PUBLIC FUNDS FROM THE NEW DEAL, TO INVEST IN LARGE INFRASTRUCTURE PROJECTS.
BUT DESPITE HIS ENORMOUS POWER, MOSES, CONTENT WITH HIS LITTLE BOAT, NAMED "BOB" AFTER HIMSELF, WILL NEVER BECOME A CAPITALIST IN THE USUAL SENSE OF THE WORD.

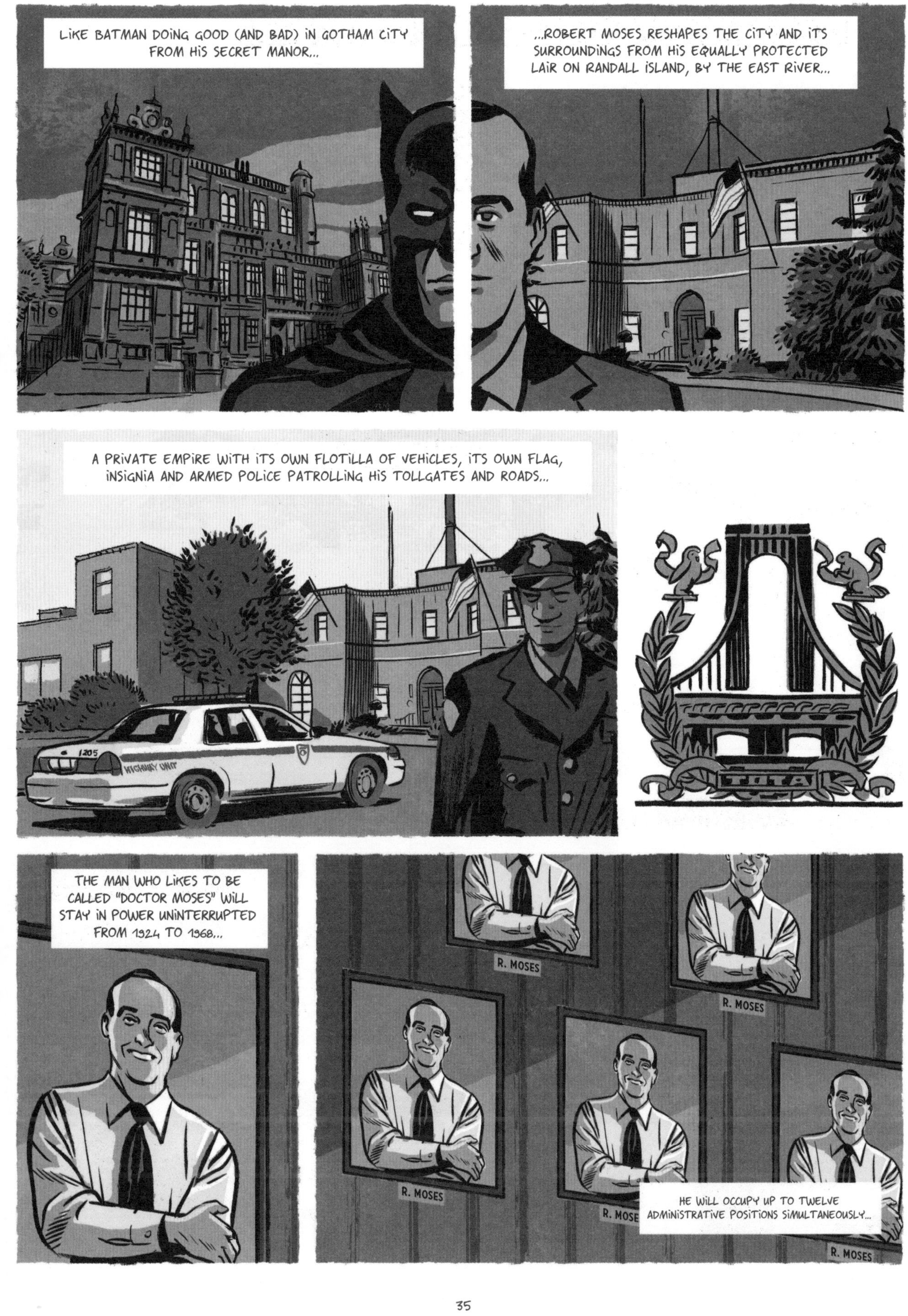
LIKE BATMAN DOING GOOD (AND BAD) IN GOTHAM CITY FROM HIS SECRET MANOR...
...ROBERT MOSES RESHAPES THE CITY AND ITS SURROUNDINGS FROM HIS EQUALLY PROTECTED LAIR ON RANDALL ISLAND, BY THE EAST RIVER...
A PRIVATE EMPIRE WITH ITS OWN FLOTILLA OF VEHICLES, ITS OWN FLAG, INSIGNIA AND ARMED POLICE PATROLLING HIS TOLLGATES AND ROADS...
1205
HIGHWAY UNIT
THE MAN WHO LIKES TO BE CALLED "DOCTOR MOSES" WILL STAY IN POWER UNINTERRUPTED FROM 1924 TO 1968...
R. MOSES
R. MOSES
R. MOSES
R. MOSE
HE WILL OCCUPY UP TO TWELVE ADMINISTRATIVE POSITIONS SIMULTANEOUSLY...
R. MOSES

EQUALING J. EDGAR HOOVER, HEAD OF THE FBI, HE WILL SEE FIVE MAYORS COME AND GO...

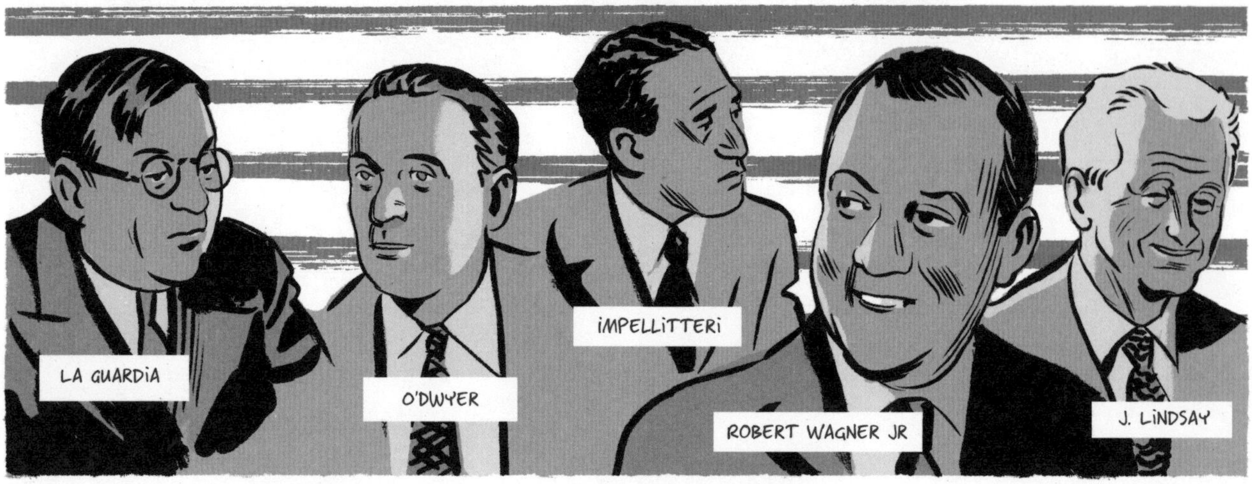
IMPELLITTERI
LA GUARDIA
O'DWYER
ROBERT WAGNER JR
J. LINDSAY

SIX GOVERNORS...

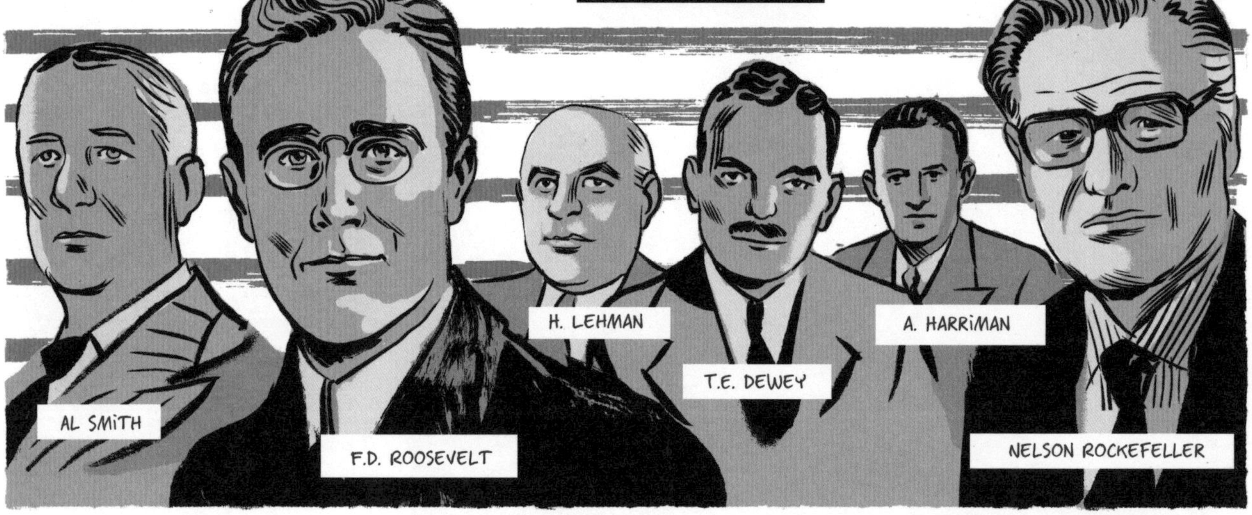
H. LEHMAN
A. HARRIMAN
T.E. DEWEY
AL SMITH
F.D. ROOSEVELT
NELSON ROCKEFELLER

SEVEN PRESIDENTS...

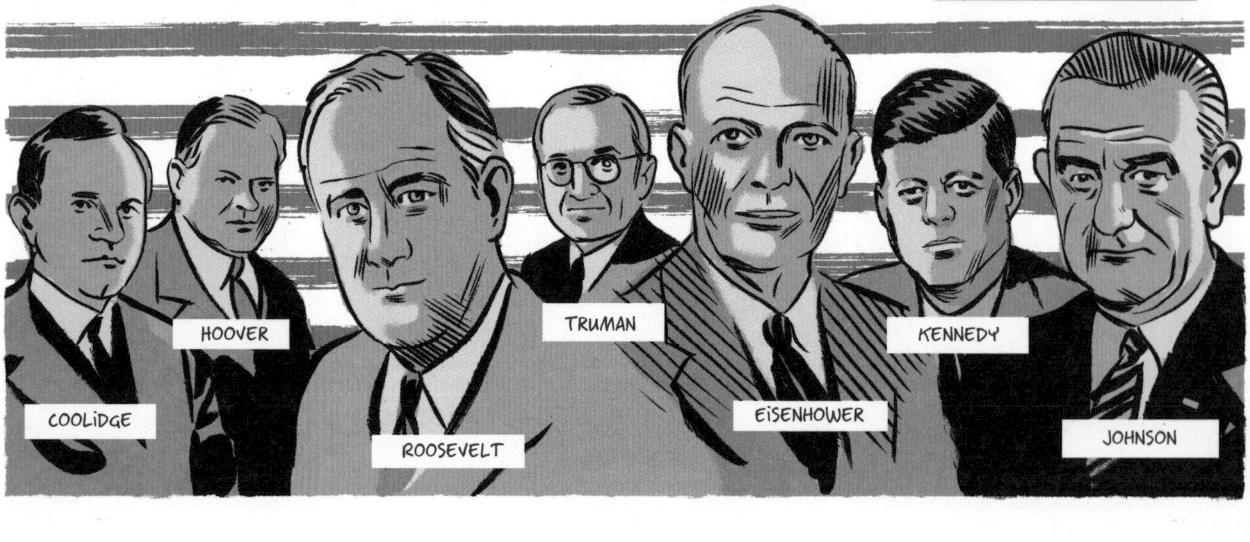
HOOVER
TRUMAN
KENNEDY
COOLIDGE
EISENHOWER
ROOSEVELT
JOHNSON

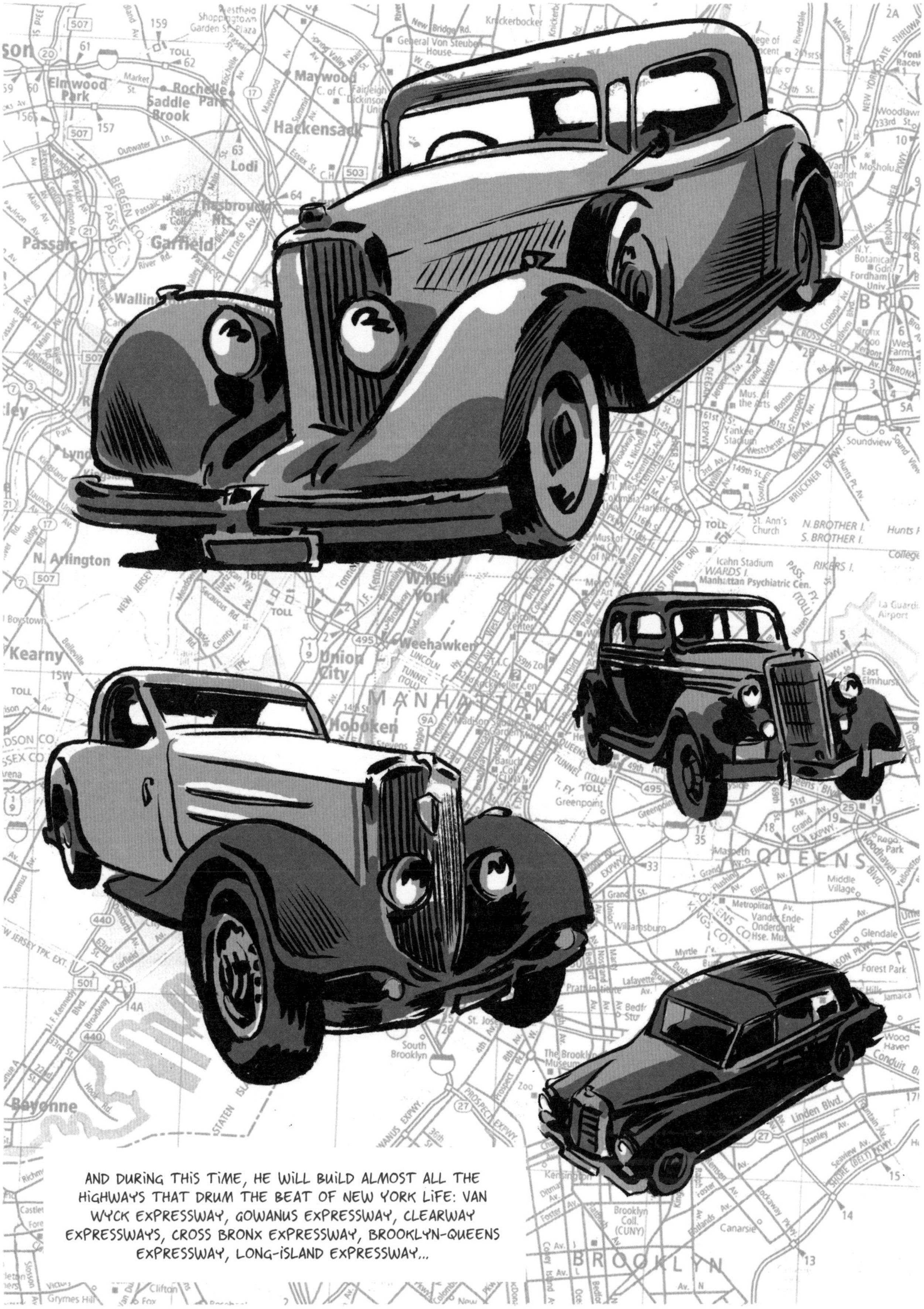
AND DURING THIS TIME, HE WILL BUILD ALMOST ALL THE HIGHWAYS THAT DRUM THE BEAT OF NEW YORK LIFE: VAN WYCK EXPRESSWAY, GOWANUS EXPRESSWAY, CLEARWAY EXPRESSWAYS, CROSS BRONX EXPRESSWAY, BROOKLYN-QUEENS EXPRESSWAY, LONG-ISLAND EXPRESSWAY...

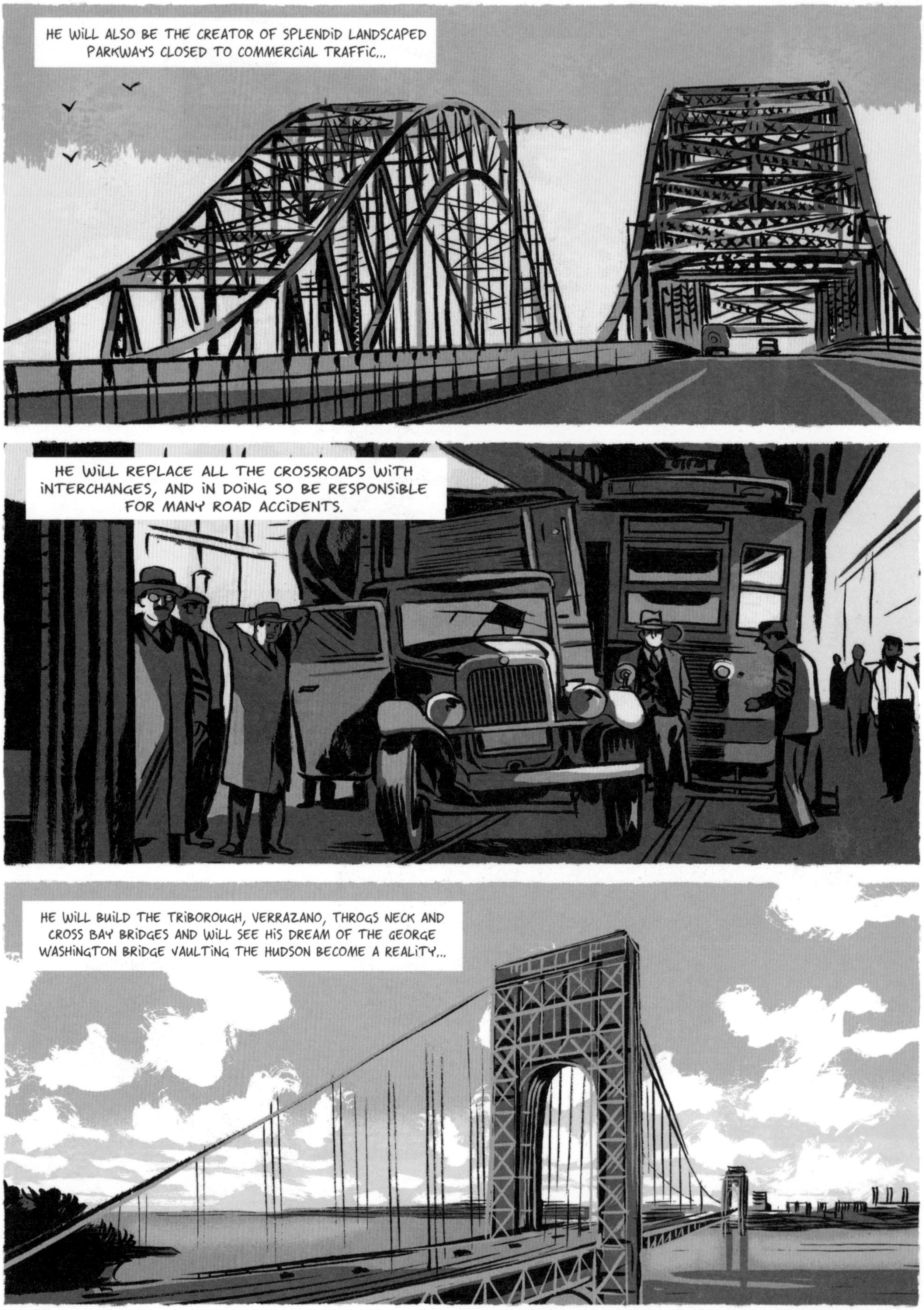
HE WILL ALSO BE THE CREATOR OF SPLENDID LANDSCAPED PARKWAYS CLOSED TO COMMERCIAL TRAFFIC...
HE WILL REPLACE ALL THE CROSSROADS WITH INTERCHANGES, AND IN DOING SO BE RESPONSIBLE FOR MANY ROAD ACCIDENTS.
HE WILL BUILD THE TRIBOROUGH, VERRAZANO, THROGS NECK AND CROSS BAY BRIDGES AND WILL SEE HIS DREAM OF THE GEORGE WASHINGTON BRIDGE VAULTING THE HUDSON BECOME A REALITY...

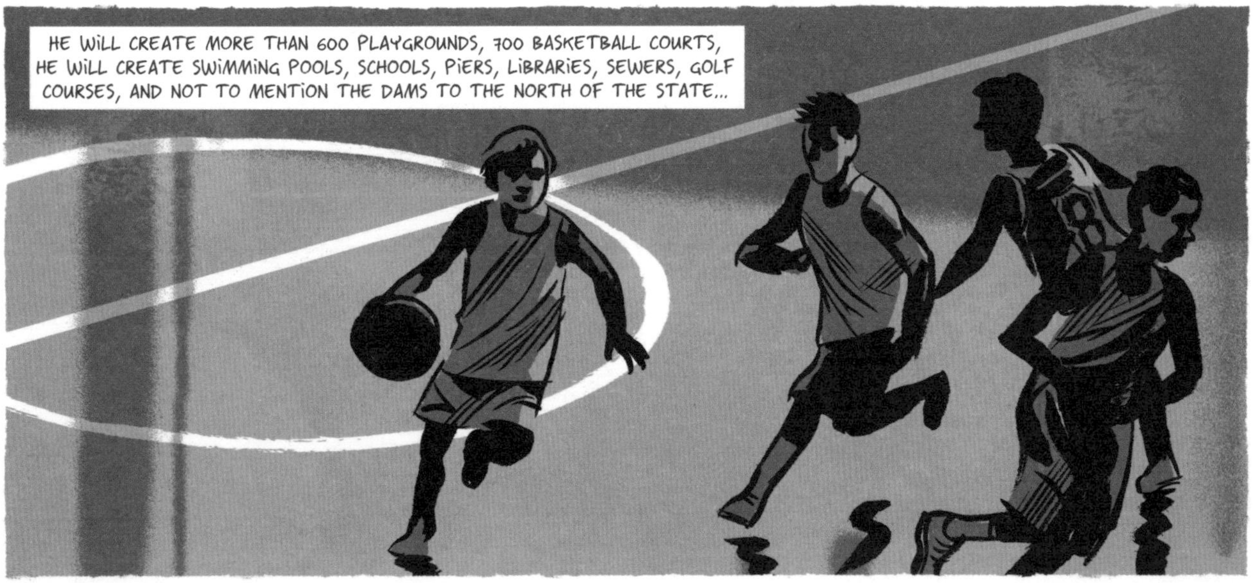
HE WILL CREATE MORE THAN 600 PLAYGROUNDS, 700 BASKETBALL COURTS, HE WILL CREATE SWIMMING POOLS, SCHOOLS, PIERS, LIBRARIES, SEWERS, GOLF COURSES, AND NOT TO MENTION THE DAMS TO THE NORTH OF THE STATE...

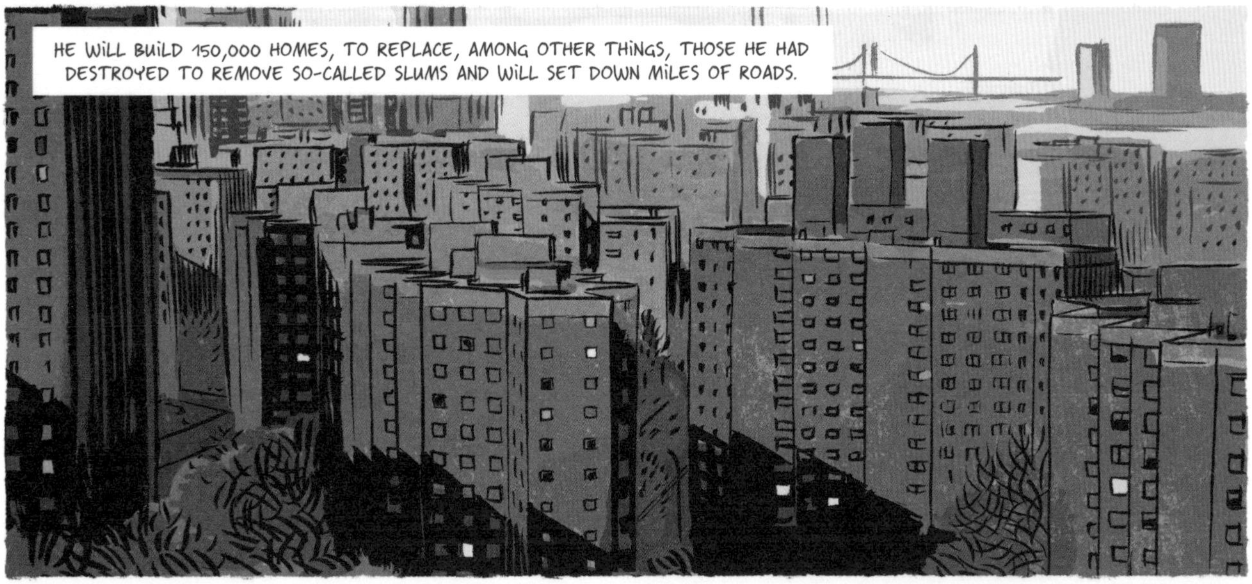
HE WILL BUILD 150,000 HOMES, TO REPLACE, AMONG OTHER THINGS, THOSE HE HAD DESTROYED TO REMOVE SO-CALLED SLUMS AND WILL SET DOWN MILES OF ROADS.

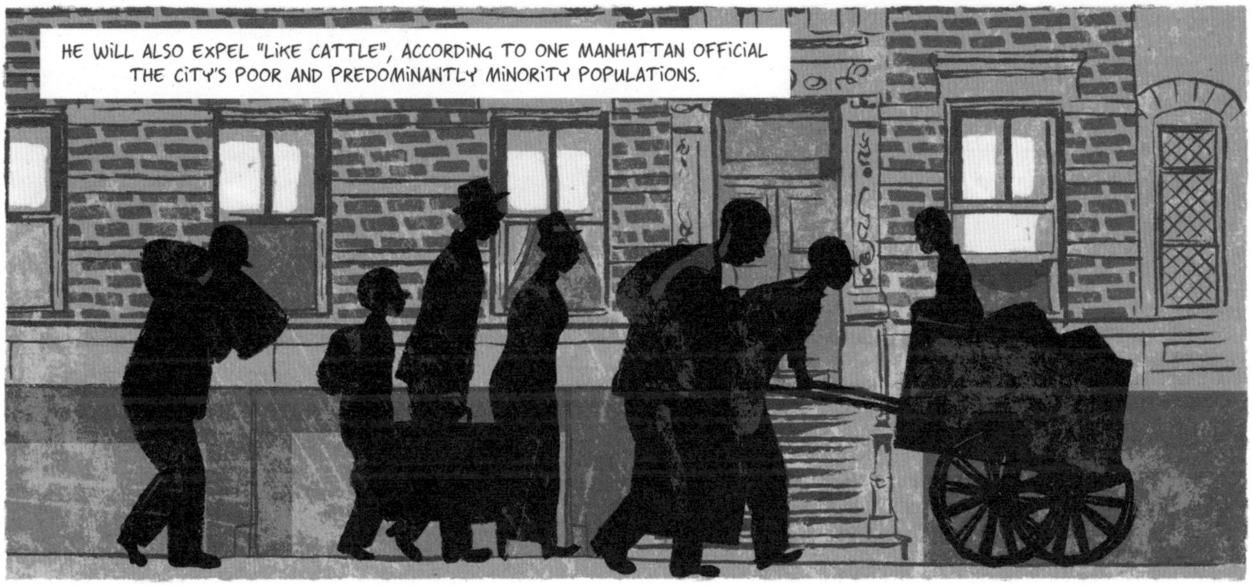
HE WILL ALSO EXPEL "LIKE CATTLE", ACCORDING TO ONE MANHATTAN OFFICIAL THE CITY'S POOR AND PREDOMINANTLY MINORITY POPULATIONS.

HE MAKES IT KNOWN THAT IN NEW YORK IT IS IMPOSSIBLE TO WALK, DRIVE, SWIM, PLAY SPORTS, SIT DOWN OR EVEN SLEEP WITHOUT MAKING USE OF A ROBERT MOSES CREATION.

IT IS, OF COURSE, ANOTHER ALL-POWERFUL BUILDER, ONE HE HIMSELF LOVED TO REFER TO, THAT HE MUST BE COMPARED TO.

THE BARON HAUSSMAN, WHO REIGNED OVER THE PARISIAN BUILDING SITE OF THE SECOND EMPIRE FOR 17 YEARS AND WHO, WITHOUT A MOMENT'S THOUGHT TO THE LOWER CLASSES, CHANGED THE CAPITAL FOREVER.

ON APRIL 30TH 1924, AGED 35, THANKS TO HIS POLITICAL CONNECTIONS, MOSES IS ELECTED PRESIDENT OF THE NEW STATE COUNCIL OF PARKS.

CLAP CLAP CLAP CLAP CLAP CLAP

IT IS THE STARTING POINT IN HIS CAREER AS A MAN OF INFLUENCE AND AS A GREAT BUILDER.

WELL, ROBERT, STILL FULL OF IDEAS, I SUPPOSE?

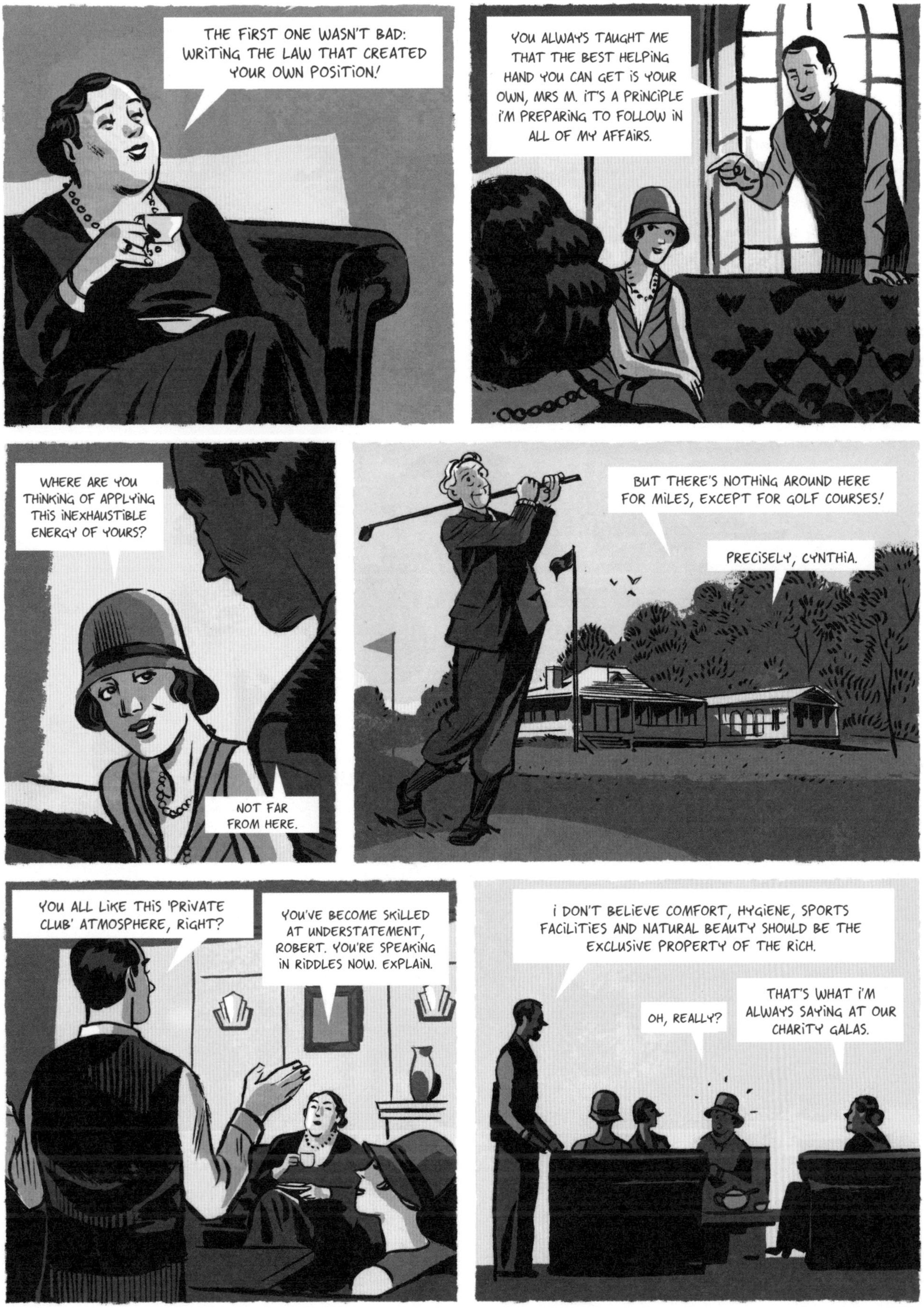
THE FIRST ONE WASN'T BAD: WRITING THE LAW THAT CREATED YOUR OWN POSITION!
YOU ALWAYS TAUGHT ME THAT THE BEST HELPING HAND YOU CAN GET IS YOUR OWN, MRS M. IT'S A PRINCIPLE I'M PREPARING TO FOLLOW IN ALL OF MY AFFAIRS.
WHERE ARE YOU THINKING OF APPLYING THIS INEXHAUSTIBLE ENERGY OF YOURS?
NOT FAR FROM HERE.
BUT THERE'S NOTHING AROUND HERE FOR MILES, EXCEPT FOR GOLF COURSES!
PRECISELY, CYNTHIA.
YOU ALL LIKE THIS 'PRIVATE CLUB' ATMOSPHERE, RIGHT?
YOU'VE BECOME SKILLED AT UNDERSTATEMENT, ROBERT. YOU'RE SPEAKING IN RIDDLES NOW. EXPLAIN.
I DON'T BELIEVE COMFORT, HYGIENE, SPORTS FACILITIES AND NATURAL BEAUTY SHOULD BE THE EXCLUSIVE PROPERTY OF THE RICH.
OH, REALLY?
THAT'S WHAT I'M ALWAYS SAYING AT OUR CHARITY GALAS.

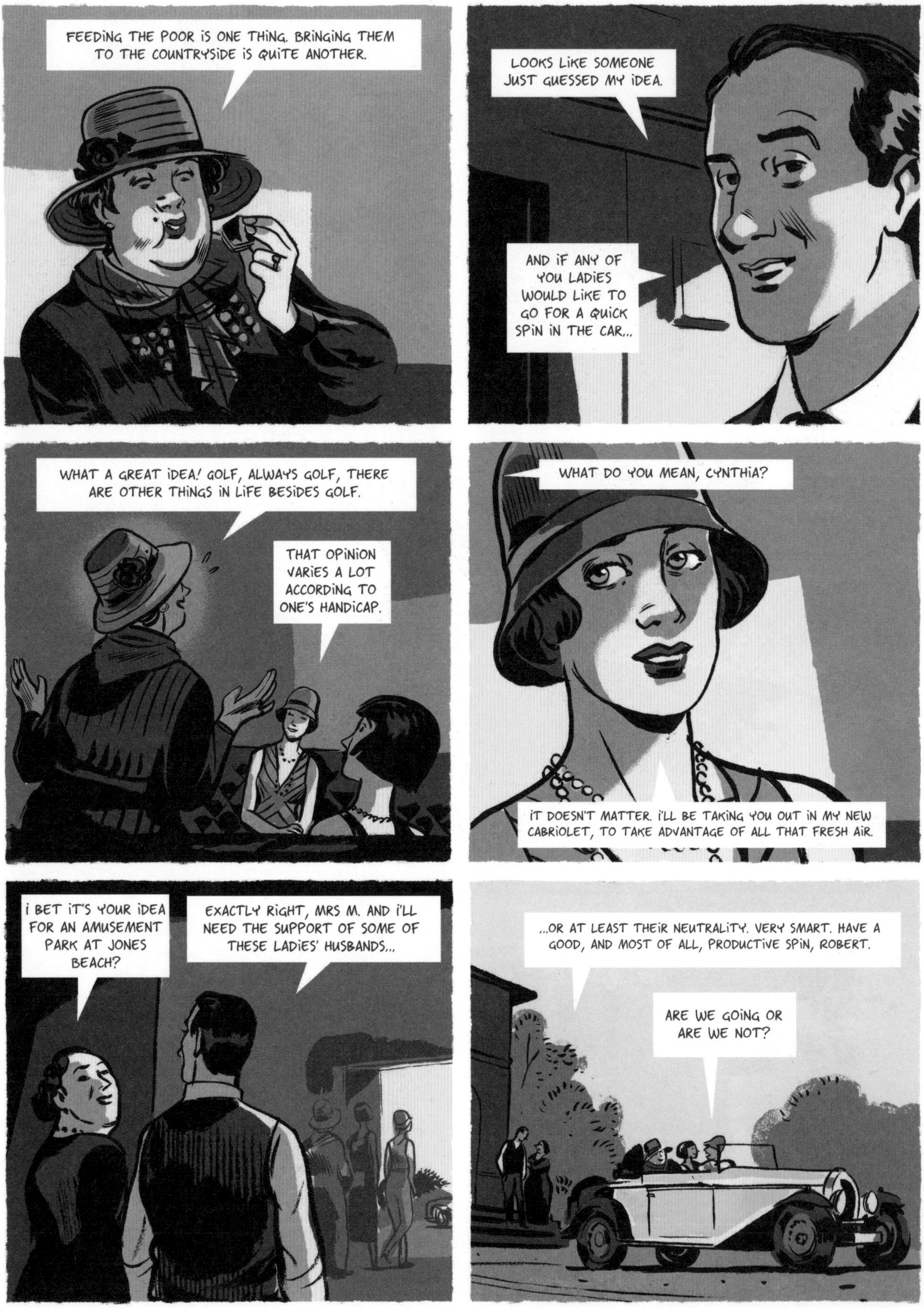
FEEDING THE POOR IS ONE THING. BRINGING THEM TO THE COUNTRYSIDE IS QUITE ANOTHER.
LOOKS LIKE SOMEONE JUST GUESSED MY IDEA.
AND IF ANY OF YOU LADIES WOULD LIKE TO GO FOR A QUICK SPIN IN THE CAR...
WHAT A GREAT IDEA! GOLF, ALWAYS GOLF, THERE ARE OTHER THINGS IN LIFE BESIDES GOLF.
THAT OPINION VARIES A LOT ACCORDING TO ONE'S HANDICAP.
WHAT DO YOU MEAN, CYNTHIA?
IT DOESN'T MATTER. I'LL BE TAKING YOU OUT IN MY NEW CABRIOLET, TO TAKE ADVANTAGE OF ALL THAT FRESH AIR.
I BET IT'S YOUR IDEA FOR AN AMUSEMENT PARK AT JONES BEACH?
EXACTLY RIGHT, MRS M. AND I'LL NEED THE SUPPORT OF SOME OF THESE LADIES' HUSBANDS...
...OR AT LEAST THEIR NEUTRALITY. VERY SMART. HAVE A GOOD, AND MOST OF ALL, PRODUCTIVE SPIN, ROBERT.
ARE WE GOING OR ARE WE NOT?

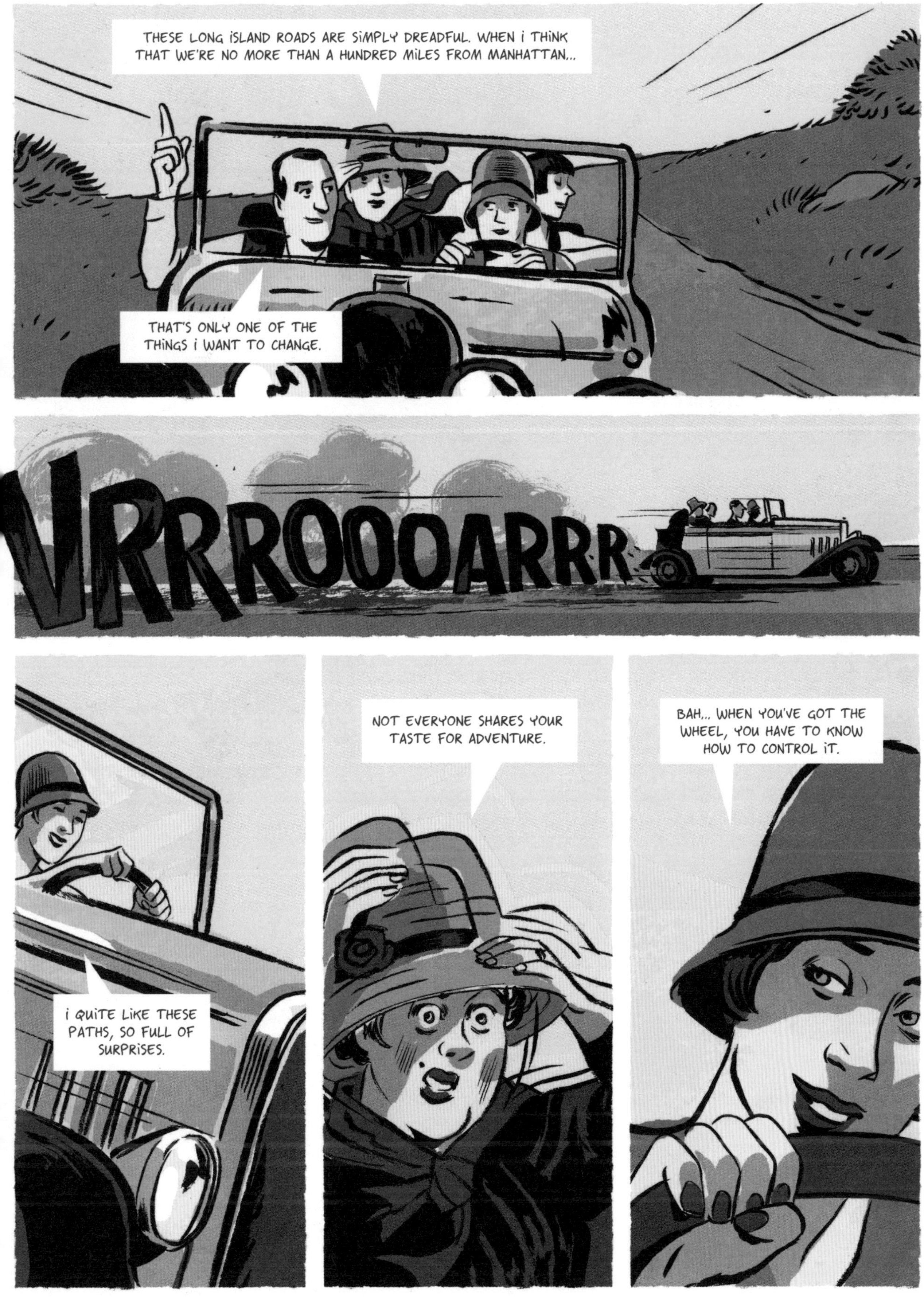
THESE LONG ISLAND ROADS ARE SIMPLY DREADFUL. WHEN I THINK THAT WE'RE NO MORE THAN A HUNDRED MILES FROM MANHATTAN...
THAT'S ONLY ONE OF THE THINGS I WANT TO CHANGE.
VRRROOOARRR
I QUITE LIKE THESE PATHS, SO FULL OF SURPRISES.
NOT EVERYONE SHARES YOUR TASTE FOR ADVENTURE.
BAH... WHEN YOU'VE GOT THE WHEEL, YOU HAVE TO KNOW HOW TO CONTROL IT.

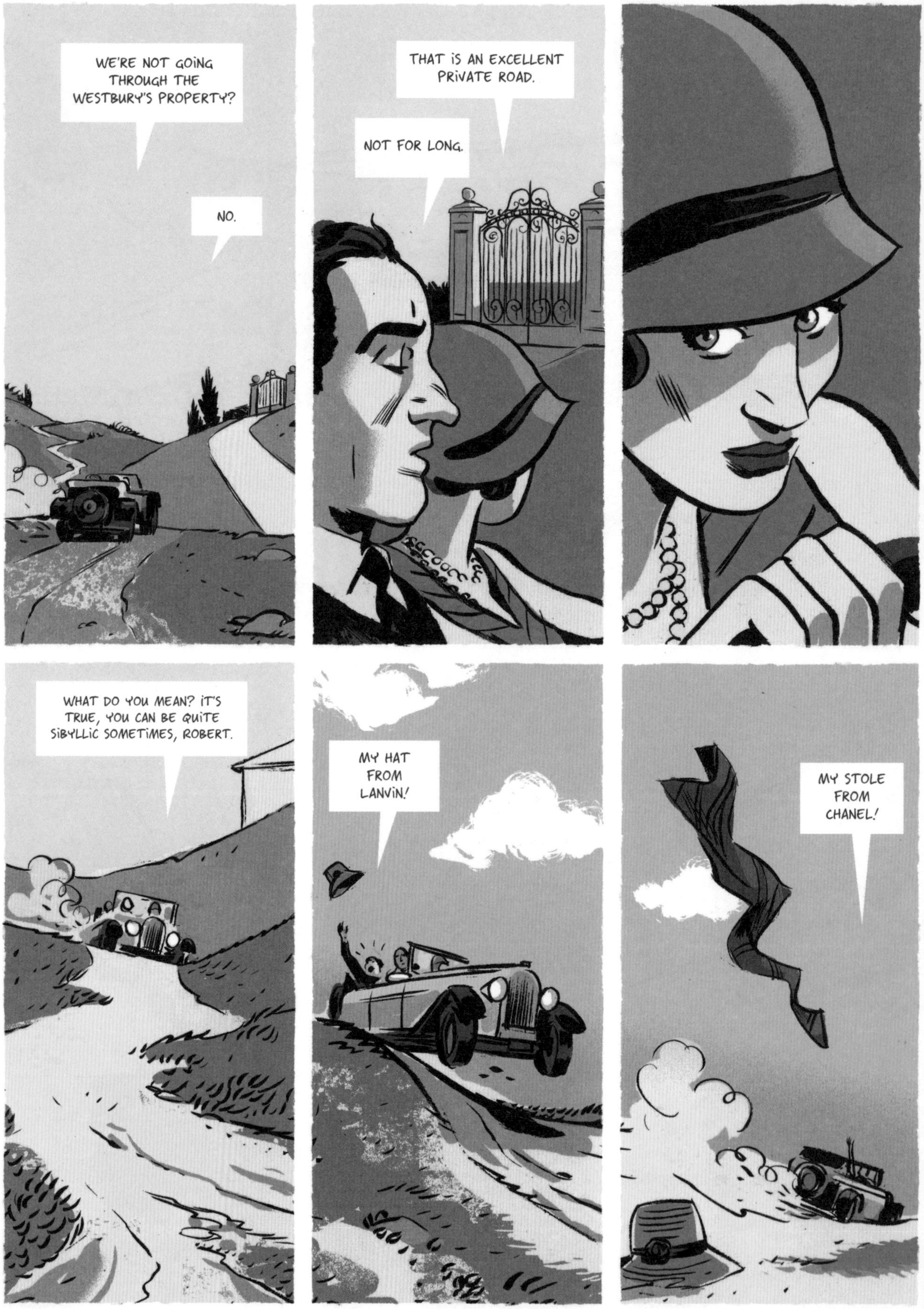
WE'RE NOT GOING THROUGH THE WESTBURY'S PROPERTY?
NO.
THAT IS AN EXCELLENT PRIVATE ROAD.
NOT FOR LONG.
WHAT DO YOU MEAN? IT'S TRUE, YOU CAN BE QUITE SIBYLLIC SOMETIMES, ROBERT.
MY HAT FROM LANVIN!
MY STOLE FROM CHANEL!

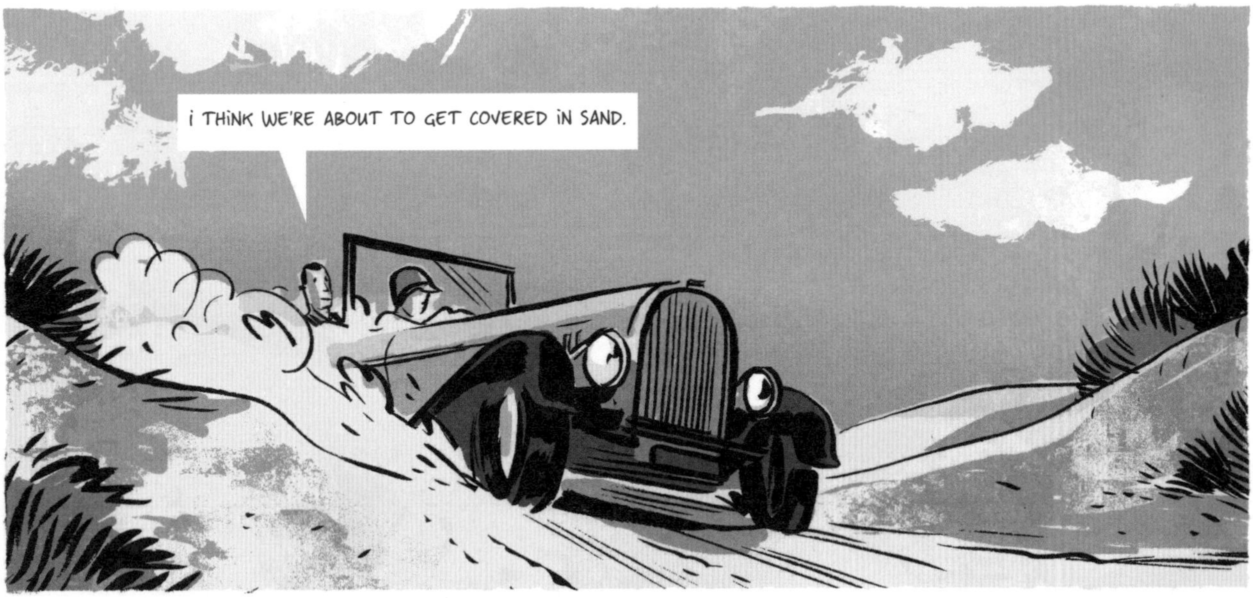
i THINK WE'RE ABOUT TO GET COVERED iN SAND.

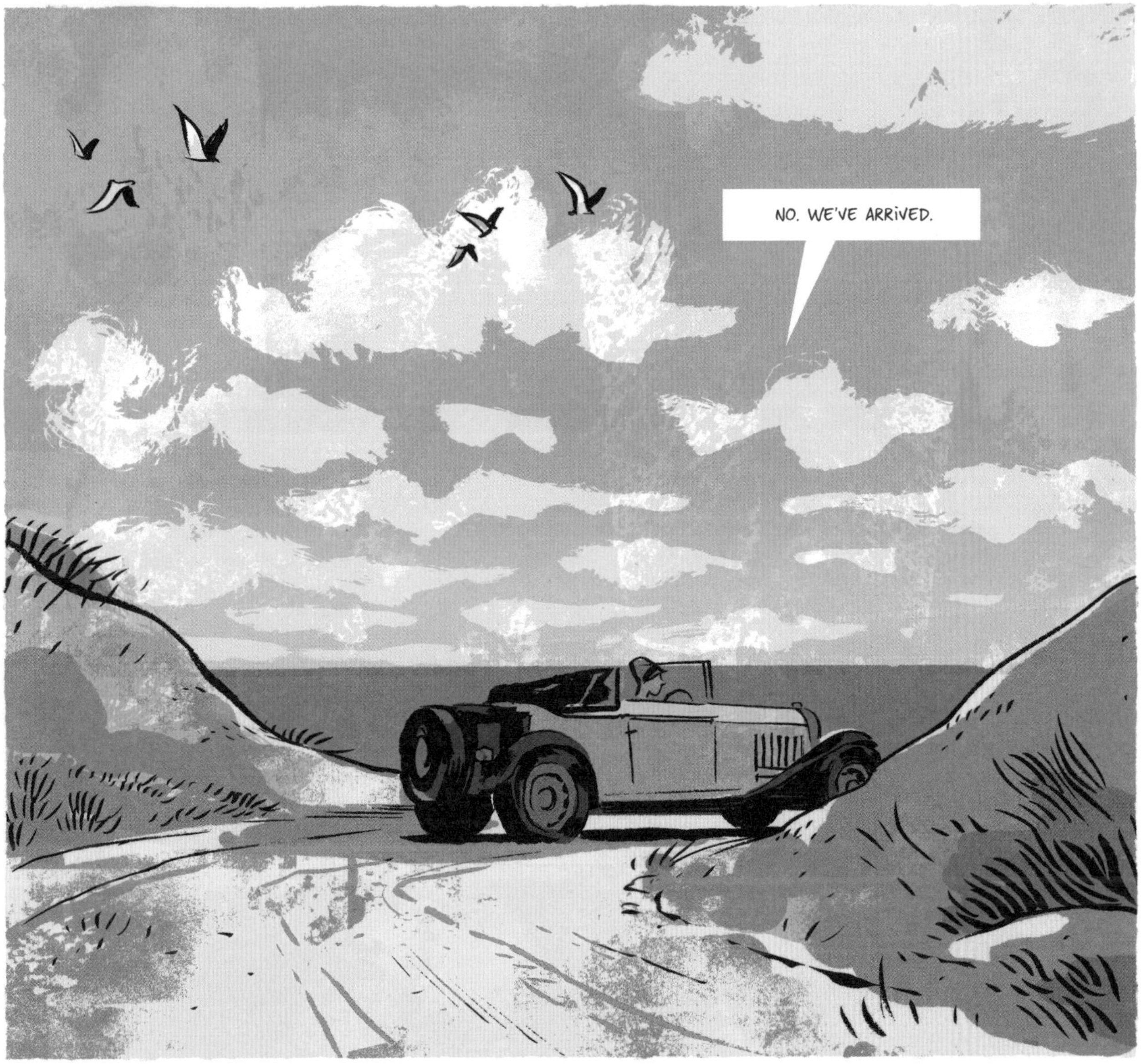
NO. WE'VE ARRiVED.

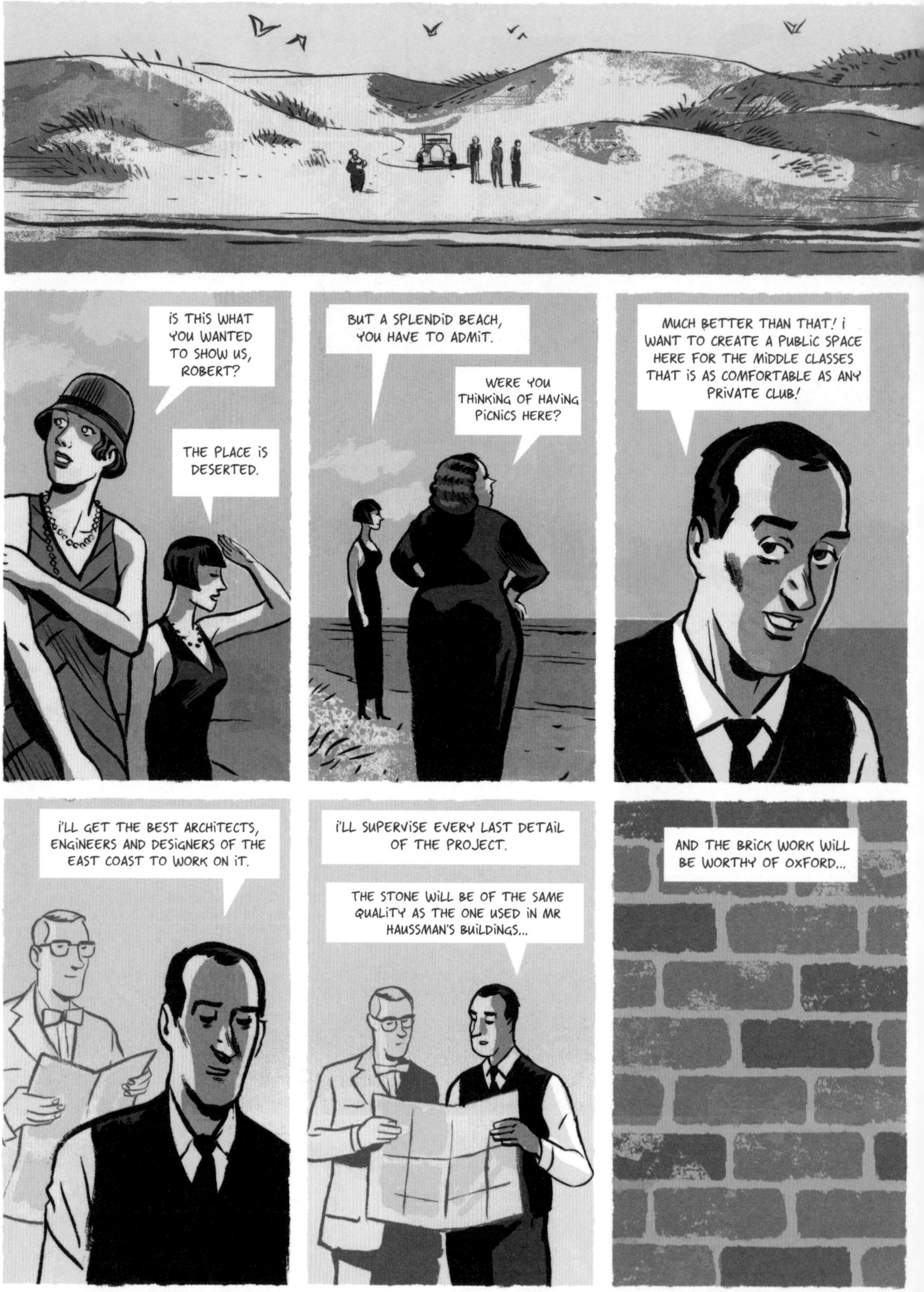
IS THIS WHAT YOU WANTED TO SHOW US, ROBERT?
THE PLACE IS DESERTED.
BUT A SPLENDID BEACH, YOU HAVE TO ADMIT.
WERE YOU THINKING OF HAVING PICNICS HERE?
MUCH BETTER THAN THAT! I WANT TO CREATE A PUBLIC SPACE HERE FOR THE MIDDLE CLASSES THAT IS AS COMFORTABLE AS ANY PRIVATE CLUB!
I'LL GET THE BEST ARCHITECTS, ENGINEERS AND DESIGNERS OF THE EAST COAST TO WORK ON IT.
I'LL SUPERVISE EVERY LAST DETAIL OF THE PROJECT.
THE STONE WILL BE OF THE SAME QUALITY AS THE ONE USED IN MR HAUSSMAN'S BUILDINGS...
AND THE BRICK WORK WILL BE WORTHY OF OXFORD...

THE MARBLE WILL BE AS BEAUTIFUL AS THAT OF A GREEK TEMPLE...

THE MOSAICS AS CAREFULLY LAID AS IN THE ORIENT...

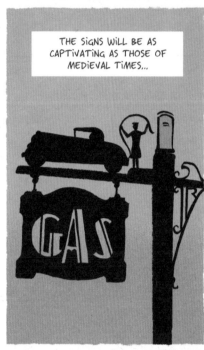

THE SIGNS WILL BE AS CAPTIVATING AS THOSE OF MEDIEVAL TIMES...

THE PUBLIC CONVENIENCES SUPERIOR TO THE ANCIENT THERMAL BATHS...

I'LL BUILD A MARITIME THEATRE FACING THE SEA...

AND THE WATER TOWERS WILL EVOKE THE TOWERS OF A TUSCAN CITYSCAPE...

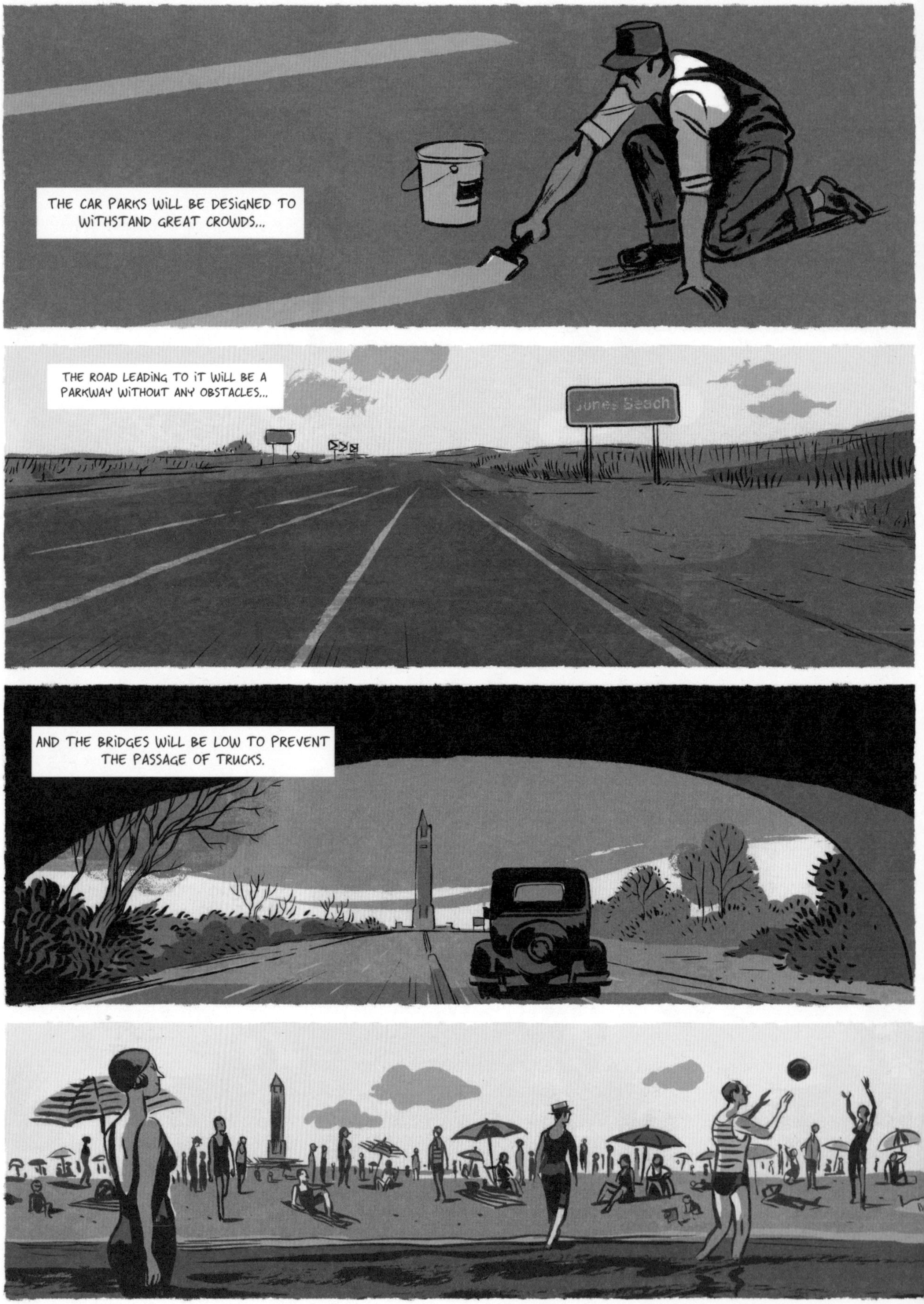
THE CAR PARKS WILL BE DESIGNED TO WITHSTAND GREAT CROWDS...
THE ROAD LEADING TO IT WILL BE A PARKWAY WITHOUT ANY OBSTACLES...
Jones Beach
AND THE BRIDGES WILL BE LOW TO PREVENT THE PASSAGE OF TRUCKS.

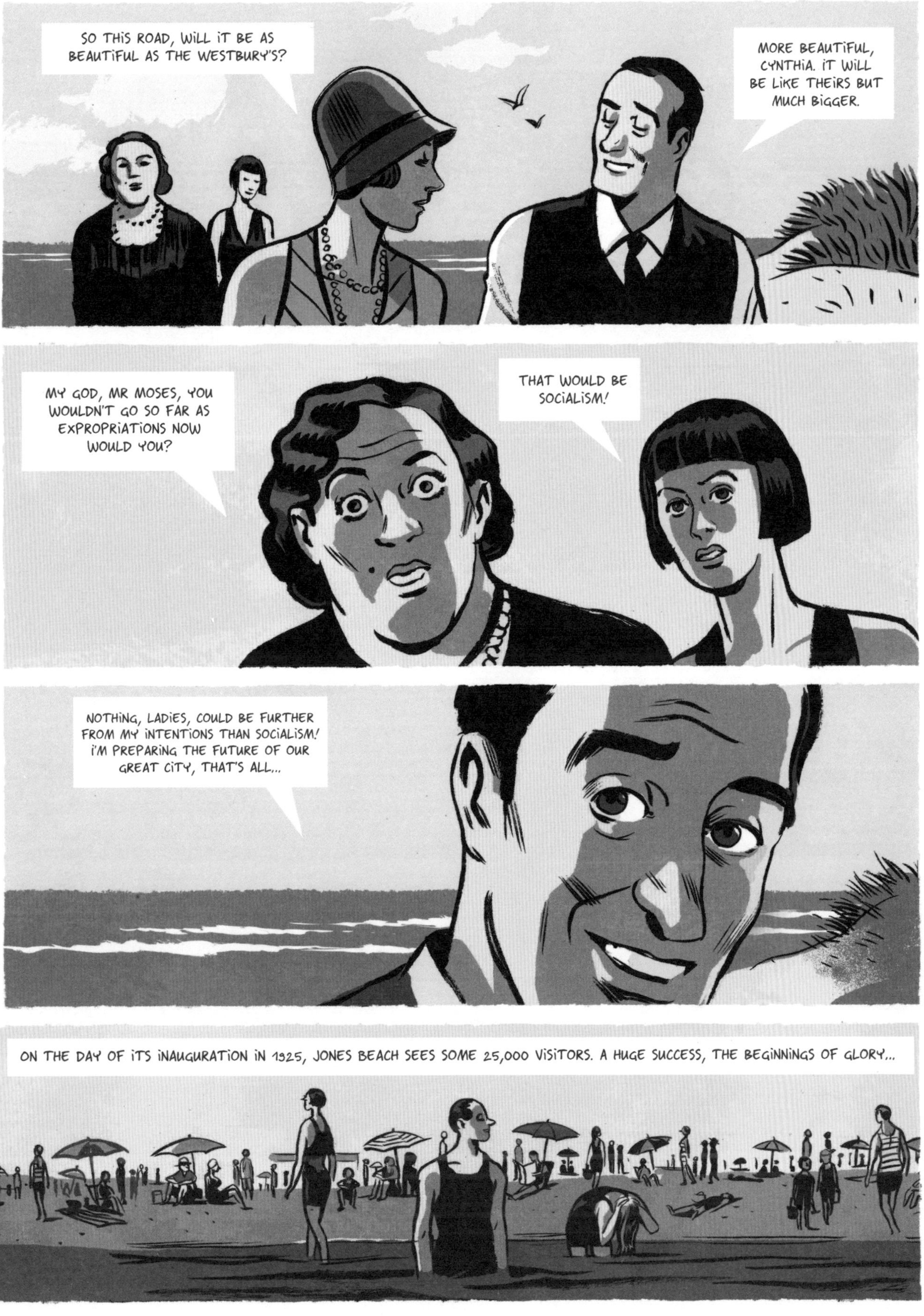

SO THIS ROAD, WILL IT BE AS BEAUTIFUL AS THE WESTBURY'S?
MORE BEAUTIFUL, CYNTHIA. IT WILL BE LIKE THEIRS BUT MUCH BIGGER.
MY GOD, MR MOSES, YOU WOULDN'T GO SO FAR AS EXPROPRIATIONS NOW WOULD YOU?
THAT WOULD BE SOCIALISM!
NOTHING, LADIES, COULD BE FURTHER FROM MY INTENTIONS THAN SOCIALISM! I'M PREPARING THE FUTURE OF OUR GREAT CITY, THAT'S ALL...
ON THE DAY OF ITS INAUGURATION IN 1925, JONES BEACH SEES SOME 25,000 VISITORS. A HUGE SUCCESS, THE BEGINNINGS OF GLORY...

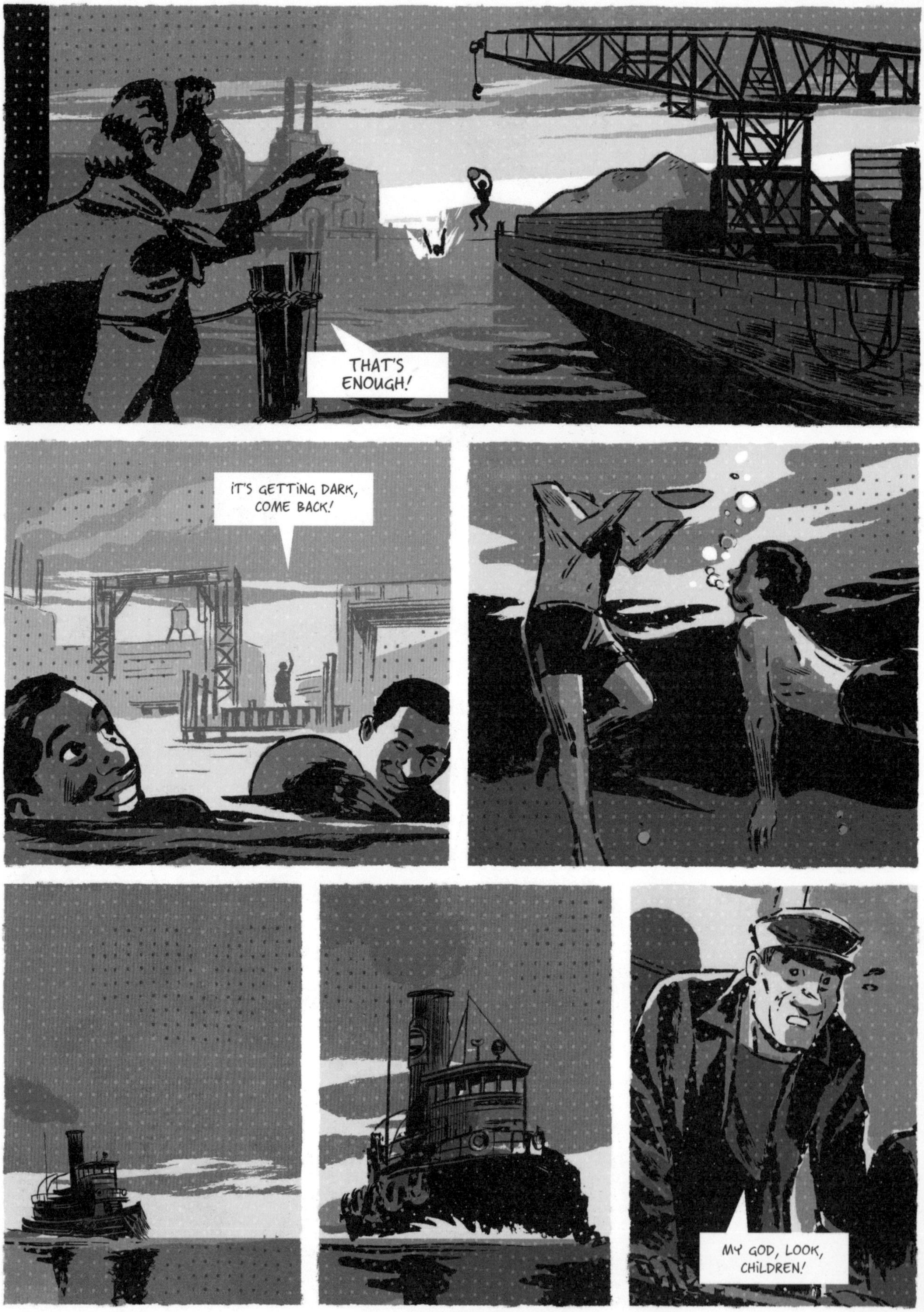
THAT'S ENOUGH!
IT'S GETTING DARK, COME BACK!
MY GOD, LOOK, CHILDREN!

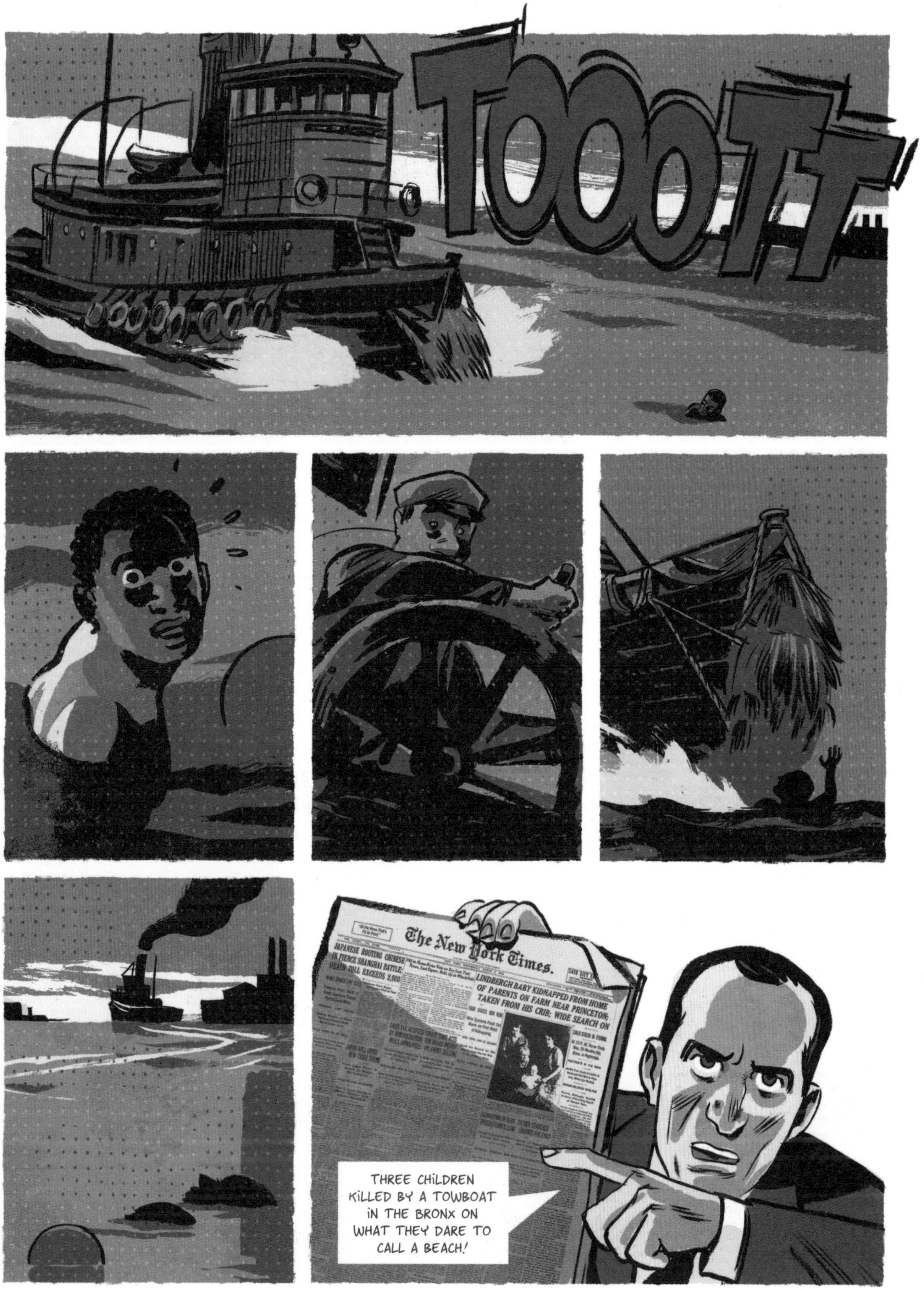
TOOOTT
The New York Times.
JAPANESE ROUTING CHINESE IN FIERCE SHANGHAI BATTLE; DEATH TOLL EXCEEDS 2,000
LINDBERGH BABY KIDNAPPED FROM HOME OF PARENTS ON FARM NEAR PRINCETON; TAKEN FROM HIS CRIB; WIDE SEARCH ON
THREE CHILDREN KILLED BY A TOWBOAT IN THE BRONX ON WHAT THEY DARE TO CALL A BEACH!

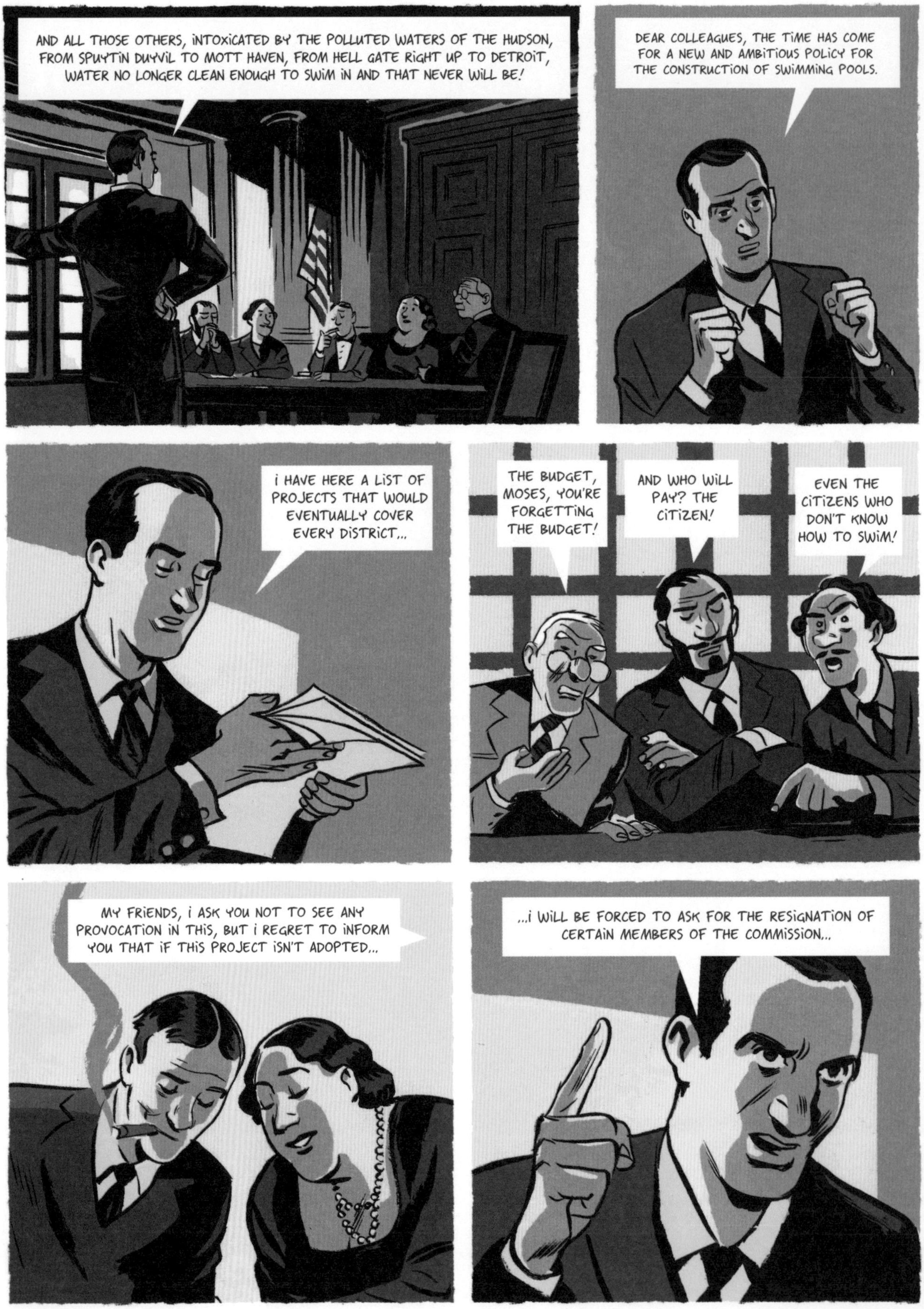
AND ALL THOSE OTHERS, INTOXICATED BY THE POLLUTED WATERS OF THE HUDSON, FROM SPUYTIN DUYVIL TO MOTT HAVEN, FROM HELL GATE RIGHT UP TO DETROIT, WATER NO LONGER CLEAN ENOUGH TO SWIM IN AND THAT NEVER WILL BE!
DEAR COLLEAGUES, THE TIME HAS COME FOR A NEW AND AMBITIOUS POLICY FOR THE CONSTRUCTION OF SWIMMING POOLS.
I HAVE HERE A LIST OF PROJECTS THAT WOULD EVENTUALLY COVER EVERY DISTRICT...
THE BUDGET, MOSES, YOU'RE FORGETTING THE BUDGET!
AND WHO WILL PAY? THE CITIZEN!
EVEN THE CITIZENS WHO DON'T KNOW HOW TO SWIM!
MY FRIENDS, I ASK YOU NOT TO SEE ANY PROVOCATION IN THIS, BUT I REGRET TO INFORM YOU THAT IF THIS PROJECT ISN'T ADOPTED...
...I WILL BE FORCED TO ASK FOR THE RESIGNATION OF CERTAIN MEMBERS OF THE COMMISSION...

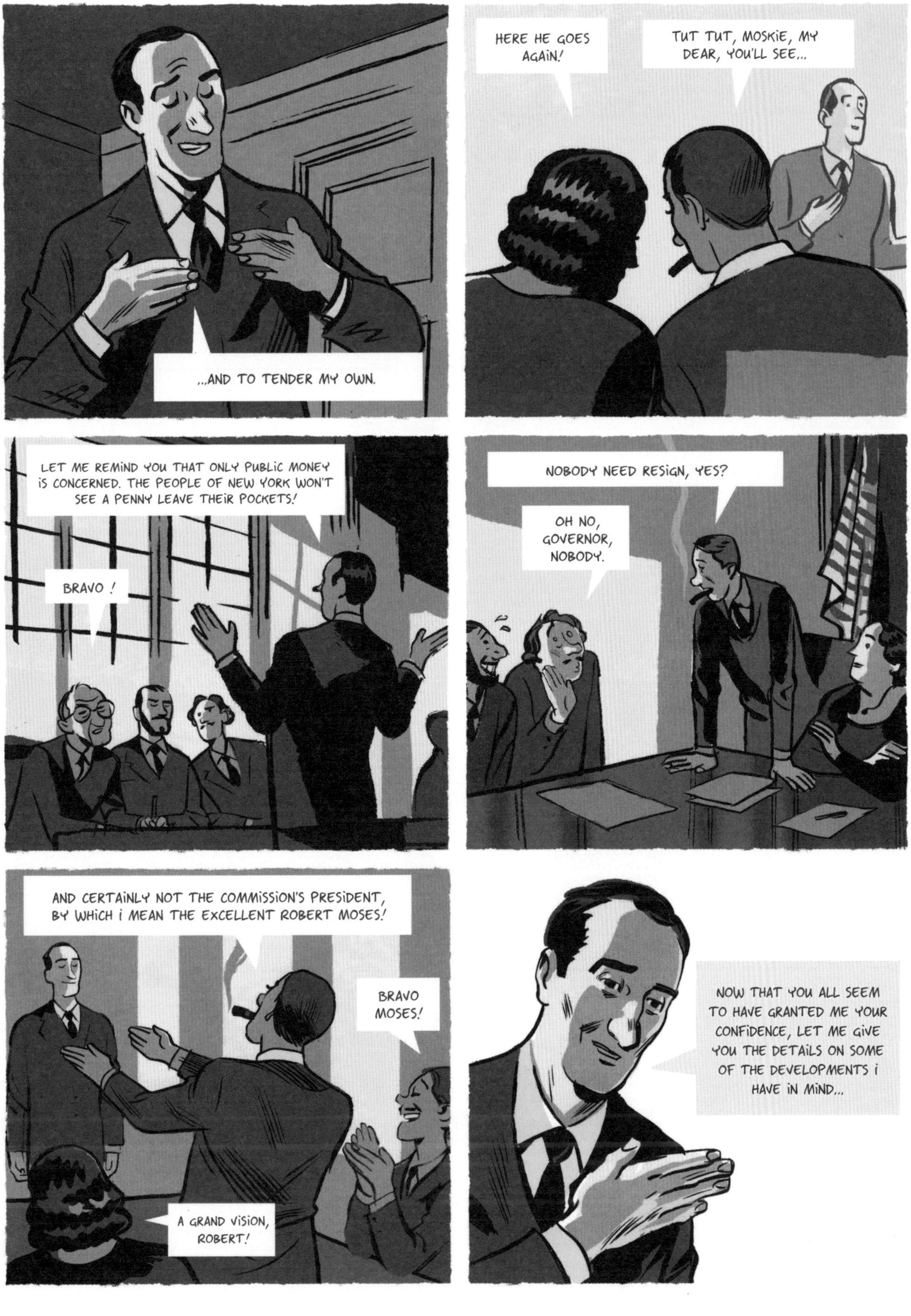
...AND TO TENDER MY OWN.
HERE HE GOES AGAIN!
TUT TUT, MOSKIE, MY DEAR, YOU'LL SEE...
LET ME REMIND YOU THAT ONLY PUBLIC MONEY IS CONCERNED. THE PEOPLE OF NEW YORK WON'T SEE A PENNY LEAVE THEIR POCKETS!
BRAVO !
NOBODY NEED RESIGN, YES?
OH NO, GOVERNOR, NOBODY.
AND CERTAINLY NOT THE COMMISSION'S PRESIDENT, BY WHICH I MEAN THE EXCELLENT ROBERT MOSES!
BRAVO MOSES!
A GRAND VISION, ROBERT!
NOW THAT YOU ALL SEEM TO HAVE GRANTED ME YOUR CONFIDENCE, LET ME GIVE YOU THE DETAILS ON SOME OF THE DEVELOPMENTS I HAVE IN MIND...

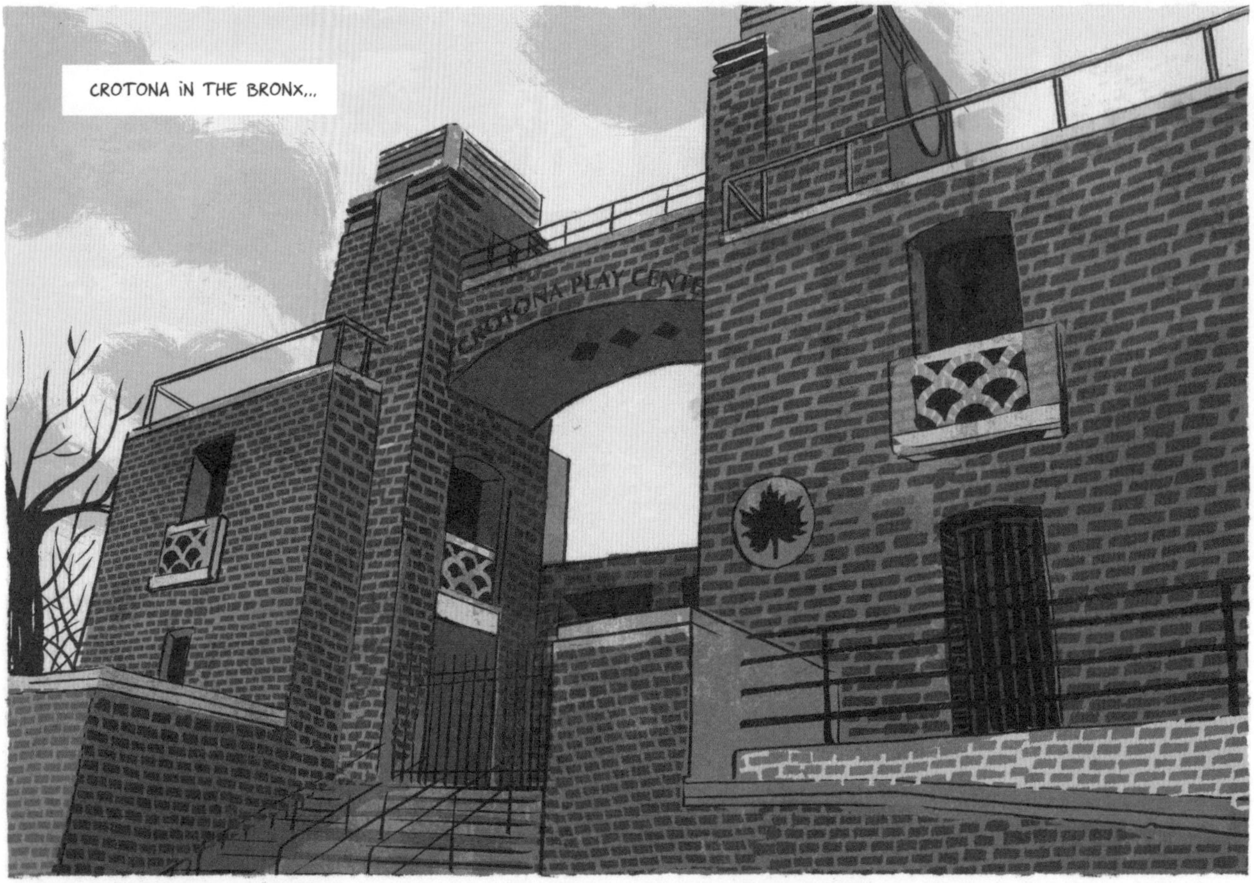
CROTONA iN THE BRONX...
CROTONA PLAY CENTE

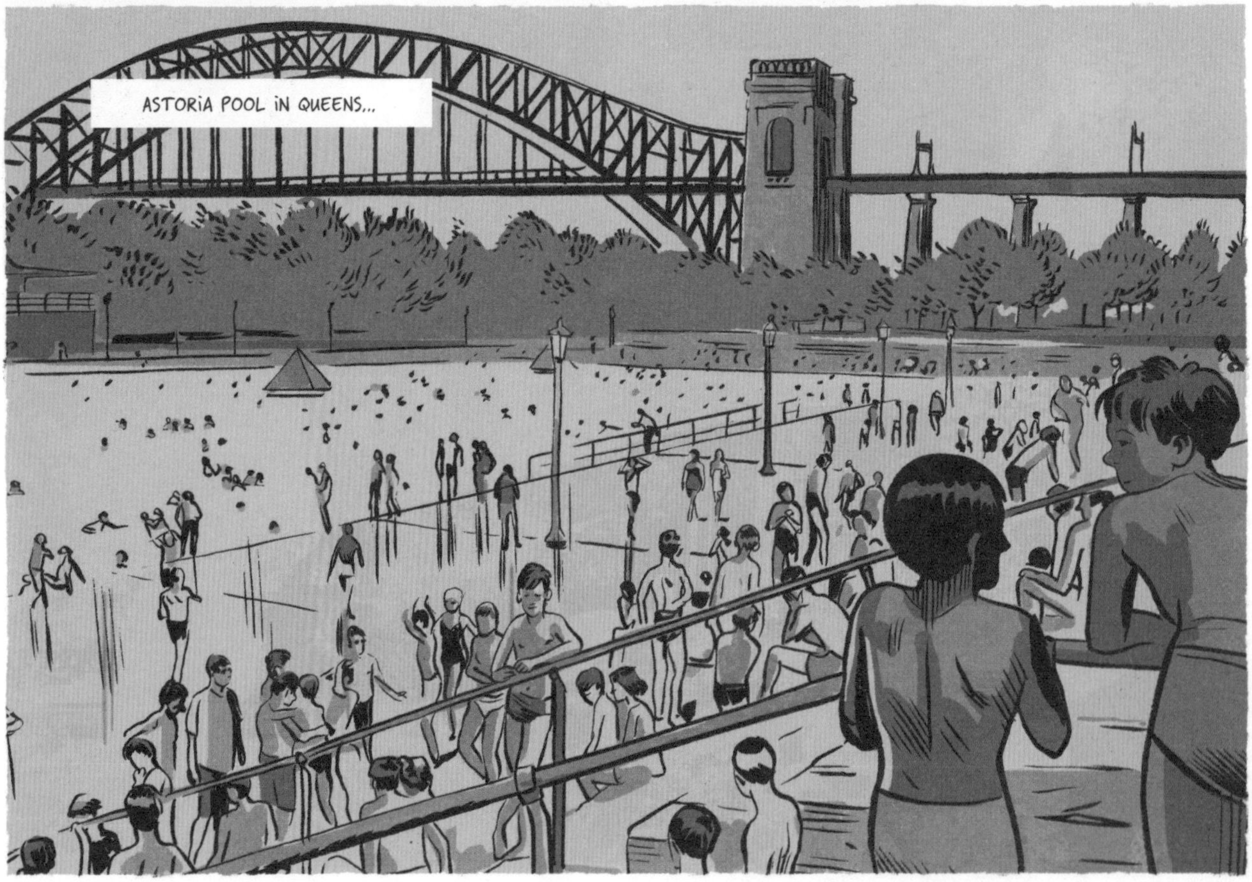
ASTORiA POOL iN QUEENS...

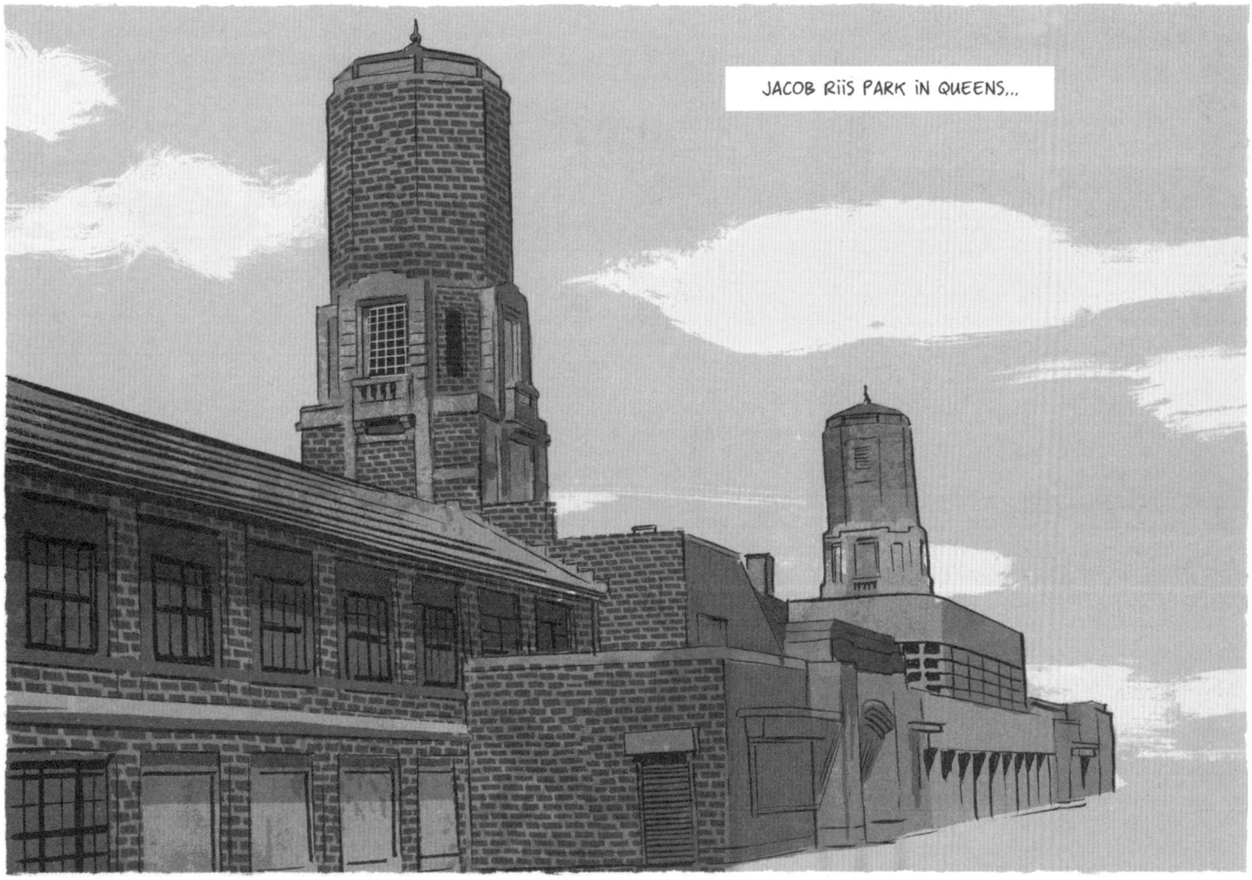
JACOB RIIS PARK IN QUEENS...

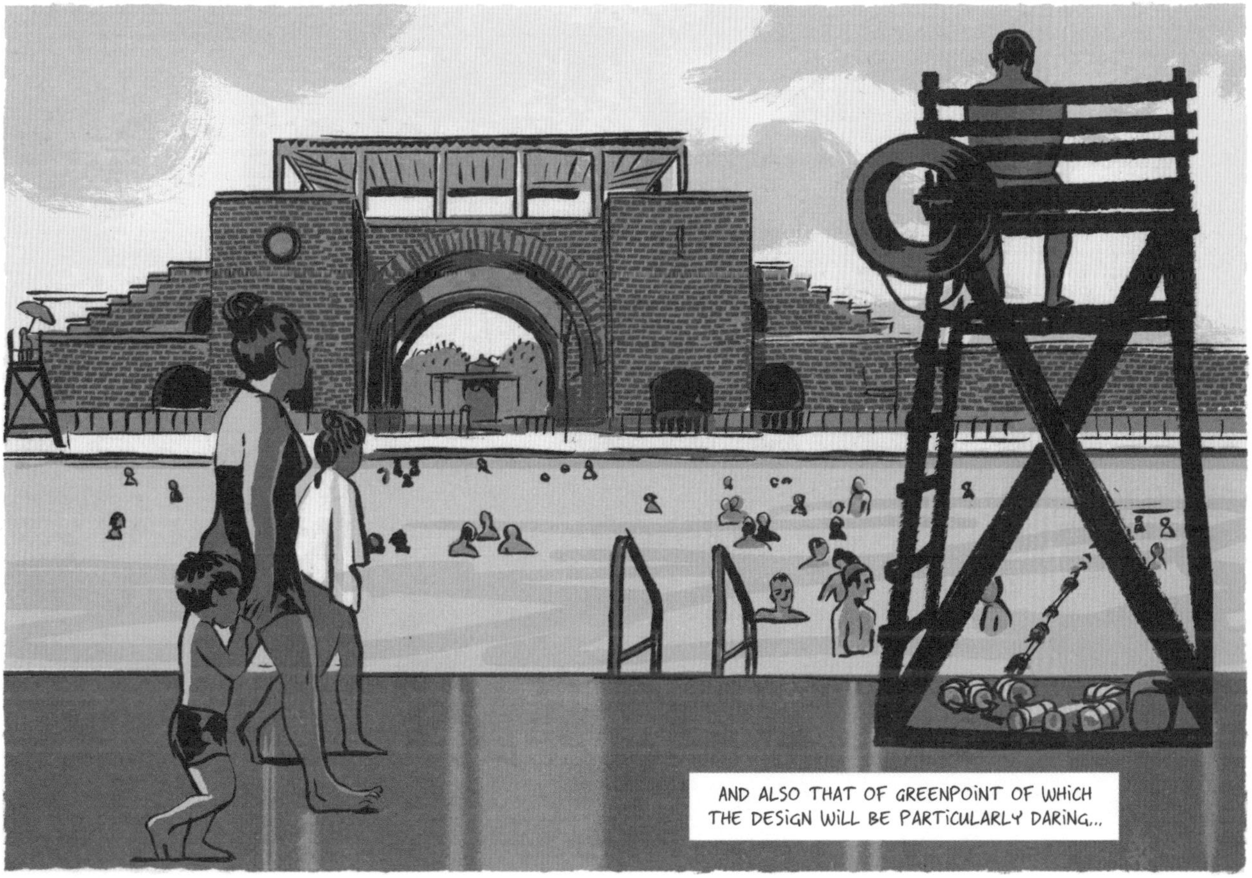
AND ALSO THAT OF GREENPOINT OF WHICH THE DESIGN WILL BE PARTICULARLY DARING...

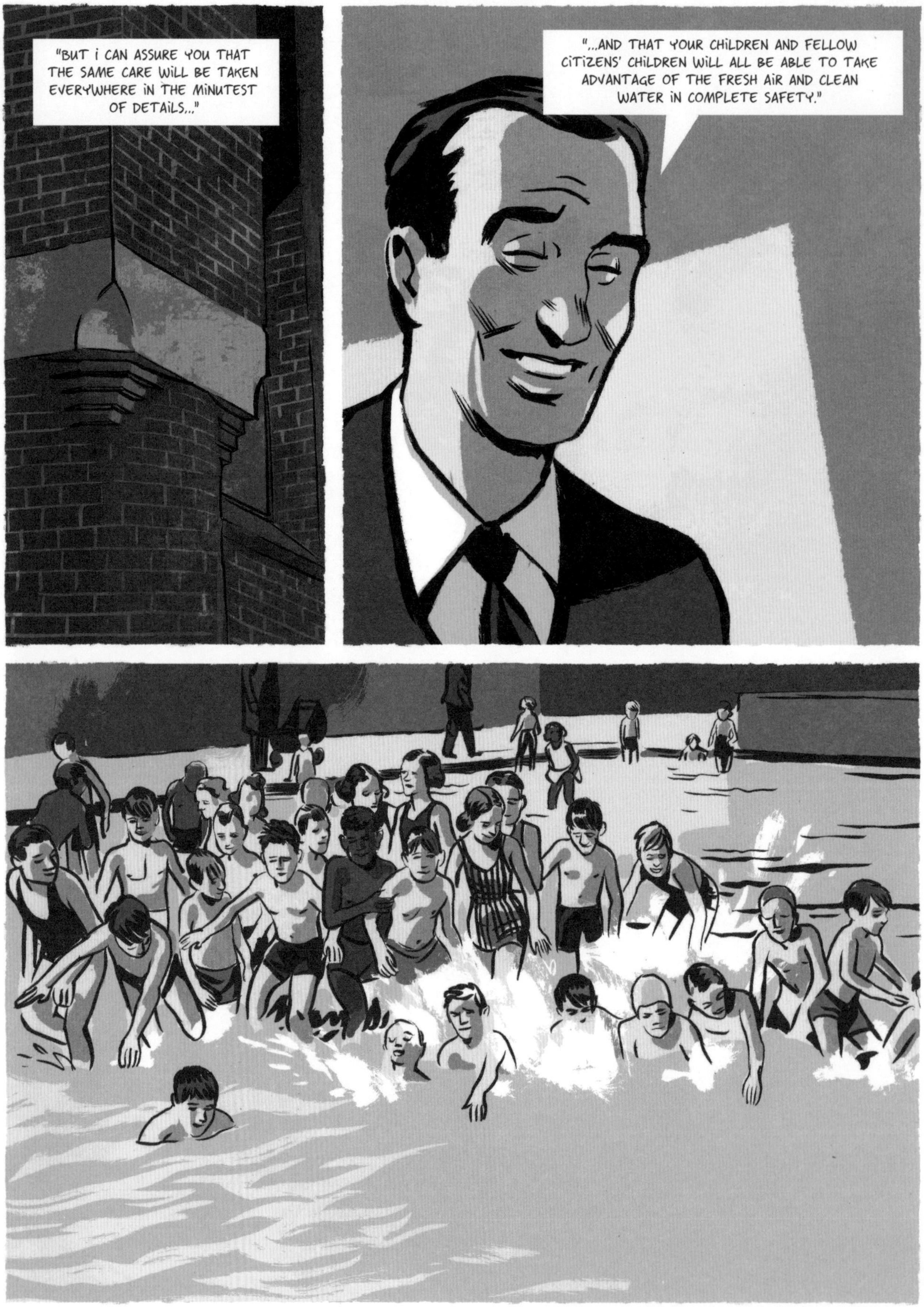
"BUT i CAN ASSURE YOU THAT THE SAME CARE WiLL BE TAKEN EVERYWHERE iN THE MiNUTEST OF DETAiLS..."
"...AND THAT YOUR CHiLDREN AND FELLOW CiTiZENS' CHiLDREN WiLL ALL BE ABLE TO TAKE ADVANTAGE OF THE FRESH AiR AND CLEAN WATER iN COMPLETE SAFETY."

# CHAPTER 3
## *The building machine*

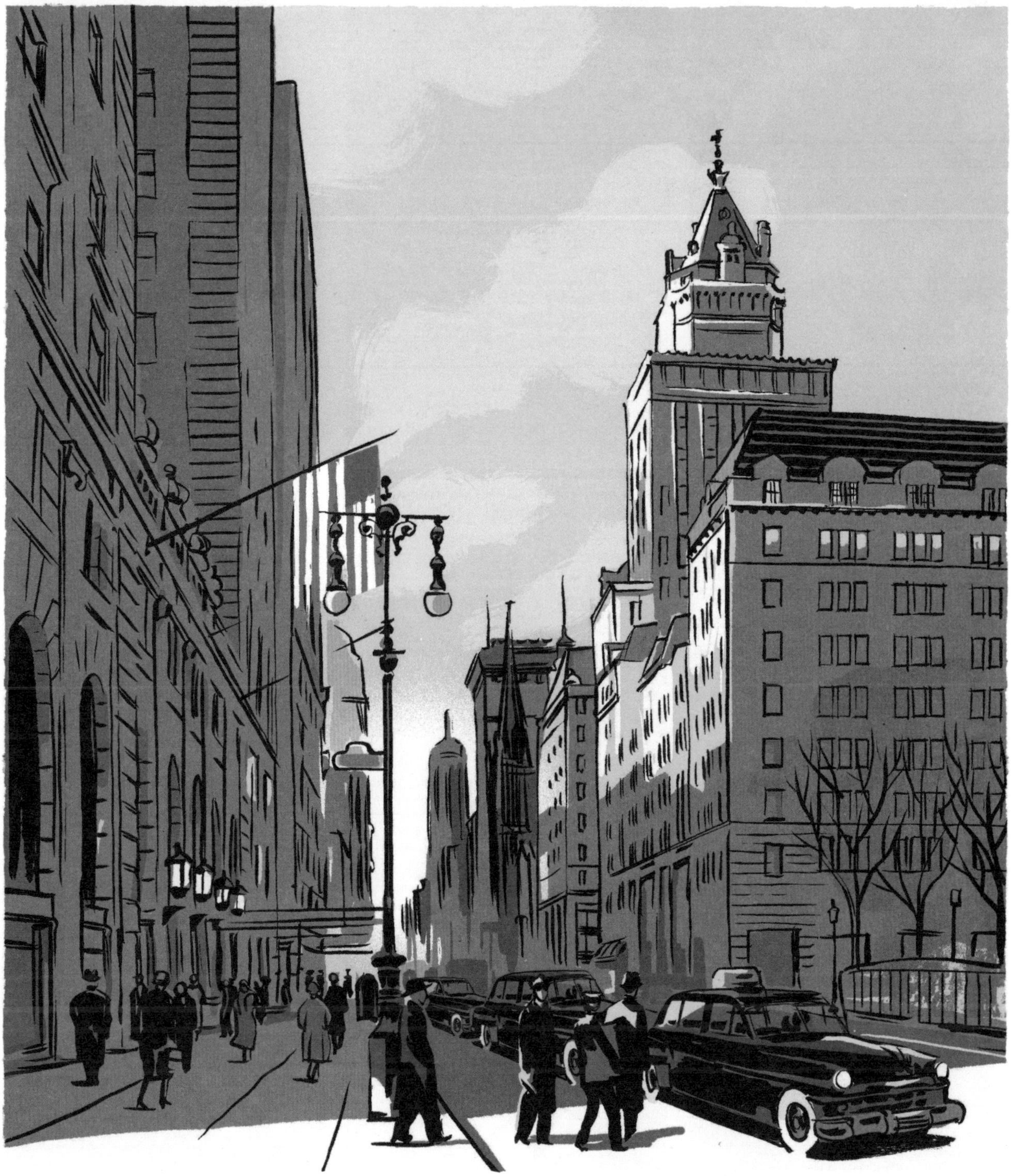

SIR, WHAT ARE WE DOING EXACTLY?
WORKING, YOUNG MAN.
ROBERT MOSES MOVES FROM SITE TO SITE AND WE ARE TO FOLLOW HIM.
AND IN THE OTHER CARS?
CRAW
ENGINEERS LIKE MYSELF, ARCHITECTS LIKE YOU, URBAN PLANNERS, FINANCIERS, ENTREPRENEURS...
AND THEY'RE ALL WORKING ON DIFFERENT PROJECTS?
THAT'S RIGHT, MY YOUNG FRIEND. DID YOU KNOW THAT AT THIS VERY MOMENT 80,000 PEOPLE ARE WORKING FOR MR MOSES IN THE STATE OF NEW YORK?
OK, THE BOSS IS FINISHED WITH OUR COLLEAGUE IN CHARGE OF THE PRELIMINARY STUDIES OF BRONX-WHITESTONE BRIDGE.

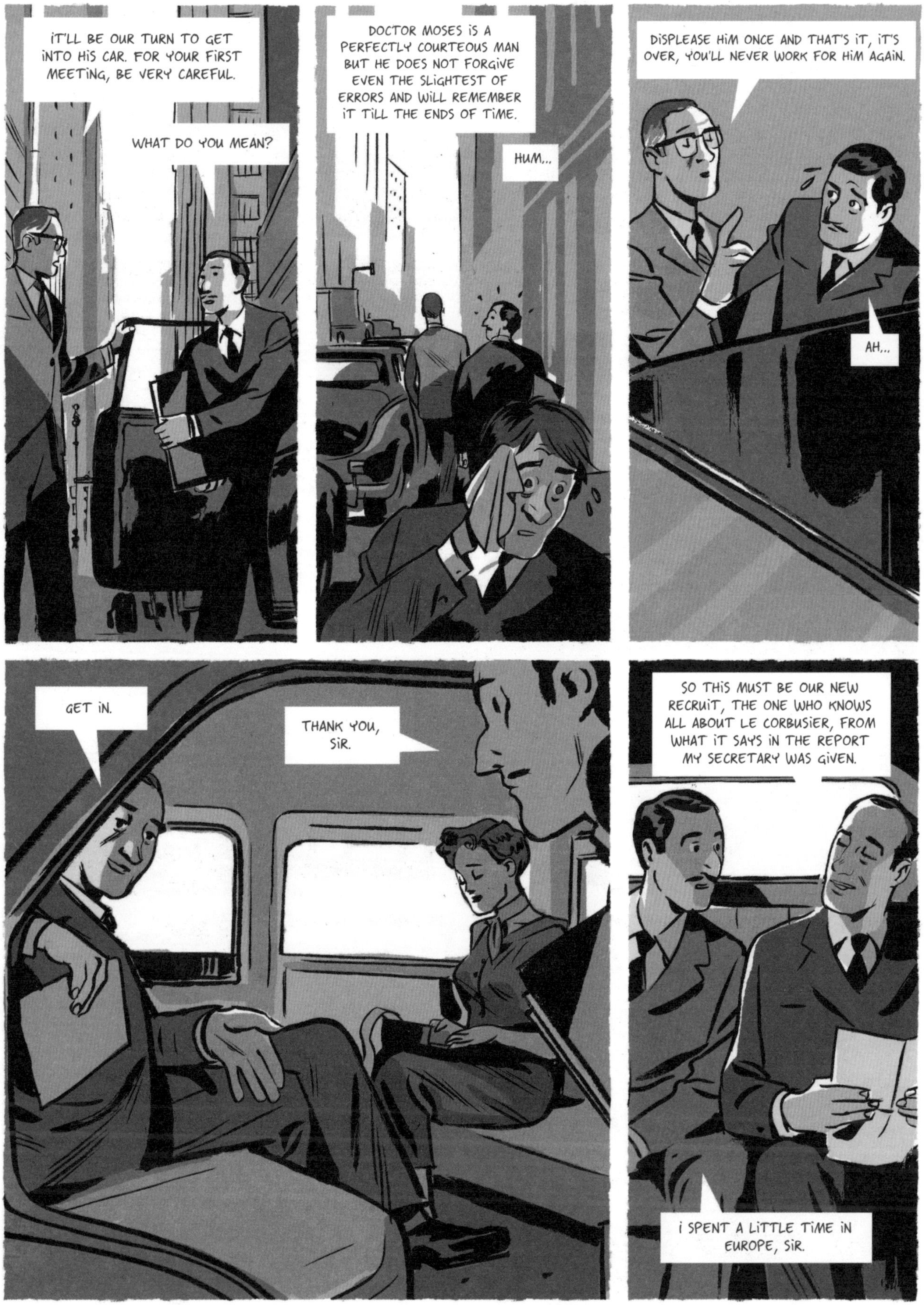
IT'LL BE OUR TURN TO GET INTO HIS CAR. FOR YOUR FIRST MEETING, BE VERY CAREFUL.
WHAT DO YOU MEAN?
DOCTOR MOSES IS A PERFECTLY COURTEOUS MAN BUT HE DOES NOT FORGIVE EVEN THE SLIGHTEST OF ERRORS AND WILL REMEMBER IT TILL THE ENDS OF TIME.
HUM...
DISPLEASE HIM ONCE AND THAT'S IT, IT'S OVER, YOU'LL NEVER WORK FOR HIM AGAIN.
AH...
GET IN.
THANK YOU, SIR.
SO THIS MUST BE OUR NEW RECRUIT, THE ONE WHO KNOWS ALL ABOUT LE CORBUSIER, FROM WHAT IT SAYS IN THE REPORT MY SECRETARY WAS GIVEN.
I SPENT A LITTLE TIME IN EUROPE, SIR.

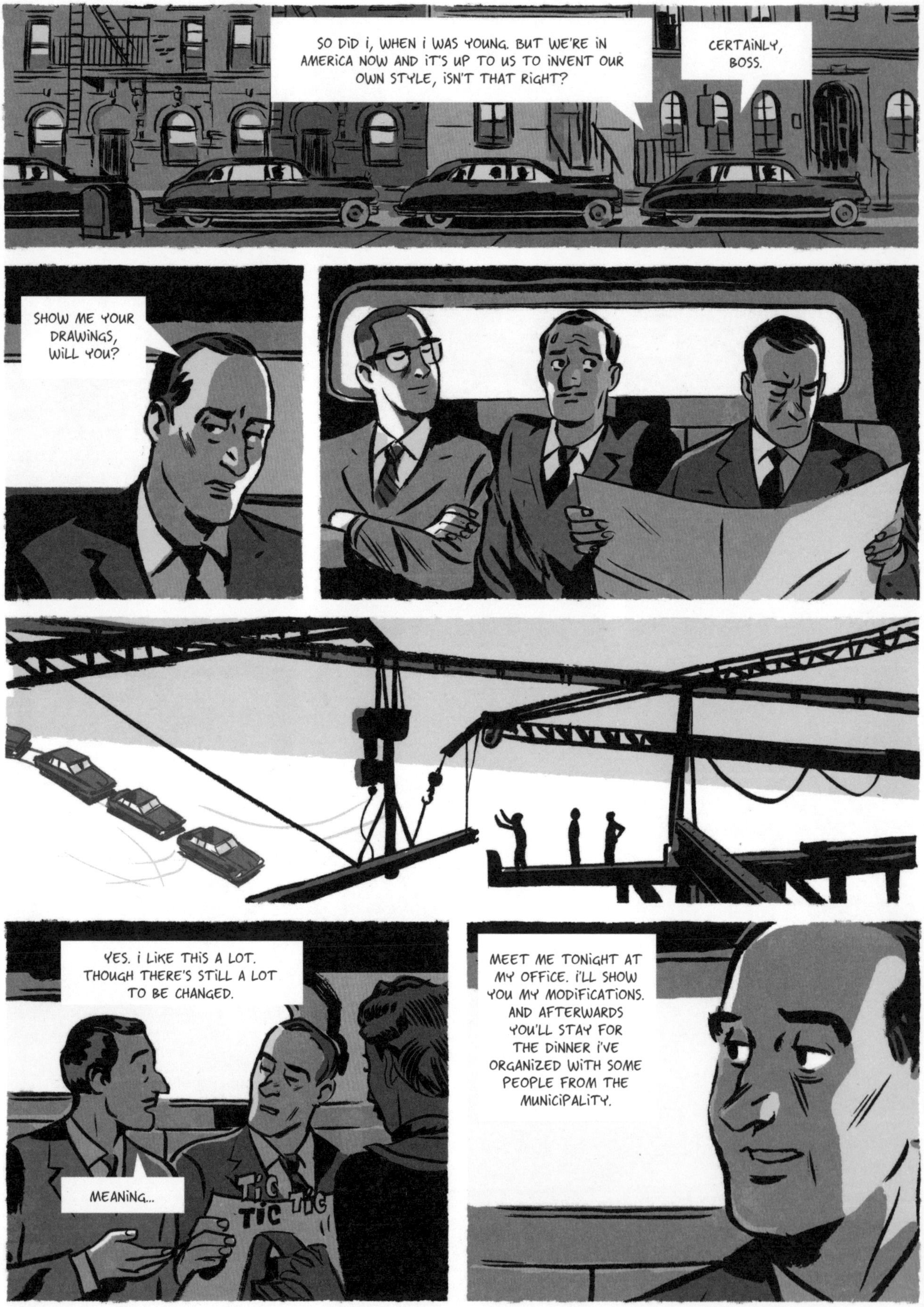
SO DID I, WHEN I WAS YOUNG. BUT WE'RE IN AMERICA NOW AND IT'S UP TO US TO INVENT OUR OWN STYLE, ISN'T THAT RIGHT?
CERTAINLY, BOSS.
SHOW ME YOUR DRAWINGS, WILL YOU?
YES. I LIKE THIS A LOT. THOUGH THERE'S STILL A LOT TO BE CHANGED.
MEANING...
TIC TIC TIC
MEET ME TONIGHT AT MY OFFICE. I'LL SHOW YOU MY MODIFICATIONS. AND AFTERWARDS YOU'LL STAY FOR THE DINNER I'VE ORGANIZED WITH SOME PEOPLE FROM THE MUNICIPALITY.

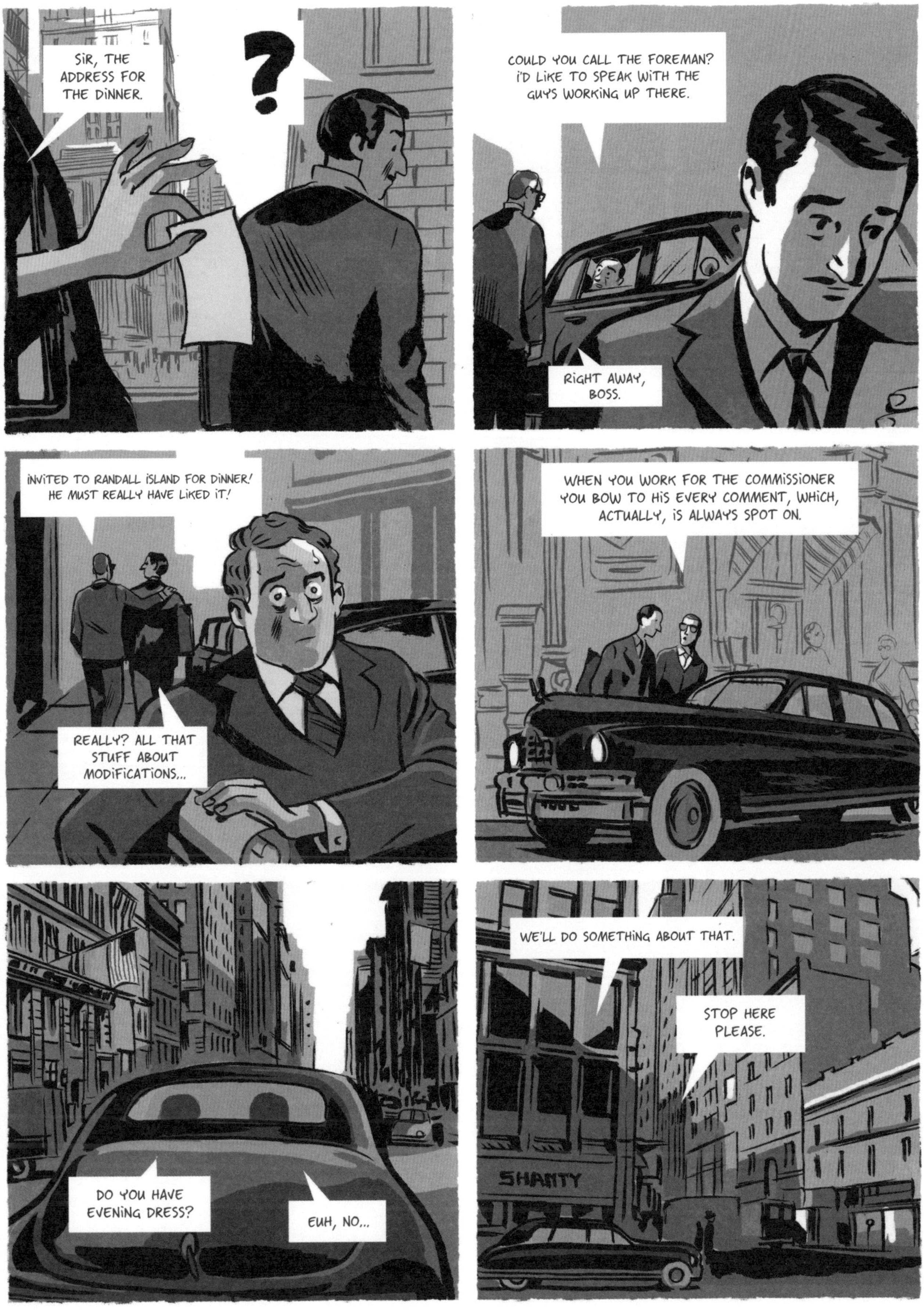
SIR, THE ADDRESS FOR THE DINNER.
?
COULD YOU CALL THE FOREMAN? I'D LIKE TO SPEAK WITH THE GUYS WORKING UP THERE.
RIGHT AWAY, BOSS.
INVITED TO RANDALL ISLAND FOR DINNER! HE MUST REALLY HAVE LIKED IT!
REALLY? ALL THAT STUFF ABOUT MODIFICATIONS...
WHEN YOU WORK FOR THE COMMISSIONER YOU BOW TO HIS EVERY COMMENT, WHICH, ACTUALLY, IS ALWAYS SPOT ON.
DO YOU HAVE EVENING DRESS?
EUH, NO...
WE'LL DO SOMETHING ABOUT THAT.
STOP HERE PLEASE.
SHANTY

TAILORING
FORMAL WEAR RENTAL
SHOEMART
REPAIR
DRESS
PUBLIC BAR
MR MOSES NEVER RECEIVES GUESTS IN RESTAURANTS, ONLY EVER AT HIS, IN THE DINING ROOM OF ONE OF HIS MANY HEADQUARTERS.
BE WARNED, IT WILL BE VERY INTERESTING, BUT VERY FORMAL.
TRIBOROUGH BRIDGE AUTHORITY
IN THE BUILDING HIDDEN AT THE HEART OF HIS TRIBOROUGH INTERCHANGE, CENTRE OF THE MOSES EMPIRE, DECORUM ISN'T THE ONLY THING...

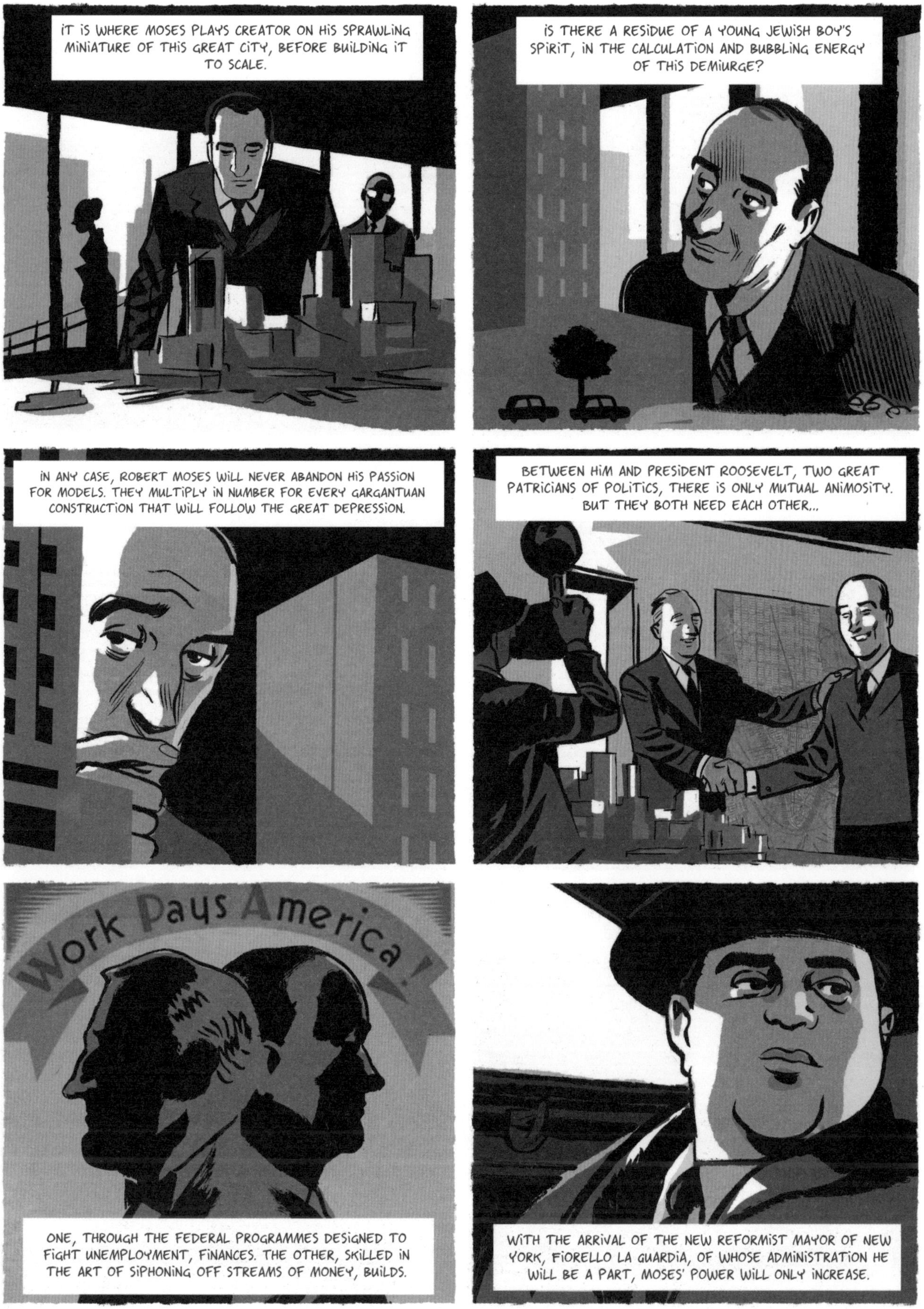
IT IS WHERE MOSES PLAYS CREATOR ON HIS SPRAWLING MINIATURE OF THIS GREAT CITY, BEFORE BUILDING IT TO SCALE.
IS THERE A RESIDUE OF A YOUNG JEWISH BOY'S SPIRIT, IN THE CALCULATION AND BUBBLING ENERGY OF THIS DEMIURGE?
IN ANY CASE, ROBERT MOSES WILL NEVER ABANDON HIS PASSION FOR MODELS. THEY MULTIPLY IN NUMBER FOR EVERY GARGANTUAN CONSTRUCTION THAT WILL FOLLOW THE GREAT DEPRESSION.
BETWEEN HIM AND PRESIDENT ROOSEVELT, TWO GREAT PATRICIANS OF POLITICS, THERE IS ONLY MUTUAL ANIMOSITY. BUT THEY BOTH NEED EACH OTHER...
Work Pays America!
ONE, THROUGH THE FEDERAL PROGRAMMES DESIGNED TO FIGHT UNEMPLOYMENT, FINANCES. THE OTHER, SKILLED IN THE ART OF SIPHONING OFF STREAMS OF MONEY, BUILDS.
WITH THE ARRIVAL OF THE NEW REFORMIST MAYOR OF NEW YORK, FIORELLO LA GUARDIA, OF WHOSE ADMINISTRATION HE WILL BE A PART, MOSES' POWER WILL ONLY INCREASE.

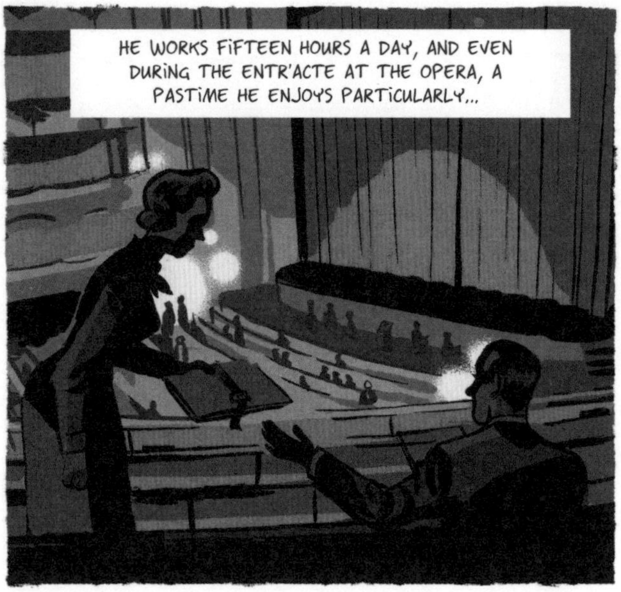
HE WORKS FIFTEEN HOURS A DAY, AND EVEN DURING THE ENTR'ACTE AT THE OPERA, A PASTIME HE ENJOYS PARTICULARLY...

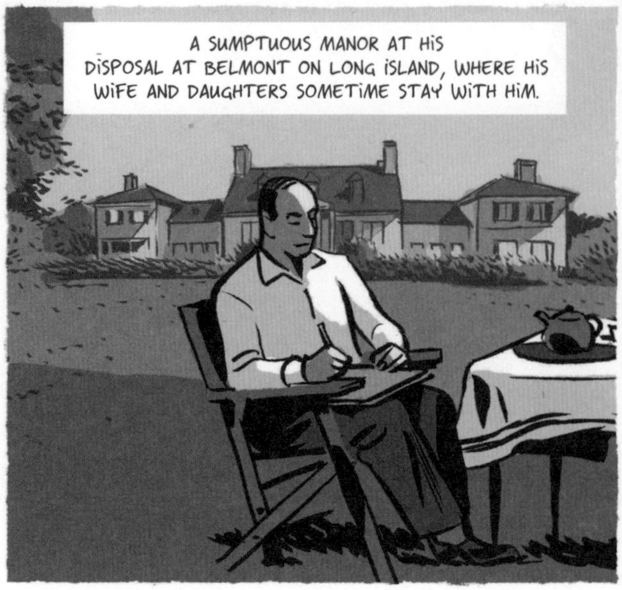
A SUMPTUOUS MANOR AT HIS DISPOSAL AT BELMONT ON LONG ISLAND, WHERE HIS WIFE AND DAUGHTERS SOMETIME STAY WITH HIM.

WHEN LEAVING A WORKPLACE, LATE AT NIGHT, HE LEAVES HIS COLLABORATORS A HUGE ENVELOPE OF TASKS...

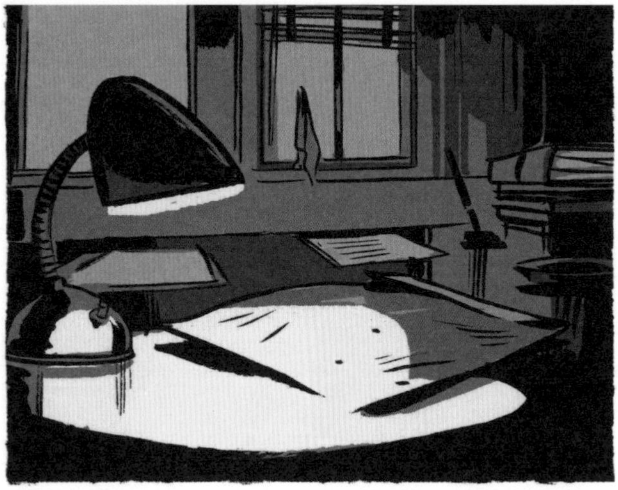

BUT HE CAN ALSO BE FOUND OUTSIDE OF THE MAYOR'S HOUSE IN NEW YORK AT DAWN, WITH ANOTHER ENVELOPE, FULL OF PAPERS TO BE SIGNED URGENTLY AND WITH, AS USUAL, THE THREAT OF RESIGNATION.

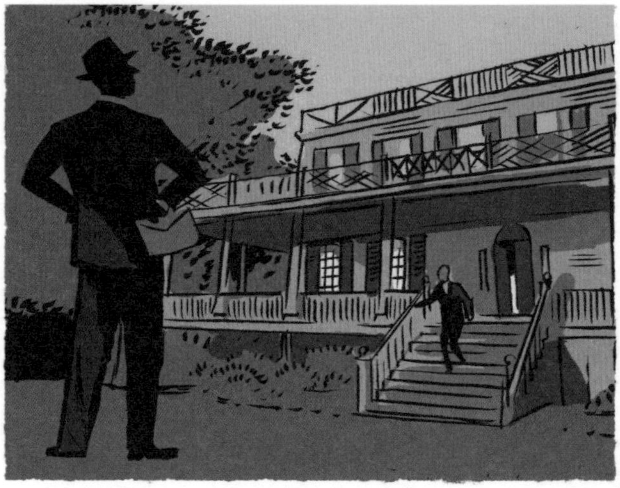

THIS IS NOT ONLY A MAN OF FILES, A CUNNING MANIPULATOR AND IMPECCABLE PLANNER, BUT ALSO HIS OWN BEST PR MACHINE...

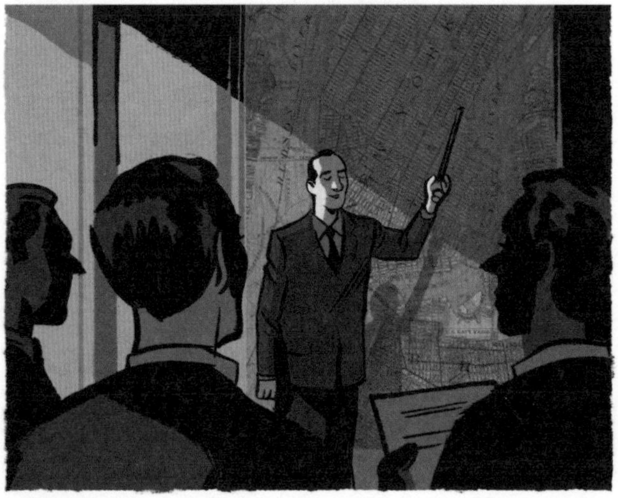

HE HAS LUXURIOUS PAMPHLETS PUBLISHED TO SHOW OFF HIS FUTURE PROJECTS AND IS ADORED BY THE PRESS, FOR WHICH HE IS A CONSTANT SOURCE OF NEWS...

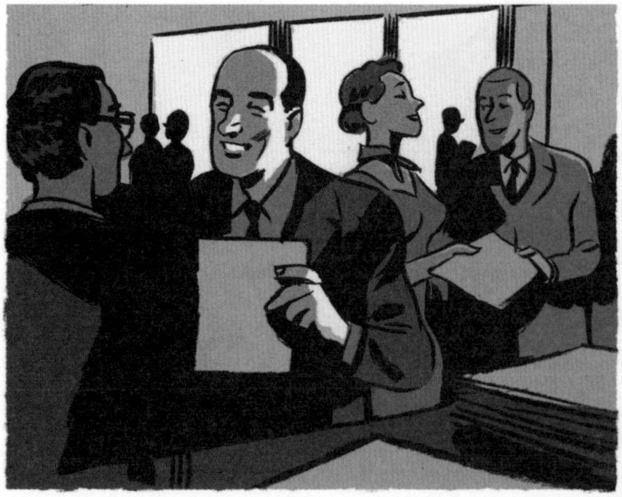

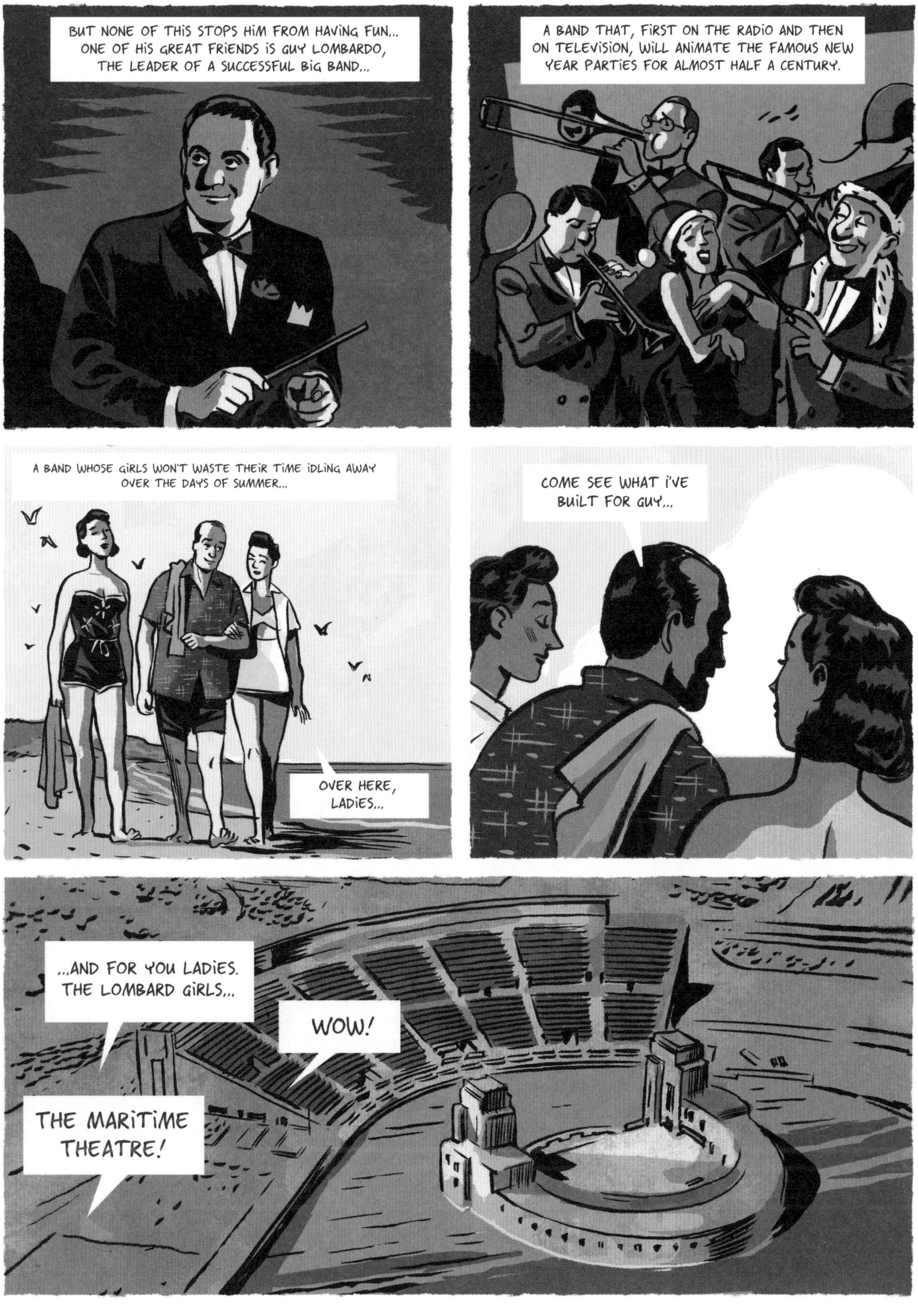
BUT NONE OF THIS STOPS HIM FROM HAVING FUN... ONE OF HIS GREAT FRIENDS IS GUY LOMBARDO, THE LEADER OF A SUCCESSFUL BIG BAND...
A BAND THAT, FIRST ON THE RADIO AND THEN ON TELEVISION, WILL ANIMATE THE FAMOUS NEW YEAR PARTIES FOR ALMOST HALF A CENTURY.
A BAND WHOSE GIRLS WON'T WASTE THEIR TIME IDLING AWAY OVER THE DAYS OF SUMMER...
OVER HERE, LADIES...
COME SEE WHAT I'VE BUILT FOR GUY...
...AND FOR YOU LADIES. THE LOMBARD GIRLS...
WOW!
THE MARITIME THEATRE!

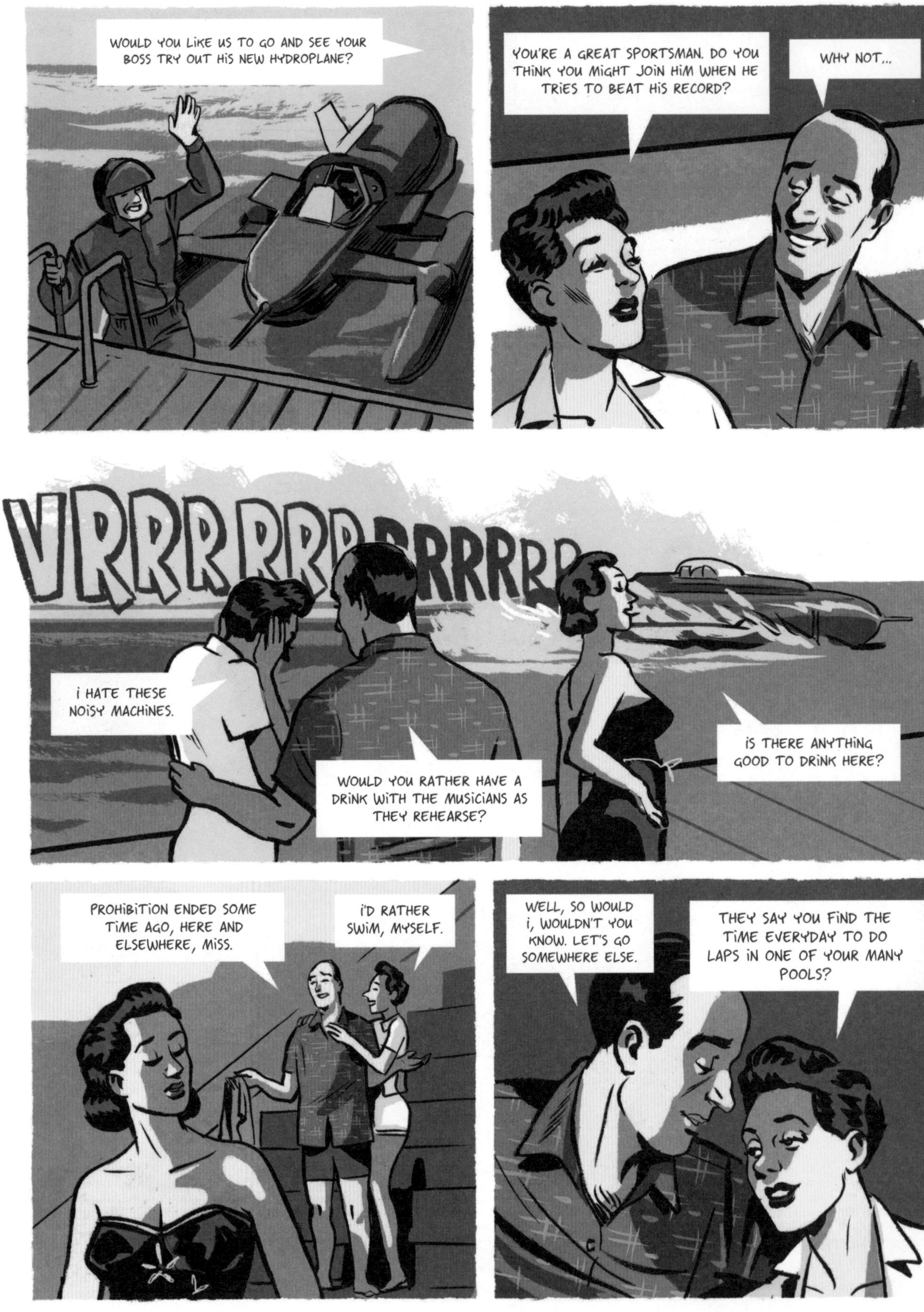

WOULD YOU LIKE US TO GO AND SEE YOUR BOSS TRY OUT HIS NEW HYDROPLANE?
YOU'RE A GREAT SPORTSMAN. DO YOU THINK YOU MIGHT JOIN HIM WHEN HE TRIES TO BEAT HIS RECORD?
WHY NOT...
VRRRRRRRRRRRR
I HATE THESE NOISY MACHINES.
WOULD YOU RATHER HAVE A DRINK WITH THE MUSICIANS AS THEY REHEARSE?
IS THERE ANYTHING GOOD TO DRINK HERE?
PROHIBITION ENDED SOME TIME AGO, HERE AND ELSEWHERE, MISS.
I'D RATHER SWIM, MYSELF.
WELL, SO WOULD I, WOULDN'T YOU KNOW. LET'S GO SOMEWHERE ELSE.
THEY SAY YOU FIND THE TIME EVERYDAY TO DO LAPS IN ONE OF YOUR MANY POOLS?

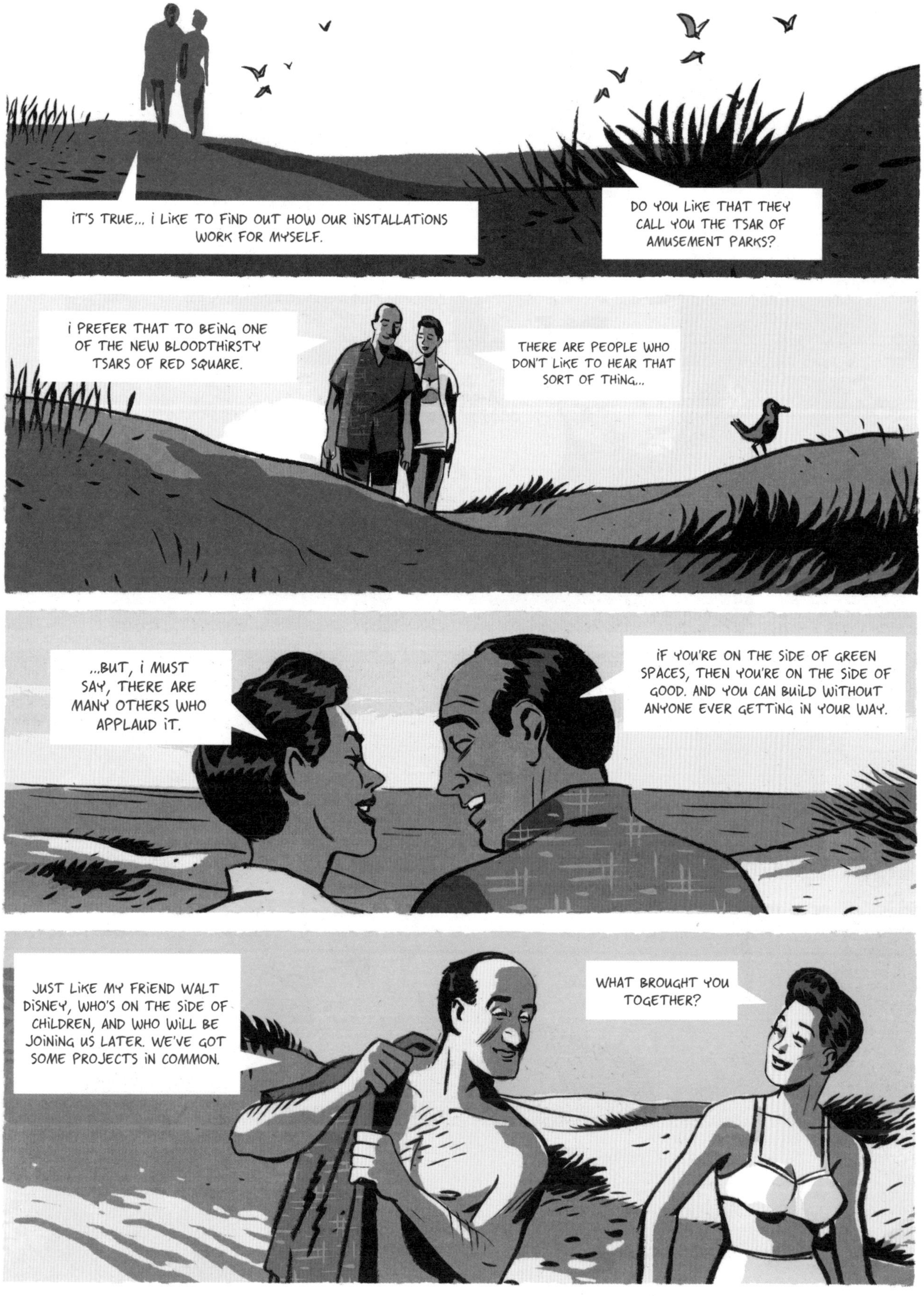

iT'S TRUE... i LiKE TO FiND OUT HOW OUR iNSTALLATiONS WORK FOR MYSELF.
DO YOU LiKE THAT THEY CALL YOU THE TSAR OF AMUSEMENT PARKS?
i PREFER THAT TO BEiNG ONE OF THE NEW BLOODTHiRSTY TSARS OF RED SQUARE.
THERE ARE PEOPLE WHO DON'T LiKE TO HEAR THAT SORT OF THiNG...
...BUT, i MUST SAY, THERE ARE MANY OTHERS WHO APPLAUD iT.
iF YOU'RE ON THE SiDE OF GREEN SPACES, THEN YOU'RE ON THE SiDE OF GOOD. AND YOU CAN BUiLD WiTHOUT ANYONE EVER GETTiNG iN YOUR WAY.
JUST LiKE MY FRiEND WALT DiSNEY, WHO'S ON THE SiDE OF CHiLDREN, AND WHO WiLL BE JOiNiNG US LATER. WE'VE GOT SOME PROJECTS iN COMMON.
WHAT BROUGHT YOU TOGETHER?

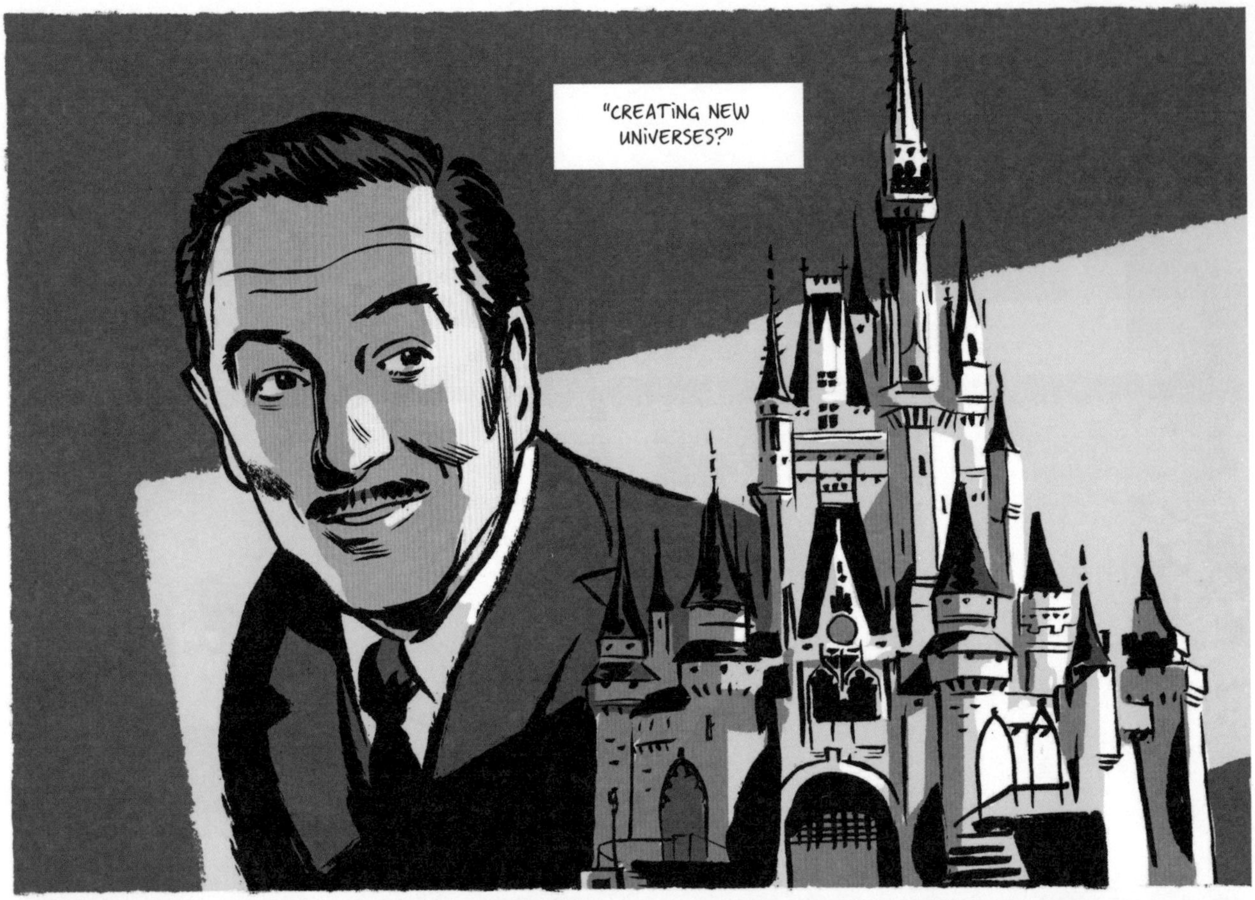
"CREATiNG NEW UNiVERSES?"

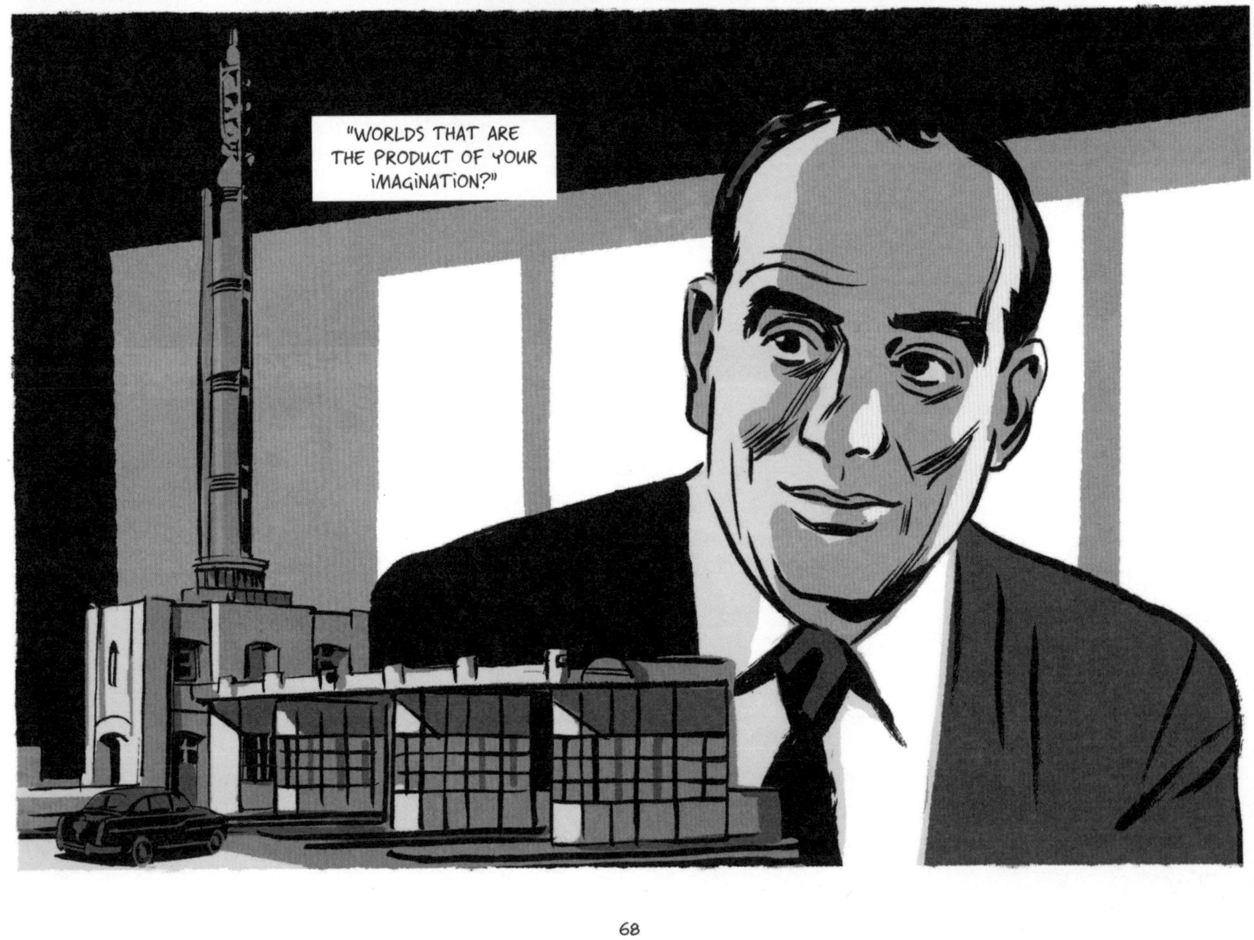
"WORLDS THAT ARE THE PRODUCT OF YOUR iMAGiNATiON?"

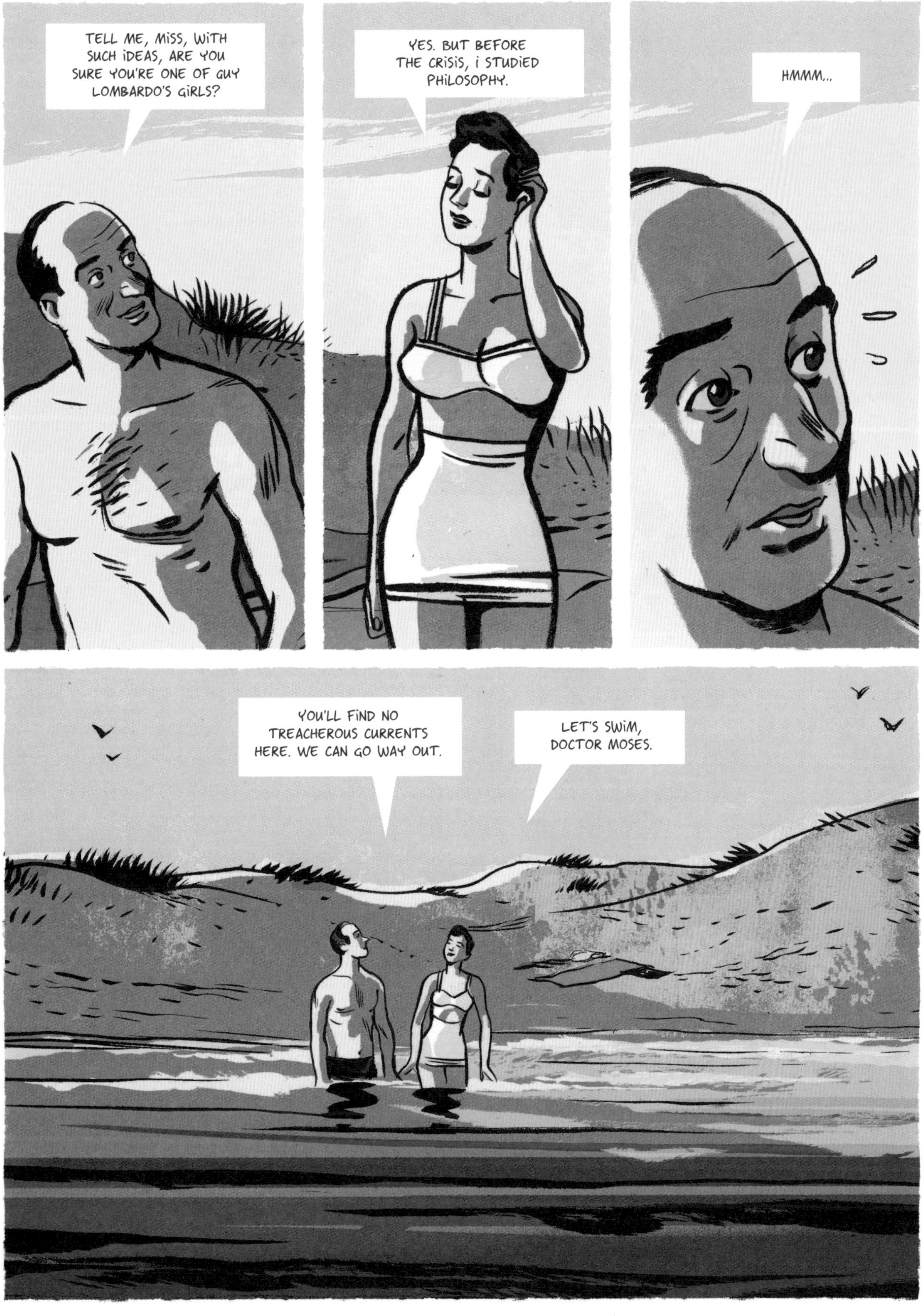
TELL ME, MISS, WITH SUCH IDEAS, ARE YOU SURE YOU'RE ONE OF GUY LOMBARDO'S GIRLS?
YES. BUT BEFORE THE CRISIS, I STUDIED PHILOSOPHY.
HMMM...
YOU'LL FIND NO TREACHEROUS CURRENTS HERE. WE CAN GO WAY OUT.
LET'S SWIM, DOCTOR MOSES.

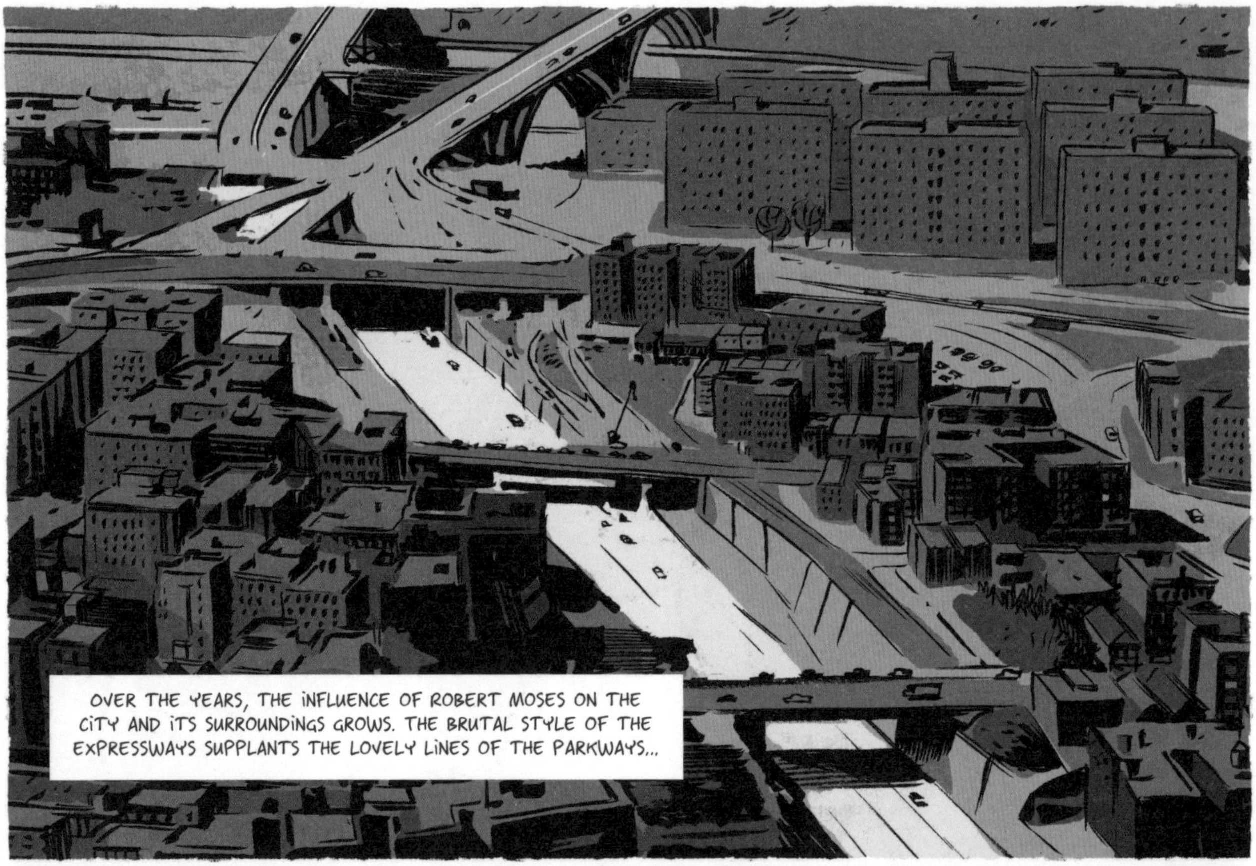
OVER THE YEARS, THE INFLUENCE OF ROBERT MOSES ON THE CITY AND ITS SURROUNDINGS GROWS. THE BRUTAL STYLE OF THE EXPRESSWAYS SUPPLANTS THE LOVELY LINES OF THE PARKWAYS...

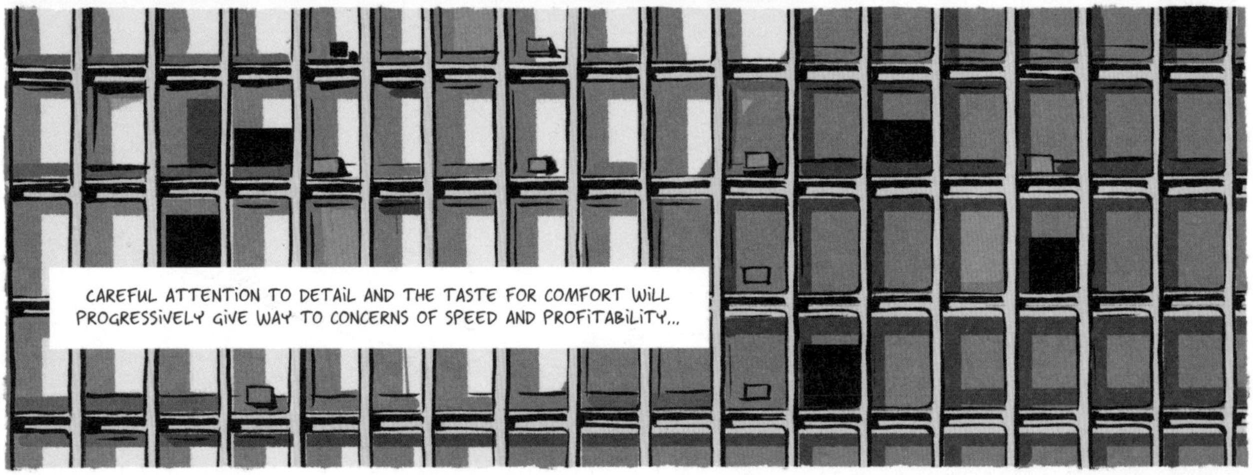
CAREFUL ATTENTION TO DETAIL AND THE TASTE FOR COMFORT WILL PROGRESSIVELY GIVE WAY TO CONCERNS OF SPEED AND PROFITABILITY...

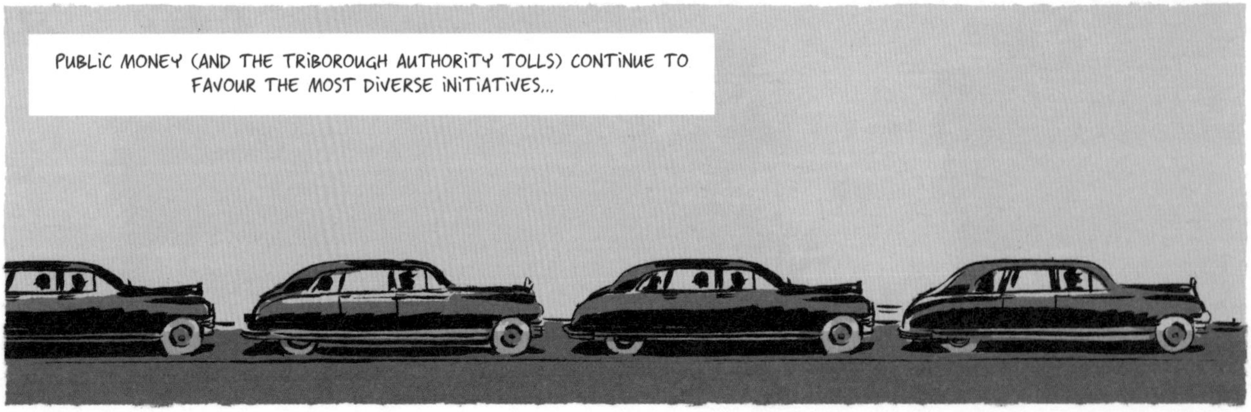
PUBLIC MONEY (AND THE TRIBOROUGH AUTHORITY TOLLS) CONTINUE TO FAVOUR THE MOST DIVERSE INITIATIVES...

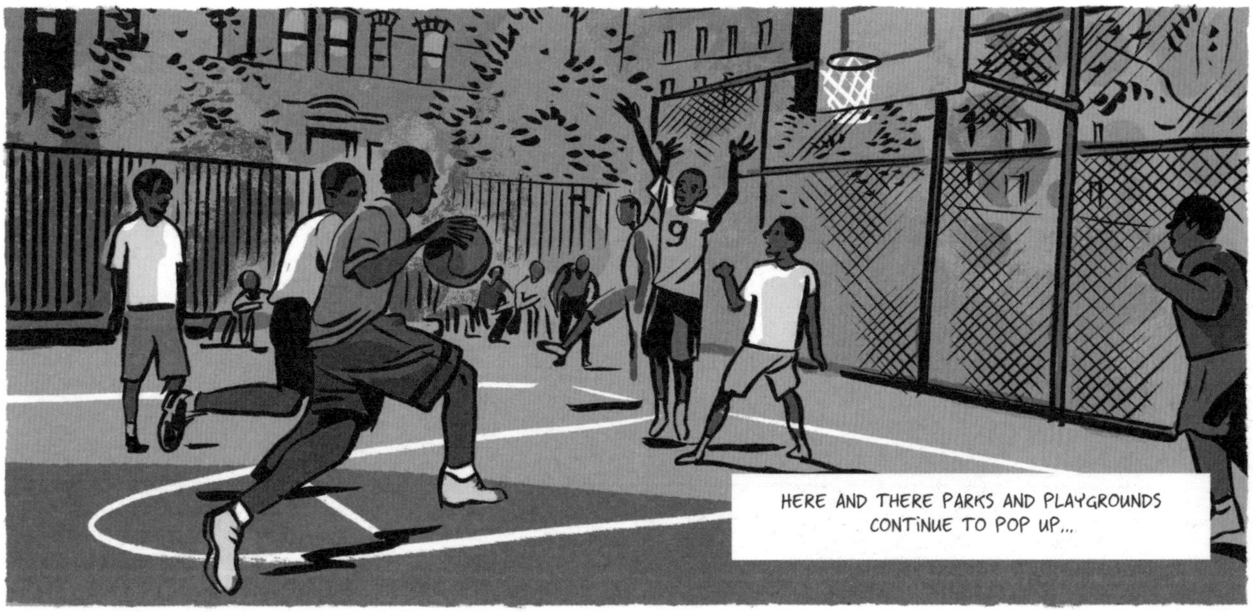
HERE AND THERE PARKS AND PLAYGROUNDS CONTINUE TO POP UP...

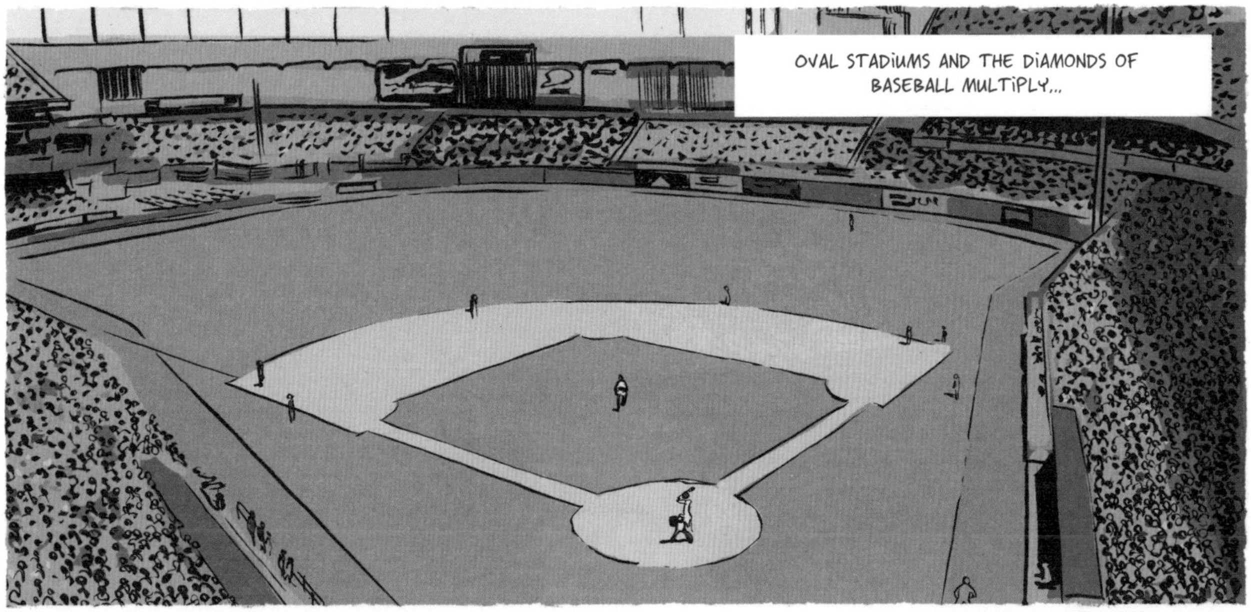
OVAL STADIUMS AND THE DIAMONDS OF BASEBALL MULTIPLY...

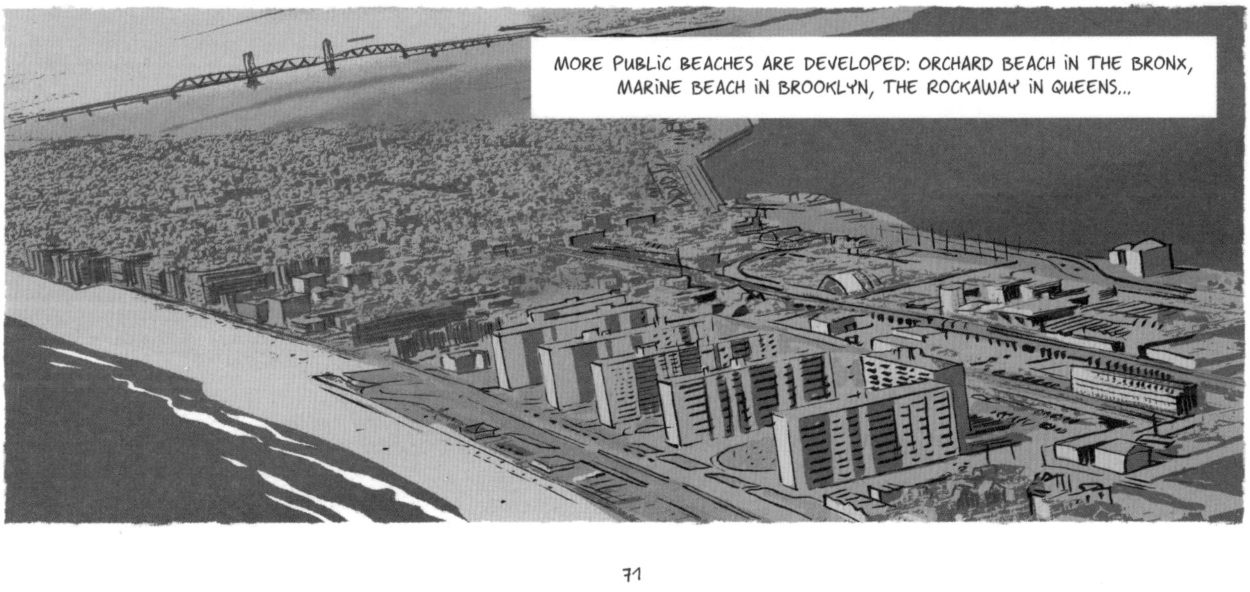
MORE PUBLIC BEACHES ARE DEVELOPED: ORCHARD BEACH IN THE BRONX, MARINE BEACH IN BROOKLYN, THE ROCKAWAY IN QUEENS...

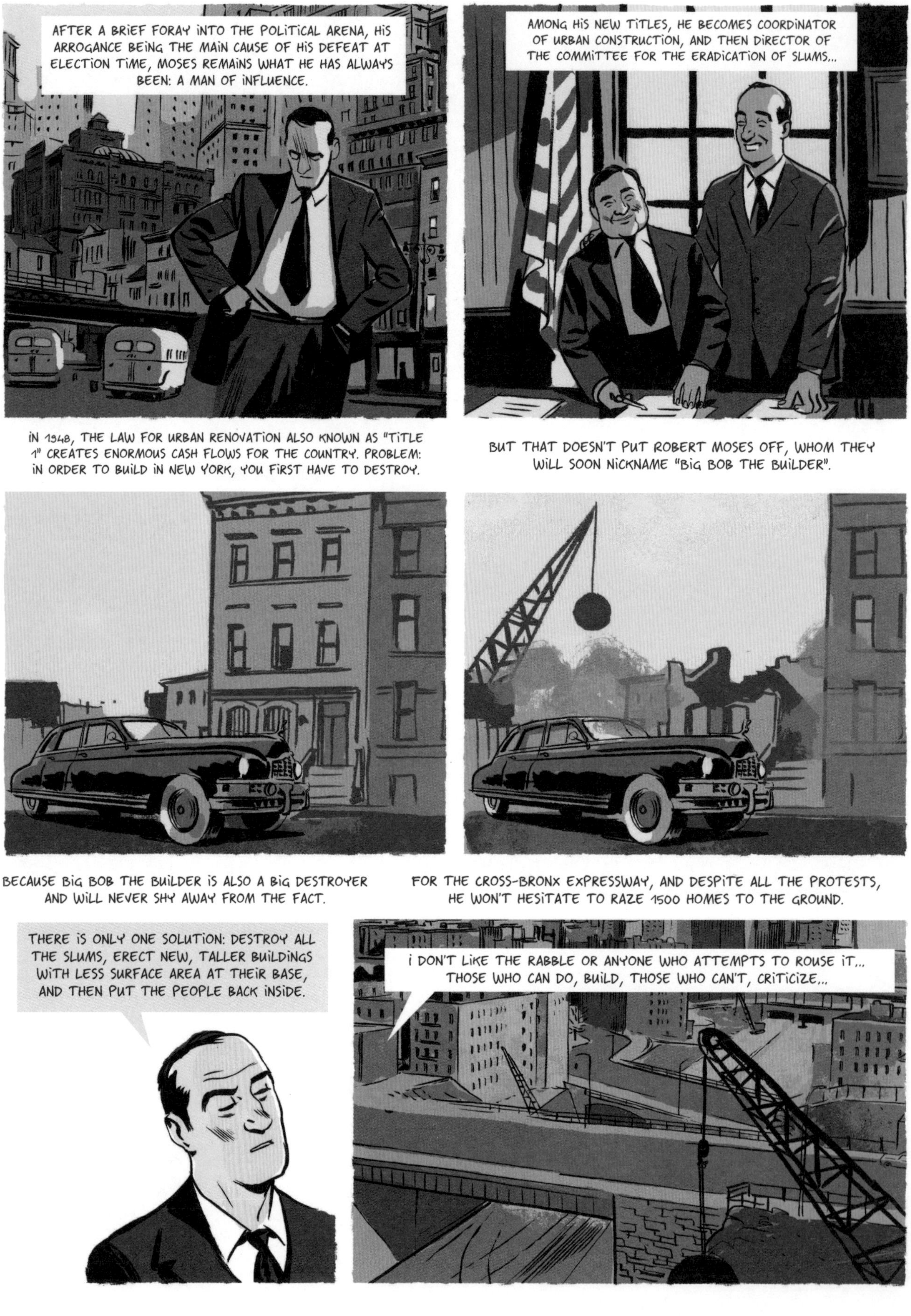
AFTER A BRIEF FORAY INTO THE POLITICAL ARENA, HIS ARROGANCE BEING THE MAIN CAUSE OF HIS DEFEAT AT ELECTION TIME, MOSES REMAINS WHAT HE HAS ALWAYS BEEN: A MAN OF INFLUENCE.
AMONG HIS NEW TITLES, HE BECOMES COORDINATOR OF URBAN CONSTRUCTION, AND THEN DIRECTOR OF THE COMMITTEE FOR THE ERADICATION OF SLUMS...
IN 1948, THE LAW FOR URBAN RENOVATION ALSO KNOWN AS "TITLE 1" CREATES ENORMOUS CASH FLOWS FOR THE COUNTRY. PROBLEM: IN ORDER TO BUILD IN NEW YORK, YOU FIRST HAVE TO DESTROY.
BUT THAT DOESN'T PUT ROBERT MOSES OFF, WHOM THEY WILL SOON NICKNAME "BIG BOB THE BUILDER".
BECAUSE BIG BOB THE BUILDER IS ALSO A BIG DESTROYER AND WILL NEVER SHY AWAY FROM THE FACT.
FOR THE CROSS-BRONX EXPRESSWAY, AND DESPITE ALL THE PROTESTS, HE WON'T HESITATE TO RAZE 1500 HOMES TO THE GROUND.
THERE IS ONLY ONE SOLUTION: DESTROY ALL THE SLUMS, ERECT NEW, TALLER BUILDINGS WITH LESS SURFACE AREA AT THEIR BASE, AND THEN PUT THE PEOPLE BACK INSIDE.
I DON'T LIKE THE RABBLE OR ANYONE WHO ATTEMPTS TO ROUSE IT... THOSE WHO CAN DO, BUILD, THOSE WHO CAN'T, CRITICIZE...

IN THE NAME OF OTHER MANHATTAN PROJECTS AND WITHOUT ANY MERCY WHATSOEVER HE ERADICATES TRADITIONALLY POOR NEIGHBOURHOODS.

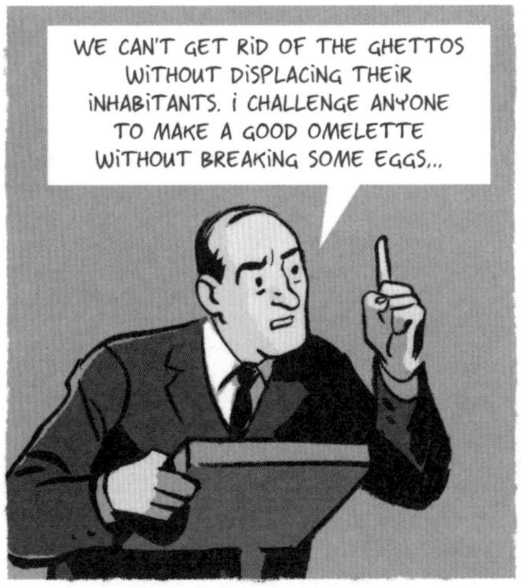
WE CAN'T GET RID OF THE GHETTOS WITHOUT DISPLACING THEIR INHABITANTS. I CHALLENGE ANYONE TO MAKE A GOOD OMELETTE WITHOUT BREAKING SOME EGGS...

UNFORTUNATELY, MOST OF MOSES' BROKEN EGGS BELONG TO NEW YORK'S MINORITIES, AND IN PARTICULAR THE AFRICAN-AMERICAN POPULATION.

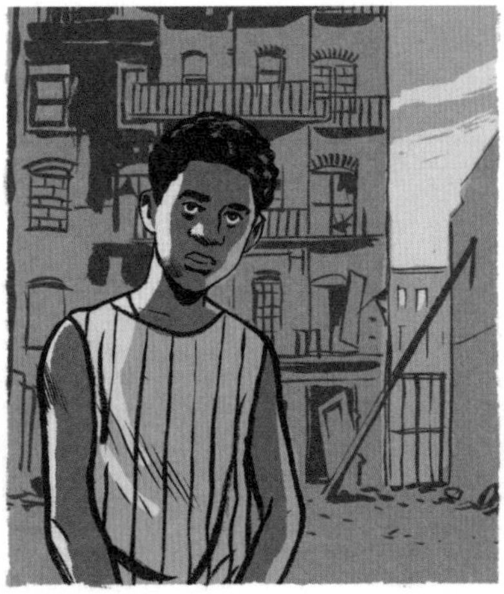

WAS MOSES A RACIST AS IT WAS LATER CLAIMED? MOST PROBABLY, LIKE MANY OF HIS GENERATION. BUT IN TRUTH, WHAT CHARACTERIZES MOSES IS HIS CONTEMPT FOR THE POOR AND THEIR SUFFERING, WHATEVER THEIR RACE...

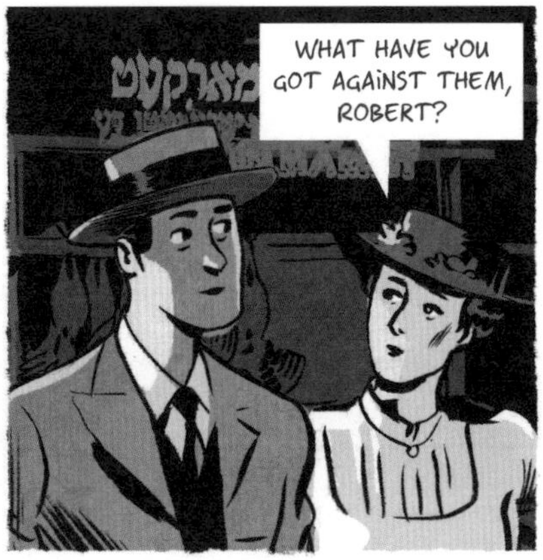
WHAT HAVE YOU GOT AGAINST THEM, ROBERT?

ON THE ONE HAND CAPABLE OF BUILDING SWIMMING POOLS FOR AFRICAN-AMERICAN CHILDREN (AND HE DID NOT REFUSE TO HEAT THE WATER TO DISSUADE THEM FROM SWIMMING, AS IT WAS CLAIMED)...

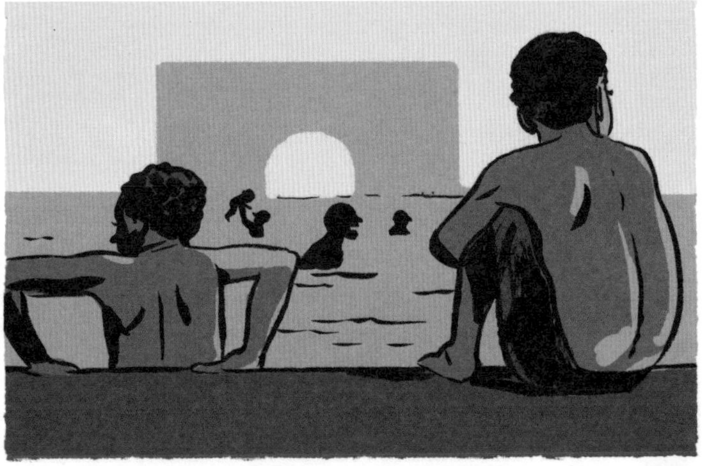

...HE IS ALSO FULLY AWARE THAT THE PARKWAYS' LOW BRIDGES PREVENTS THE DISADVANTAGED CLASSES FROM ACCESSING THE PUBLIC HIGHWAYS IN THEIR CARS...

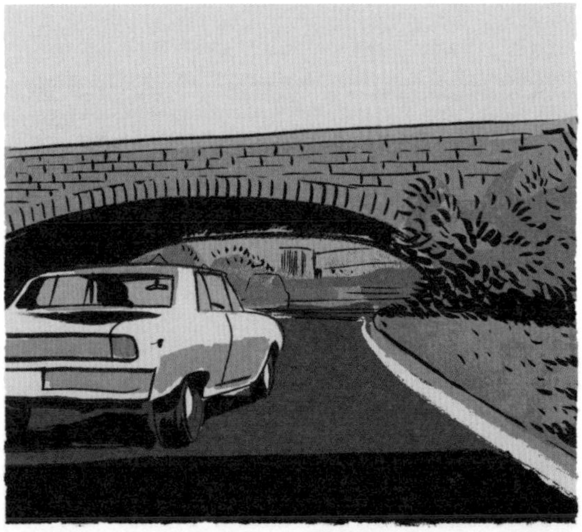

BUT AT THE SAME TIME HE FURIOUSLY ATTACKS THE ULTRA-RICH WHO COLONIZED LONG ISLAND...

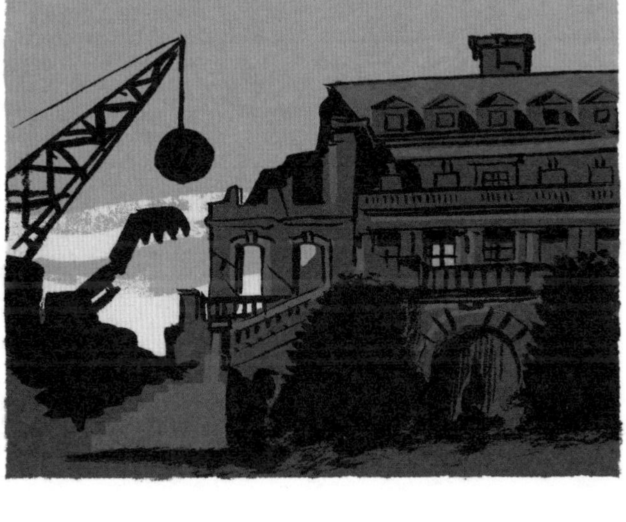

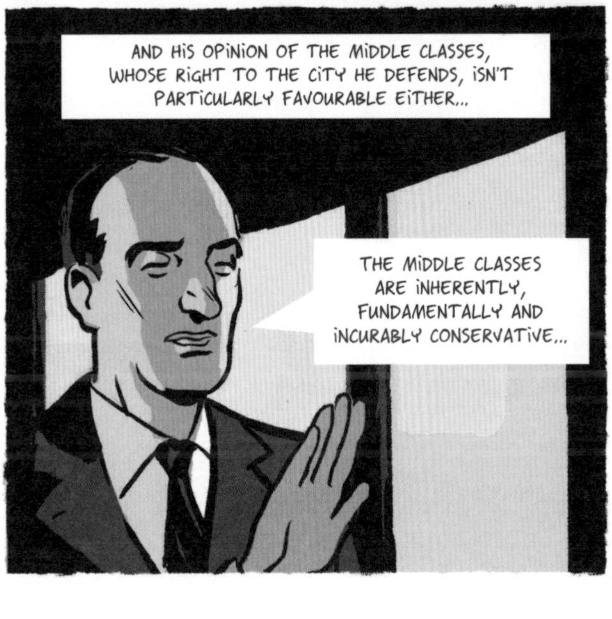
AND HIS OPINION OF THE MIDDLE CLASSES, WHOSE RIGHT TO THE CITY HE DEFENDS, ISN'T PARTICULARLY FAVOURABLE EITHER...
THE MIDDLE CLASSES ARE INHERENTLY, FUNDAMENTALLY AND INCURABLY CONSERVATIVE...

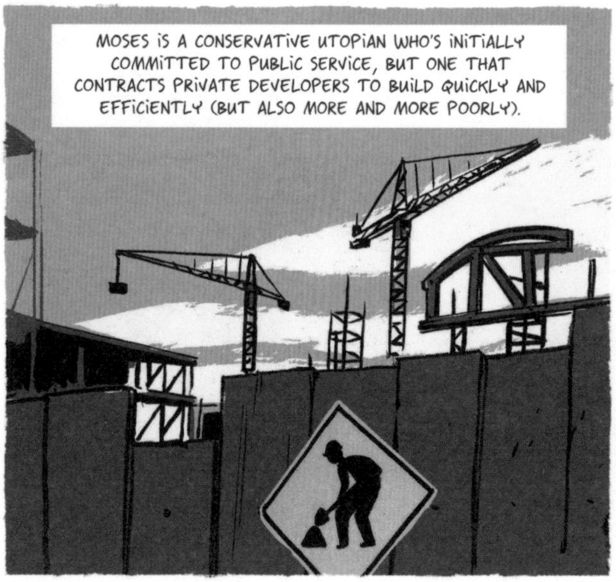
MOSES IS A CONSERVATIVE UTOPIAN WHO'S INITIALLY COMMITTED TO PUBLIC SERVICE, BUT ONE THAT CONTRACTS PRIVATE DEVELOPERS TO BUILD QUICKLY AND EFFICIENTLY (BUT ALSO MORE AND MORE POORLY).

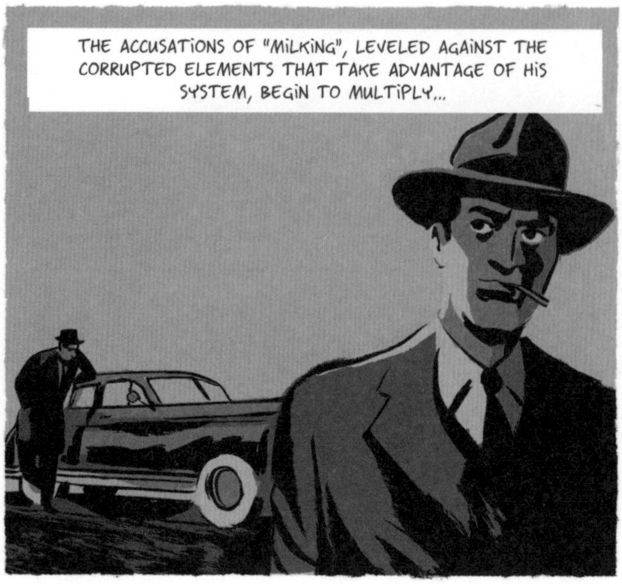
THE ACCUSATIONS OF "MILKING", LEVELED AGAINST THE CORRUPTED ELEMENTS THAT TAKE ADVANTAGE OF HIS SYSTEM, BEGIN TO MULTIPLY...

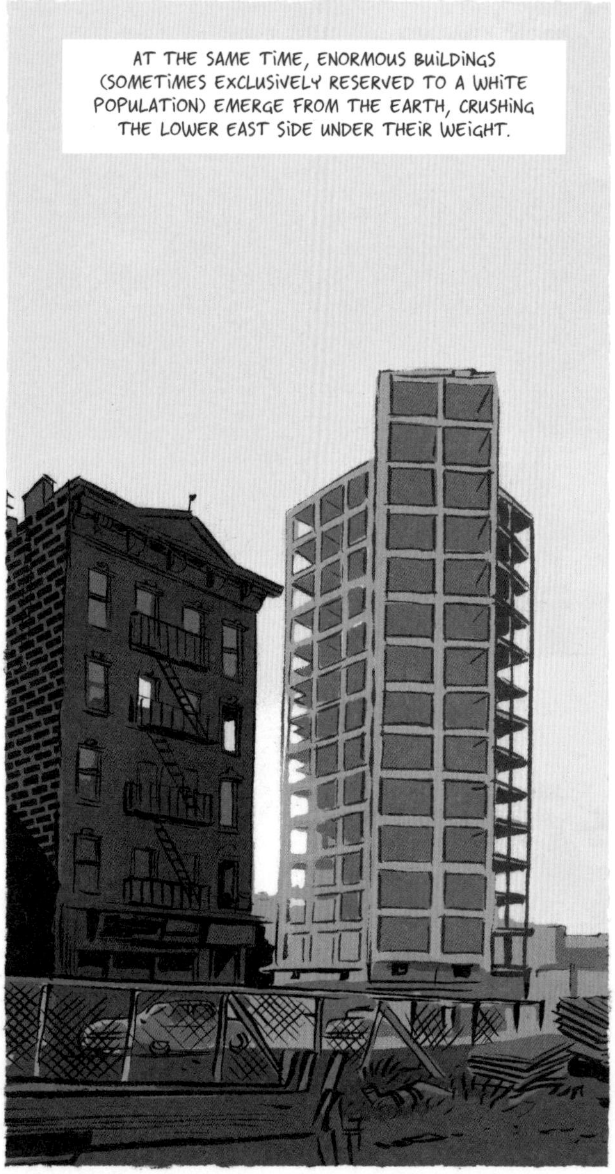
AT THE SAME TIME, ENORMOUS BUILDINGS (SOMETIMES EXCLUSIVELY RESERVED TO A WHITE POPULATION) EMERGE FROM THE EARTH, CRUSHING THE LOWER EAST SIDE UNDER THEIR WEIGHT.

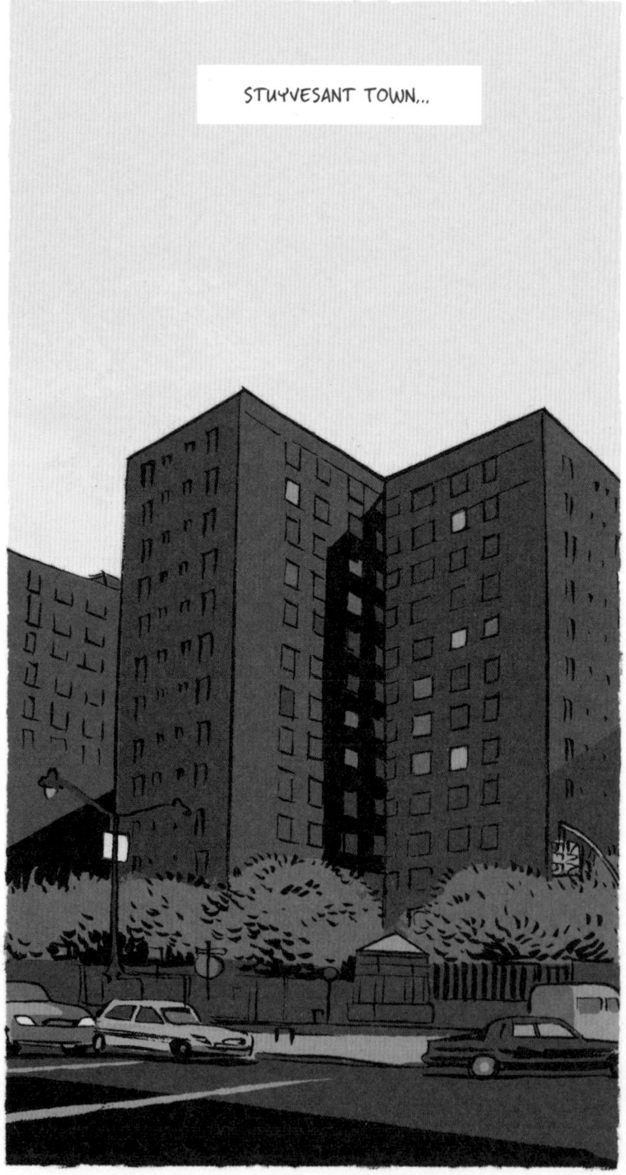
STUYVESANT TOWN...

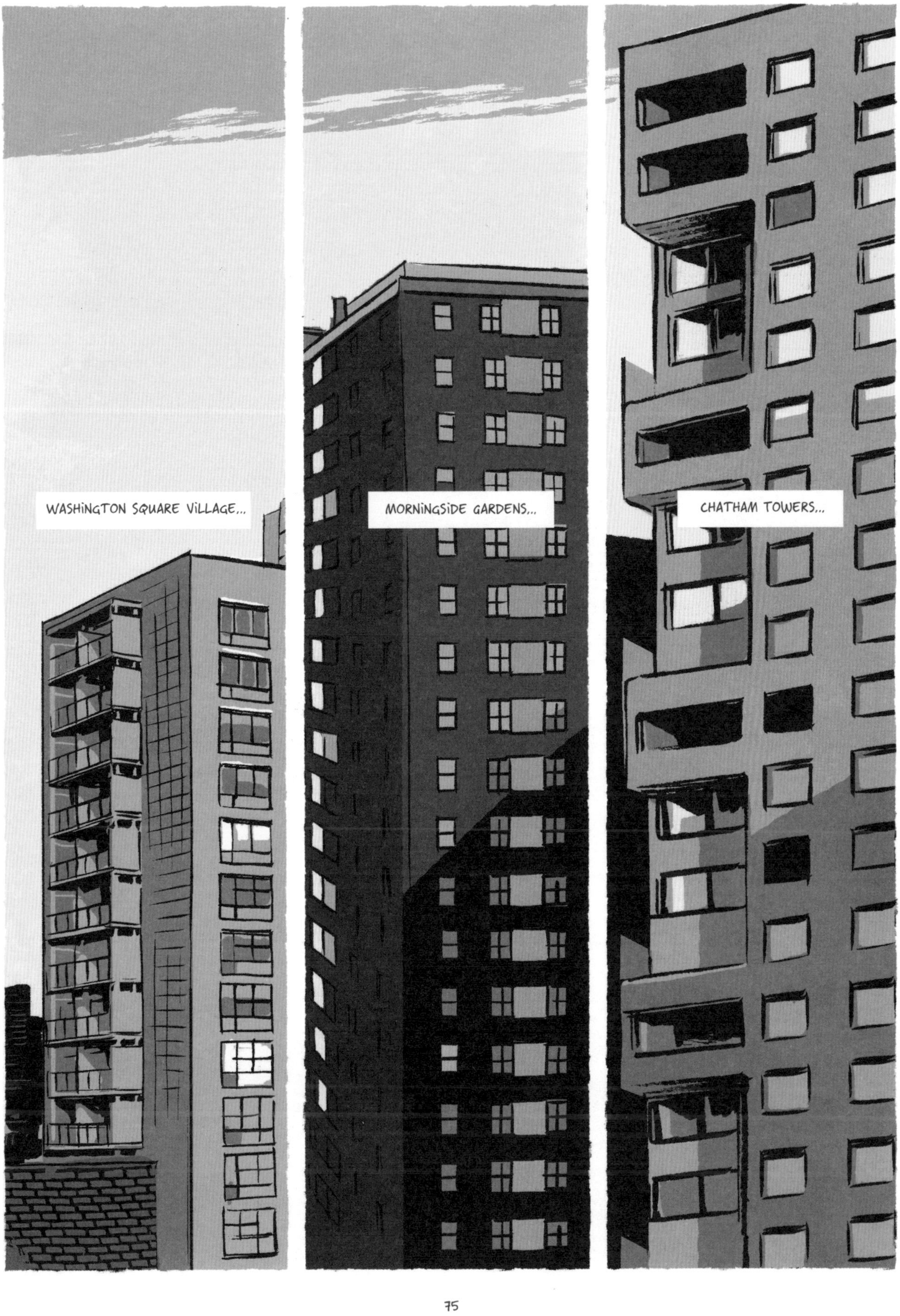
WASHINGTON SQUARE VILLAGE...
MORNINGSIDE GARDENS...
CHATHAM TOWERS...

SOME REFERRED TO A KIND OF "MACHO URBAN PLANNING" IN RELATION TO ROBERT MOSES AND HIS BAND OF DISCIPLES.

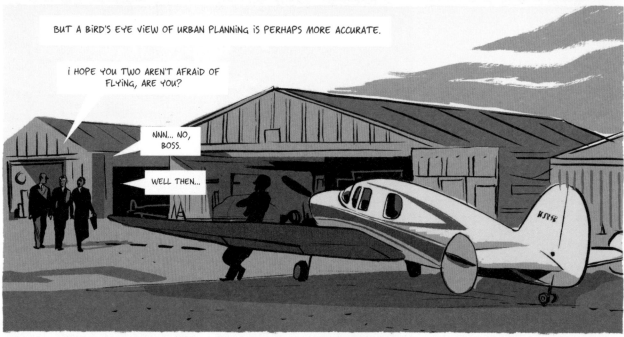

BUT A BIRD'S EYE VIEW OF URBAN PLANNING IS PERHAPS MORE ACCURATE.

I HOPE YOU TWO AREN'T AFRAID OF FLYING, ARE YOU?

NNN... NO, BOSS.

WELL THEN...

JUST A COUPLE MORE SIGNATURES BEFORE YOU TAKE OFF TO THE GREAT NORTH, BOSS...

LET'S NOT EXAGGERATE, IT'S ONLY THE NORTH OF THE STATE.

IT'S NOT AS WELL HEATED AS THE PACKARD IN THERE...

THANK YOU.

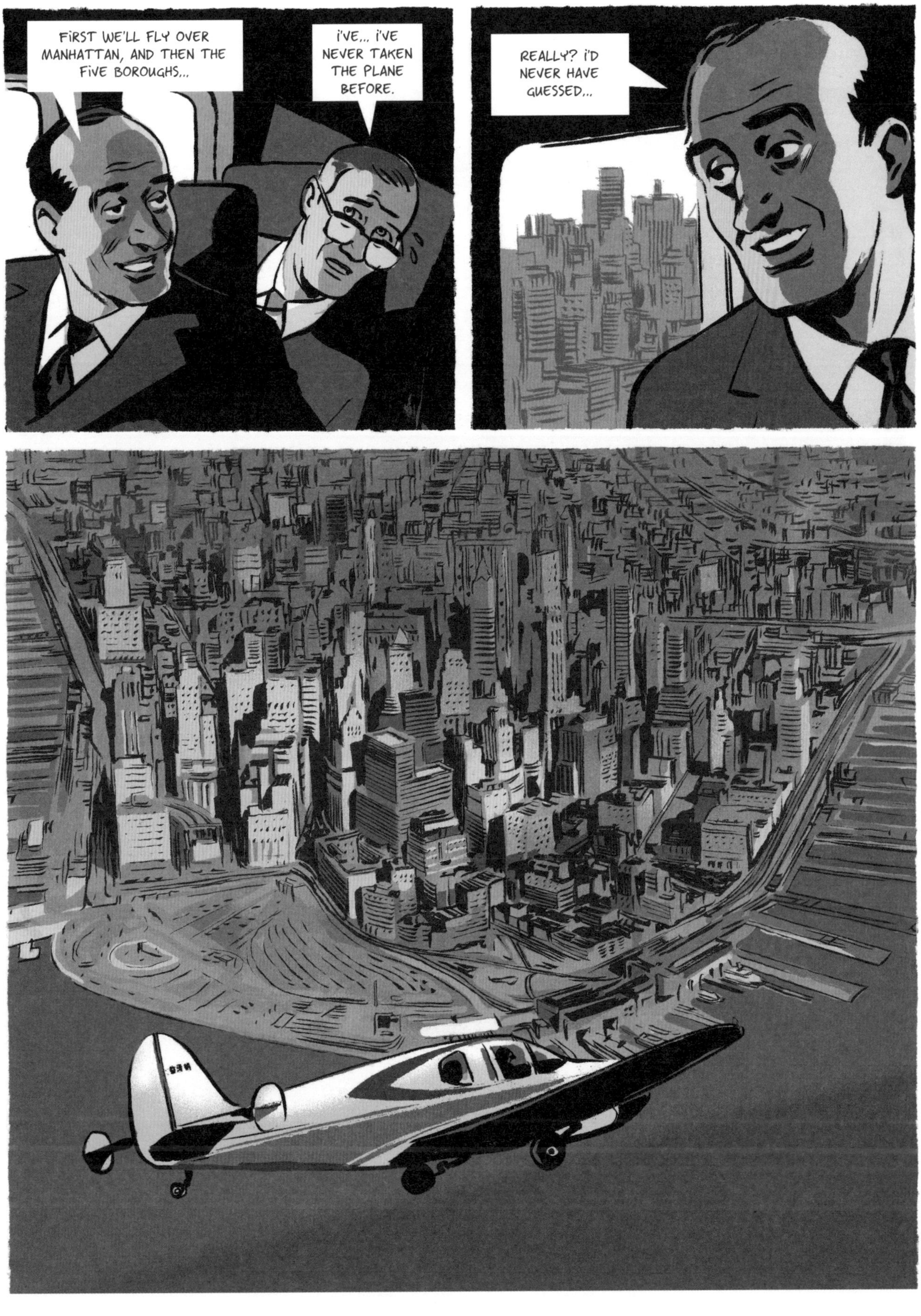
FIRST WE'LL FLY OVER MANHATTAN, AND THEN THE FIVE BOROUGHS...
I'VE... I'VE NEVER TAKEN THE PLANE BEFORE.
REALLY? I'D NEVER HAVE GUESSED...

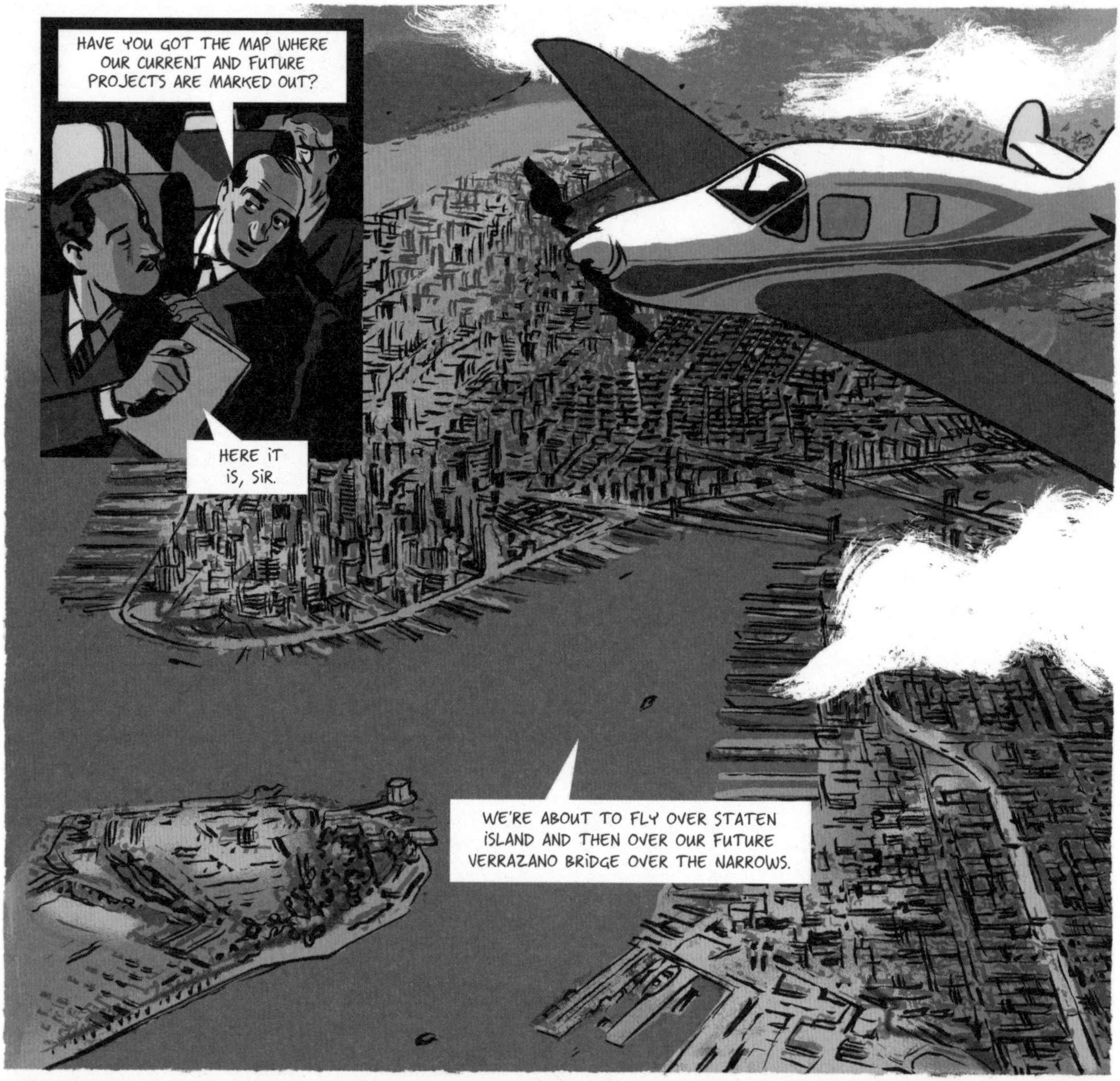
HAVE YOU GOT THE MAP WHERE OUR CURRENT AND FUTURE PROJECTS ARE MARKED OUT?
HERE iT iS, SiR.
WE'RE ABOUT TO FLY OVER STATEN iSLAND AND THEN OVER OUR FUTURE VERRAZANO BRiDGE OVER THE NARROWS.

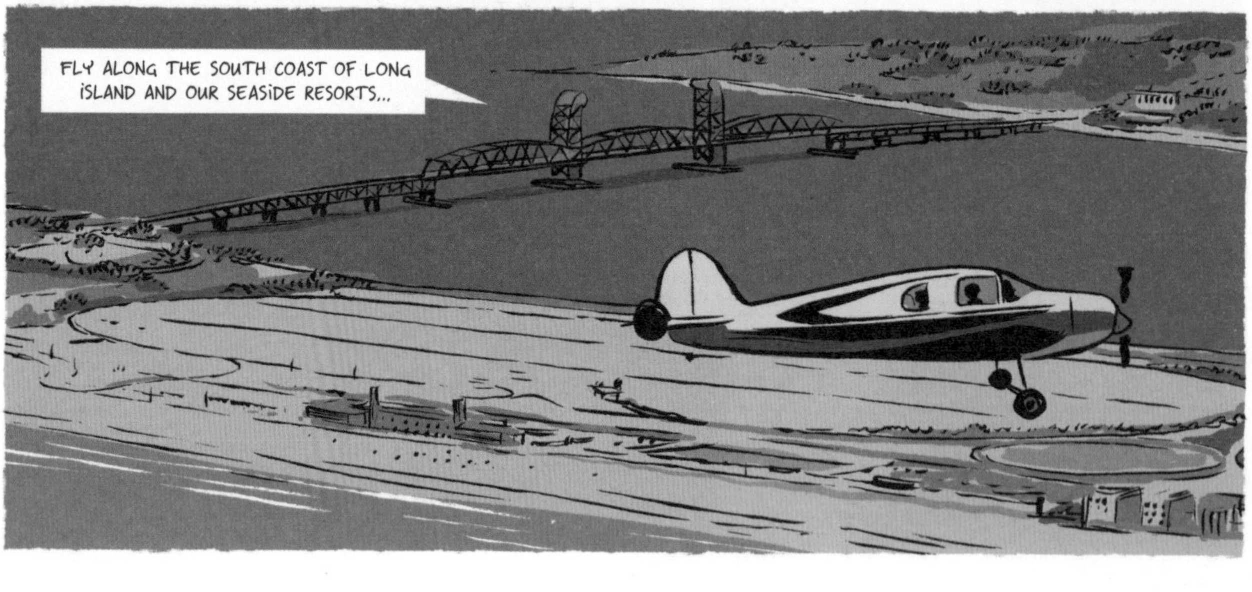
FLY ALONG THE SOUTH COAST OF LONG iSLAND AND OUR SEASiDE RESORTS...

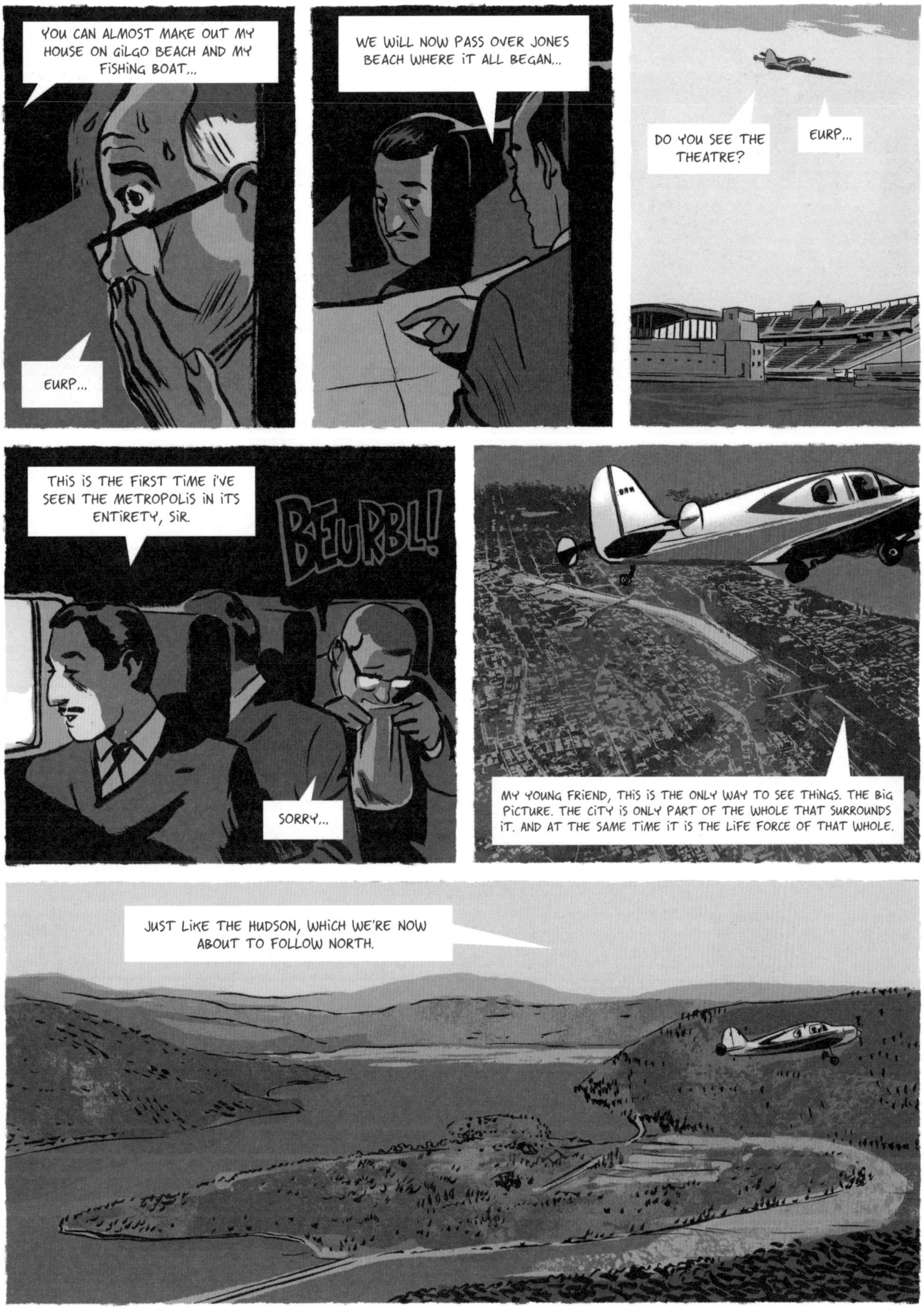

YOU CAN ALMOST MAKE OUT MY HOUSE ON GILGO BEACH AND MY FISHING BOAT...
EURP...
WE WILL NOW PASS OVER JONES BEACH WHERE IT ALL BEGAN...
DO YOU SEE THE THEATRE?
EURP...
THIS IS THE FIRST TIME I'VE SEEN THE METROPOLIS IN ITS ENTIRETY, SIR.
BEURBL!
SORRY...
MY YOUNG FRIEND, THIS IS THE ONLY WAY TO SEE THINGS. THE BIG PICTURE. THE CITY IS ONLY PART OF THE WHOLE THAT SURROUNDS IT. AND AT THE SAME TIME IT IS THE LIFE FORCE OF THAT WHOLE.
JUST LIKE THE HUDSON, WHICH WE'RE NOW ABOUT TO FOLLOW NORTH.

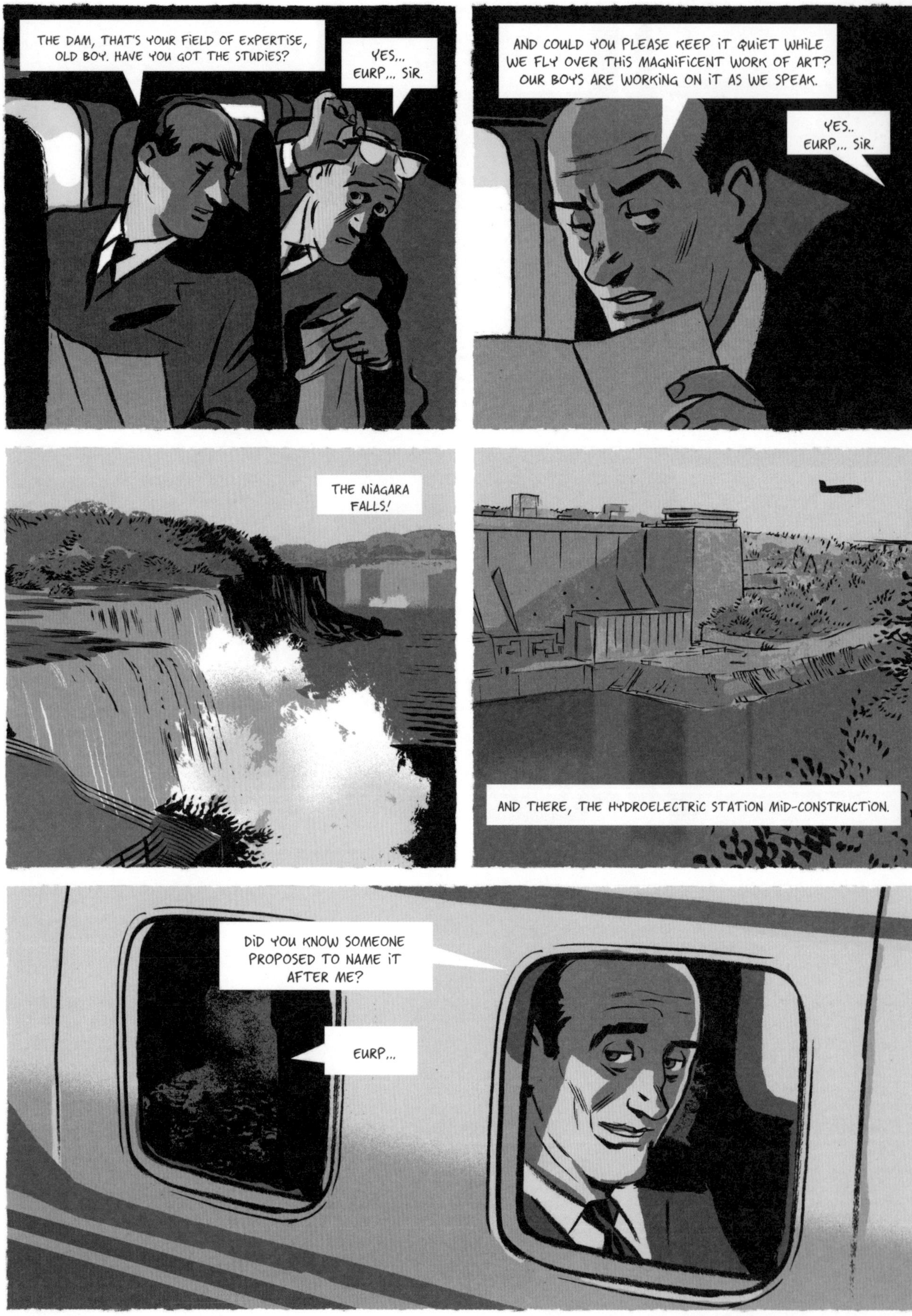
THE DAM, THAT'S YOUR FIELD OF EXPERTISE, OLD BOY. HAVE YOU GOT THE STUDIES?
YES... EURP... SIR.
AND COULD YOU PLEASE KEEP IT QUIET WHILE WE FLY OVER THIS MAGNIFICENT WORK OF ART? OUR BOYS ARE WORKING ON IT AS WE SPEAK.
YES.. EURP... SIR.
THE NIAGARA FALLS!
AND THERE, THE HYDROELECTRIC STATION MID-CONSTRUCTION.
DID YOU KNOW SOMEONE PROPOSED TO NAME IT AFTER ME?
EURP...

# CHAPTER 4

## Jane vs LOMEX

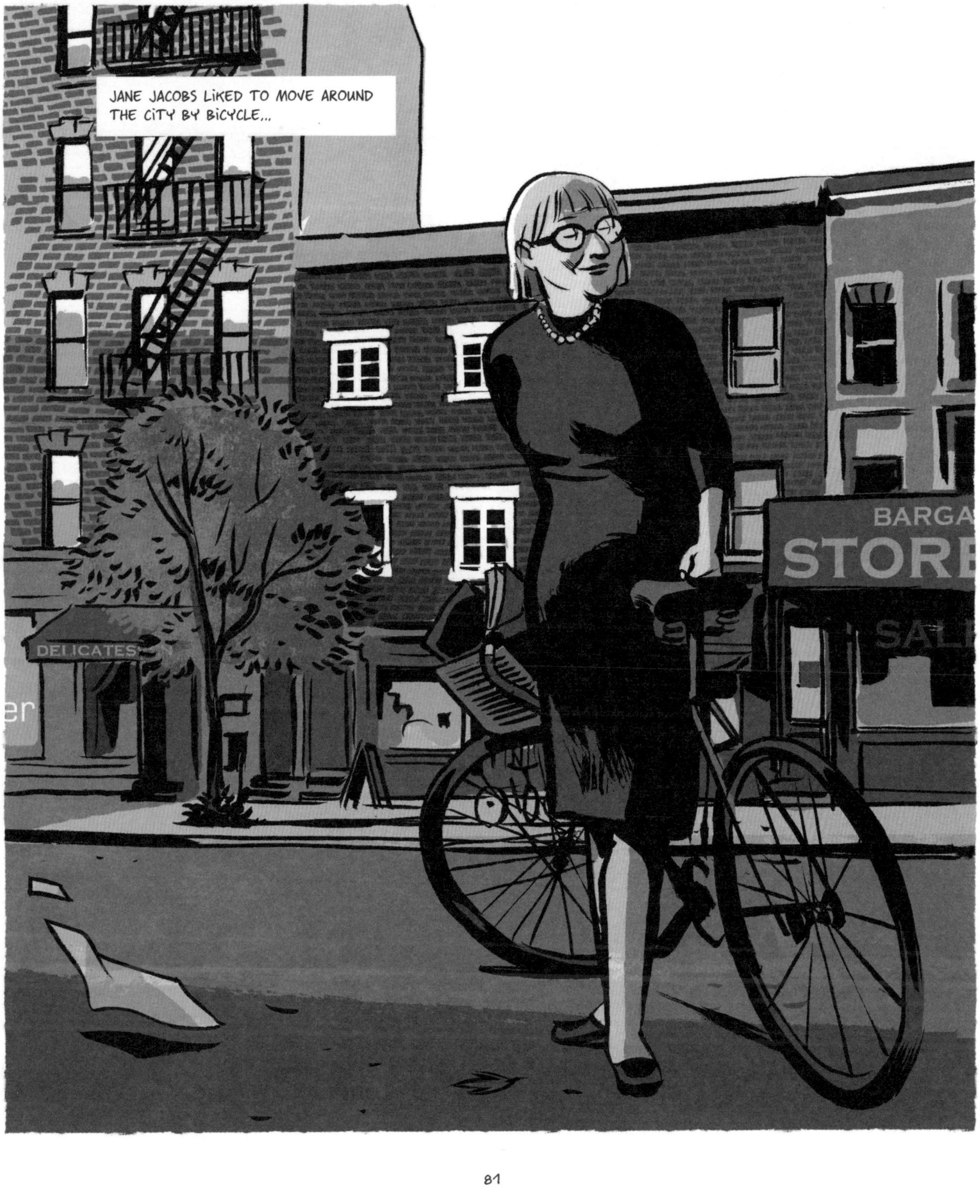
JANE JACOBS LIKED TO MOVE AROUND THE CITY BY BICYCLE...
BARGA
STORE
DELICATES

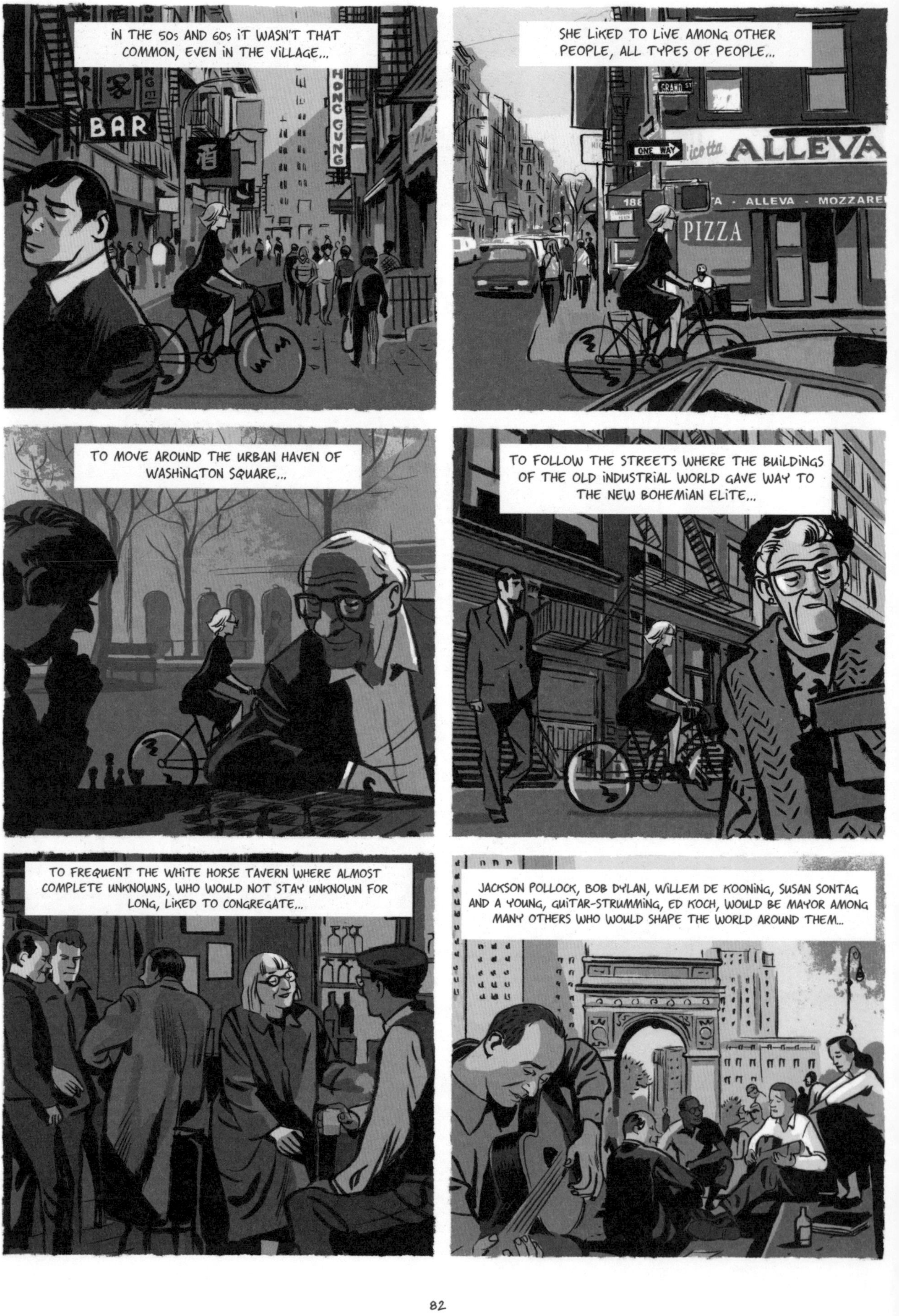
IN THE 50s AND 60s IT WASN'T THAT COMMON, EVEN IN THE VILLAGE...
BAR
HONG GUNG
SHE LIKED TO LIVE AMONG OTHER PEOPLE, ALL TYPES OF PEOPLE...
GRAND ST
ONE WAY
ALLEVA
PIZZA
TO MOVE AROUND THE URBAN HAVEN OF WASHINGTON SQUARE...
TO FOLLOW THE STREETS WHERE THE BUILDINGS OF THE OLD INDUSTRIAL WORLD GAVE WAY TO THE NEW BOHEMIAN ELITE...
TO FREQUENT THE WHITE HORSE TAVERN WHERE ALMOST COMPLETE UNKNOWNS, WHO WOULD NOT STAY UNKNOWN FOR LONG, LIKED TO CONGREGATE...
JACKSON POLLOCK, BOB DYLAN, WILLEM DE KOONING, SUSAN SONTAG AND A YOUNG, GUITAR-STRUMMING, ED KOCH, WOULD BE MAYOR AMONG MANY OTHERS WHO WOULD SHAPE THE WORLD AROUND THEM...

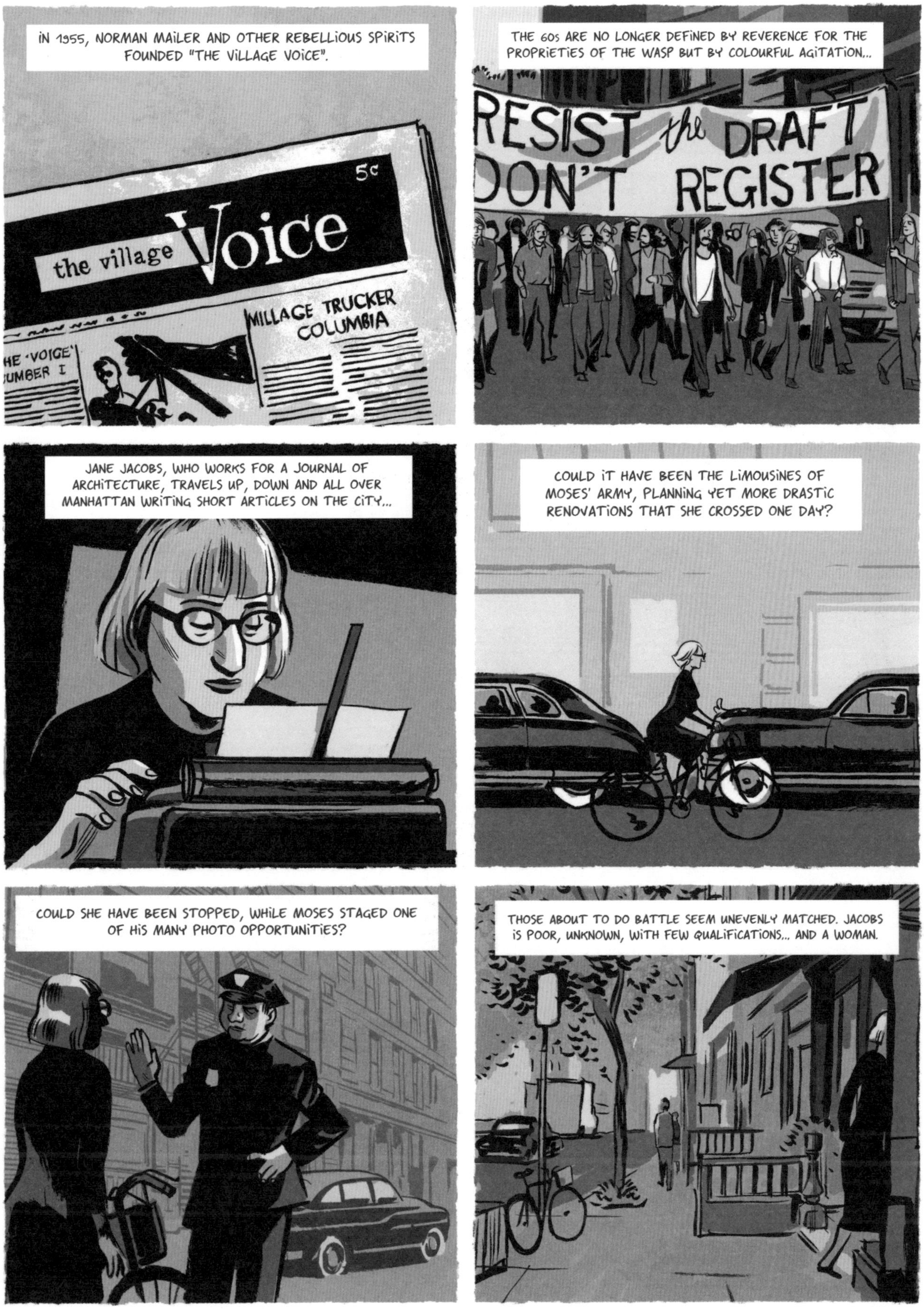

IN 1955, NORMAN MAILER AND OTHER REBELLIOUS SPIRITS FOUNDED "THE VILLAGE VOICE".
5c
the village Voice
VILLAGE TRUCKER
COLUMBIA
THE 60s ARE NO LONGER DEFINED BY REVERENCE FOR THE PROPRIETIES OF THE WASP BUT BY COLOURFUL AGITATION...
RESIST the DRAFT
DON'T REGISTER
JANE JACOBS, WHO WORKS FOR A JOURNAL OF ARCHITECTURE, TRAVELS UP, DOWN AND ALL OVER MANHATTAN WRITING SHORT ARTICLES ON THE CITY...
COULD IT HAVE BEEN THE LIMOUSINES OF MOSES' ARMY, PLANNING YET MORE DRASTIC RENOVATIONS THAT SHE CROSSED ONE DAY?
COULD SHE HAVE BEEN STOPPED, WHILE MOSES STAGED ONE OF HIS MANY PHOTO OPPORTUNITIES?
THOSE ABOUT TO DO BATTLE SEEM UNEVENLY MATCHED. JACOBS IS POOR, UNKNOWN, WITH FEW QUALIFICATIONS... AND A WOMAN.

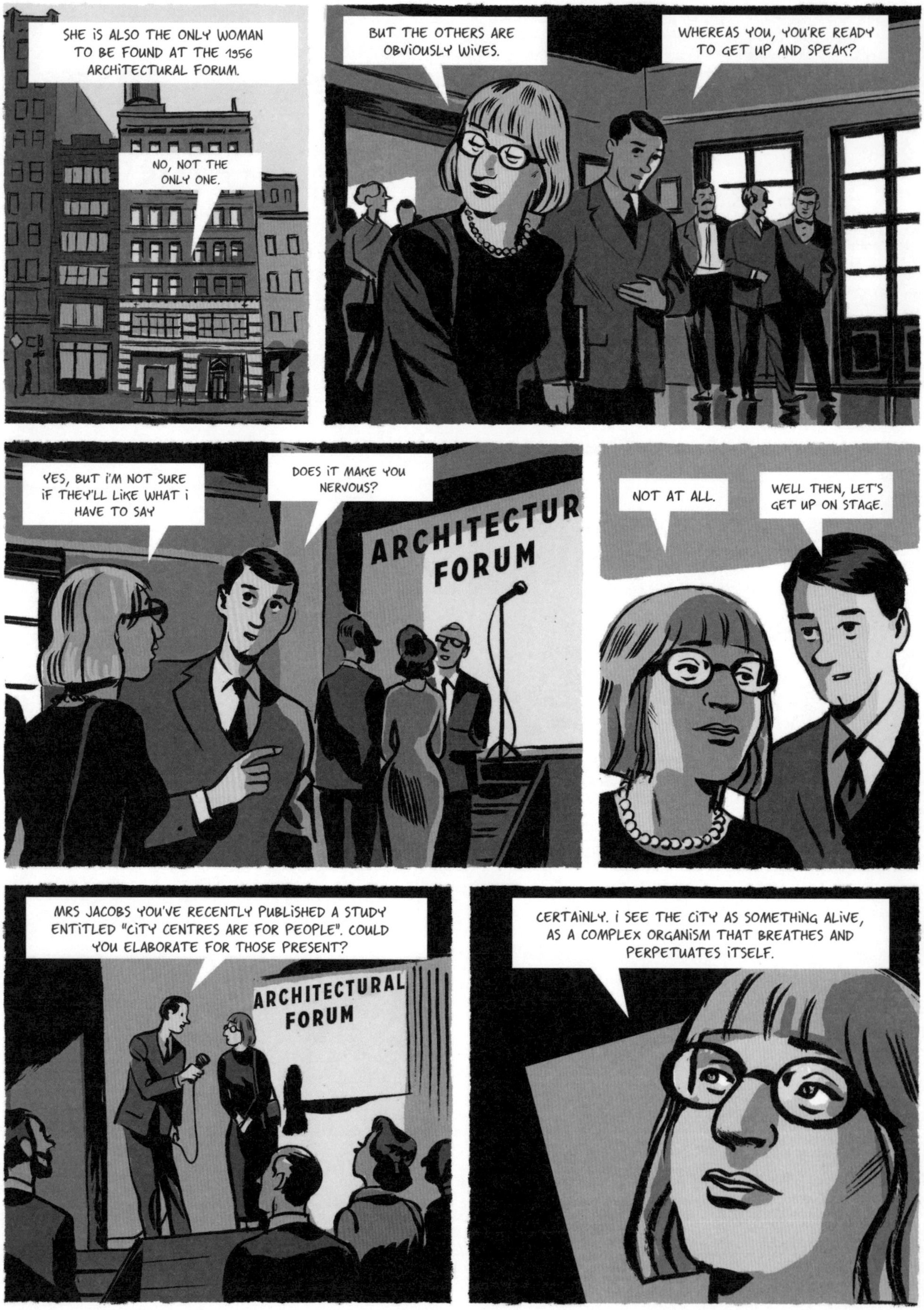
SHE iS ALSO THE ONLY WOMAN TO BE FOUND AT THE 1956 ARCHiTECTURAL FORUM.
NO, NOT THE ONLY ONE.
BUT THE OTHERS ARE OBViOUSLY WiVES.
WHEREAS YOU, YOU'RE READY TO GET UP AND SPEAK?
YES, BUT i'M NOT SURE iF THEY'LL LiKE WHAT i HAVE TO SAY
DOES iT MAKE YOU NERVOUS?
ARCHITECTUR FORUM
NOT AT ALL.
WELL THEN, LET'S GET UP ON STAGE.
MRS JACOBS YOU'VE RECENTLY PUBLiSHED A STUDY ENTiTLED "CiTY CENTRES ARE FOR PEOPLE". COULD YOU ELABORATE FOR THOSE PRESENT?
ARCHITECTURAL FORUM
CERTAiNLY. i SEE THE CiTY AS SOMETHiNG ALiVE, AS A COMPLEX ORGANiSM THAT BREATHES AND PERPETUATES iTSELF.

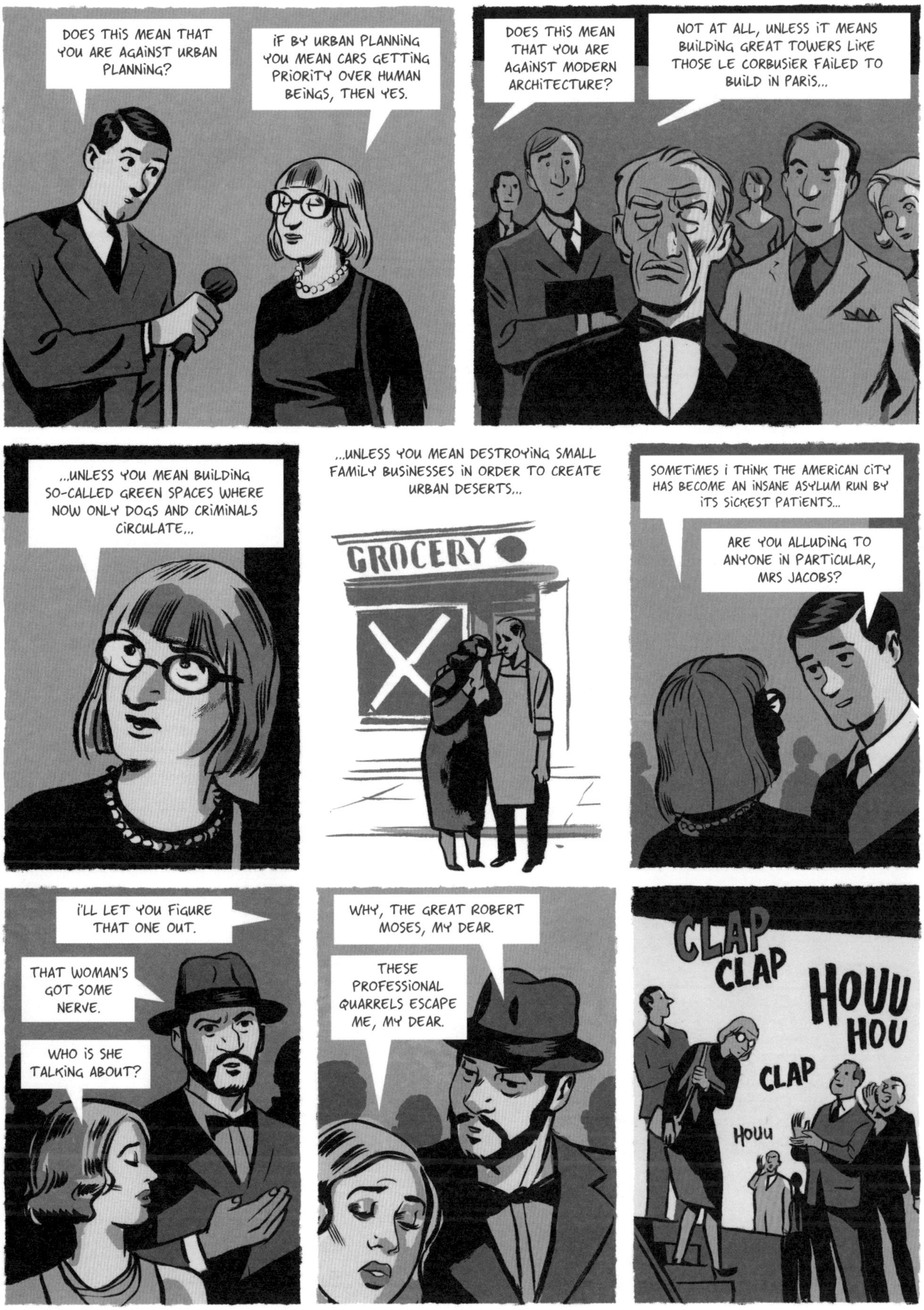
DOES THIS MEAN THAT YOU ARE AGAINST URBAN PLANNING?
IF BY URBAN PLANNING YOU MEAN CARS GETTING PRIORITY OVER HUMAN BEINGS, THEN YES.
DOES THIS MEAN THAT YOU ARE AGAINST MODERN ARCHITECTURE?
NOT AT ALL, UNLESS IT MEANS BUILDING GREAT TOWERS LIKE THOSE LE CORBUSIER FAILED TO BUILD IN PARIS...
...UNLESS YOU MEAN BUILDING SO-CALLED GREEN SPACES WHERE NOW ONLY DOGS AND CRIMINALS CIRCULATE...
...UNLESS YOU MEAN DESTROYING SMALL FAMILY BUSINESSES IN ORDER TO CREATE URBAN DESERTS...
GROCERY
SOMETIMES I THINK THE AMERICAN CITY HAS BECOME AN INSANE ASYLUM RUN BY ITS SICKEST PATIENTS...
ARE YOU ALLUDING TO ANYONE IN PARTICULAR, MRS JACOBS?
I'LL LET YOU FIGURE THAT ONE OUT.
THAT WOMAN'S GOT SOME NERVE.
WHO IS SHE TALKING ABOUT?
WHY, THE GREAT ROBERT MOSES, MY DEAR.
THESE PROFESSIONAL QUARRELS ESCAPE ME, MY DEAR.
CLAP
CLAP
HOUU
HOU
CLAP
HOUU

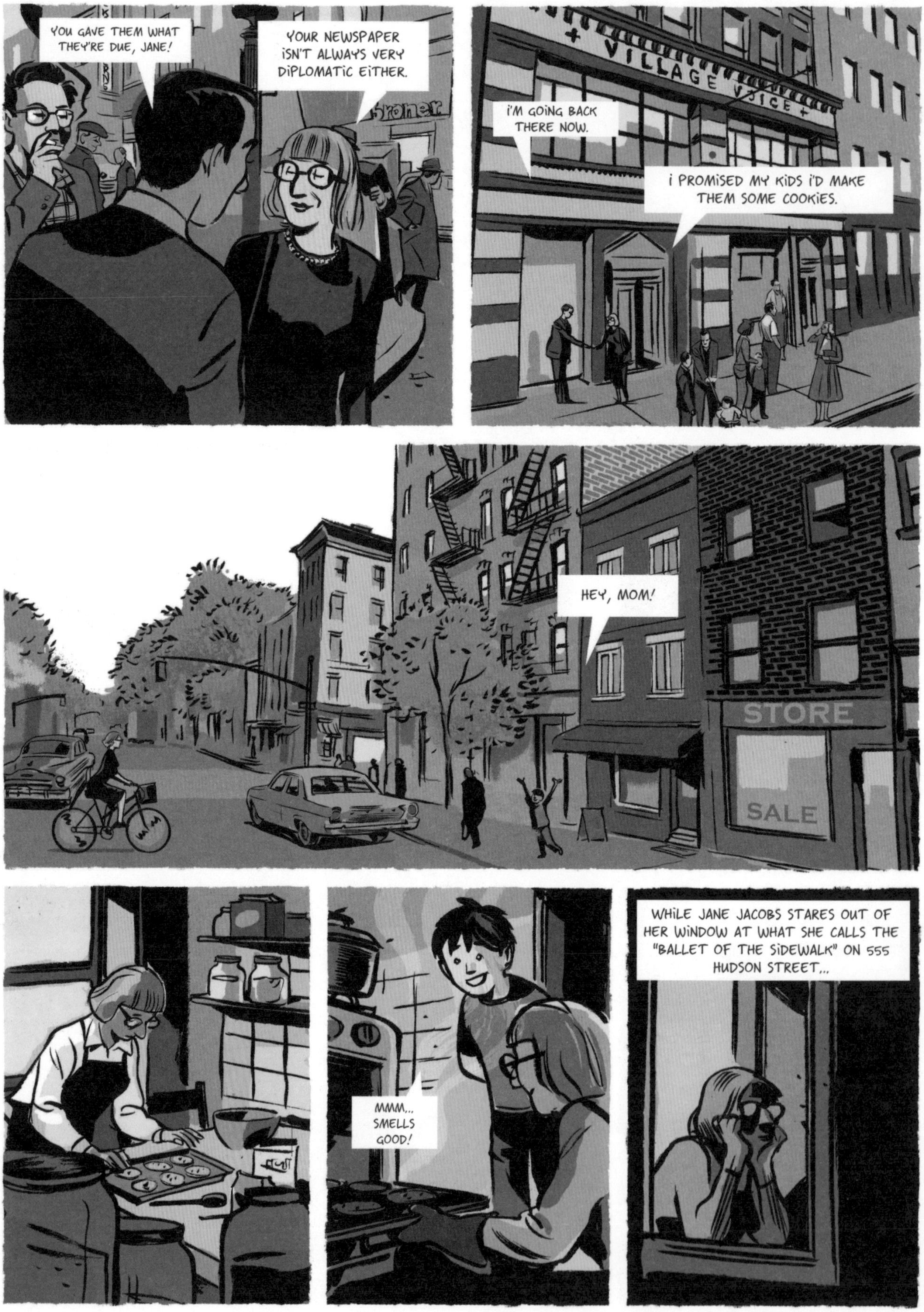
YOU GAVE THEM WHAT THEY'RE DUE, JANE!
YOUR NEWSPAPER iSN'T ALWAYS VERY DiPLOMATiC EiTHER.
VILLAGE VOICE
i'M GOiNG BACK THERE NOW.
i PROMiSED MY KiDS i'D MAKE THEM SOME COOKiES.
HEY, MOM!
STORE
SALE
MMM... SMELLS GOOD!
WHiLE JANE JACOBS STARES OUT OF HER WiNDOW AT WHAT SHE CALLS THE "BALLET OF THE SiDEWALK" ON 555 HUDSON STREET...

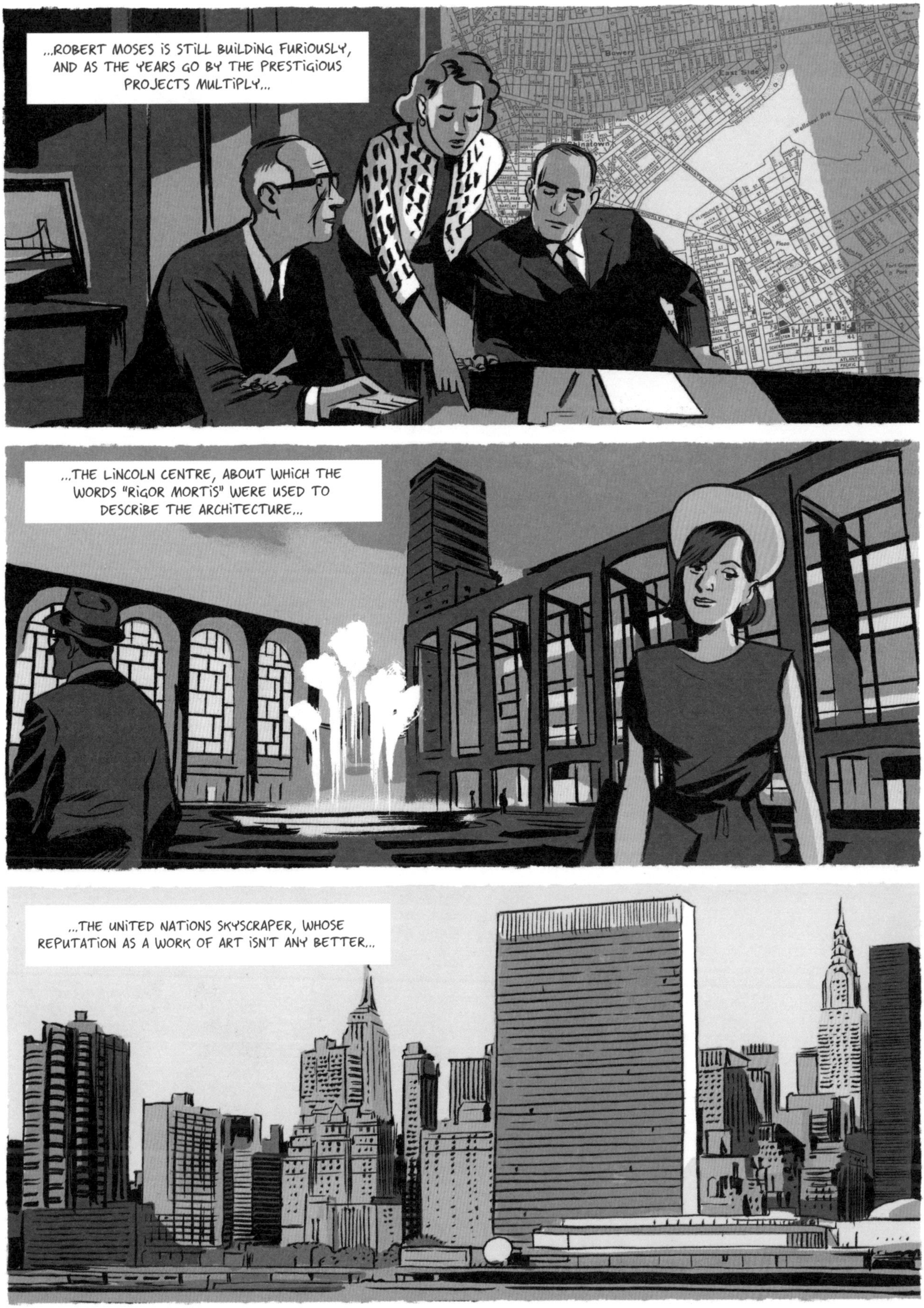
...ROBERT MOSES IS STILL BUILDING FURIOUSLY, AND AS THE YEARS GO BY THE PRESTIGIOUS PROJECTS MULTIPLY...
...THE LINCOLN CENTRE, ABOUT WHICH THE WORDS "RIGOR MORTIS" WERE USED TO DESCRIBE THE ARCHITECTURE...
...THE UNITED NATIONS SKYSCRAPER, WHOSE REPUTATION AS A WORK OF ART ISN'T ANY BETTER...

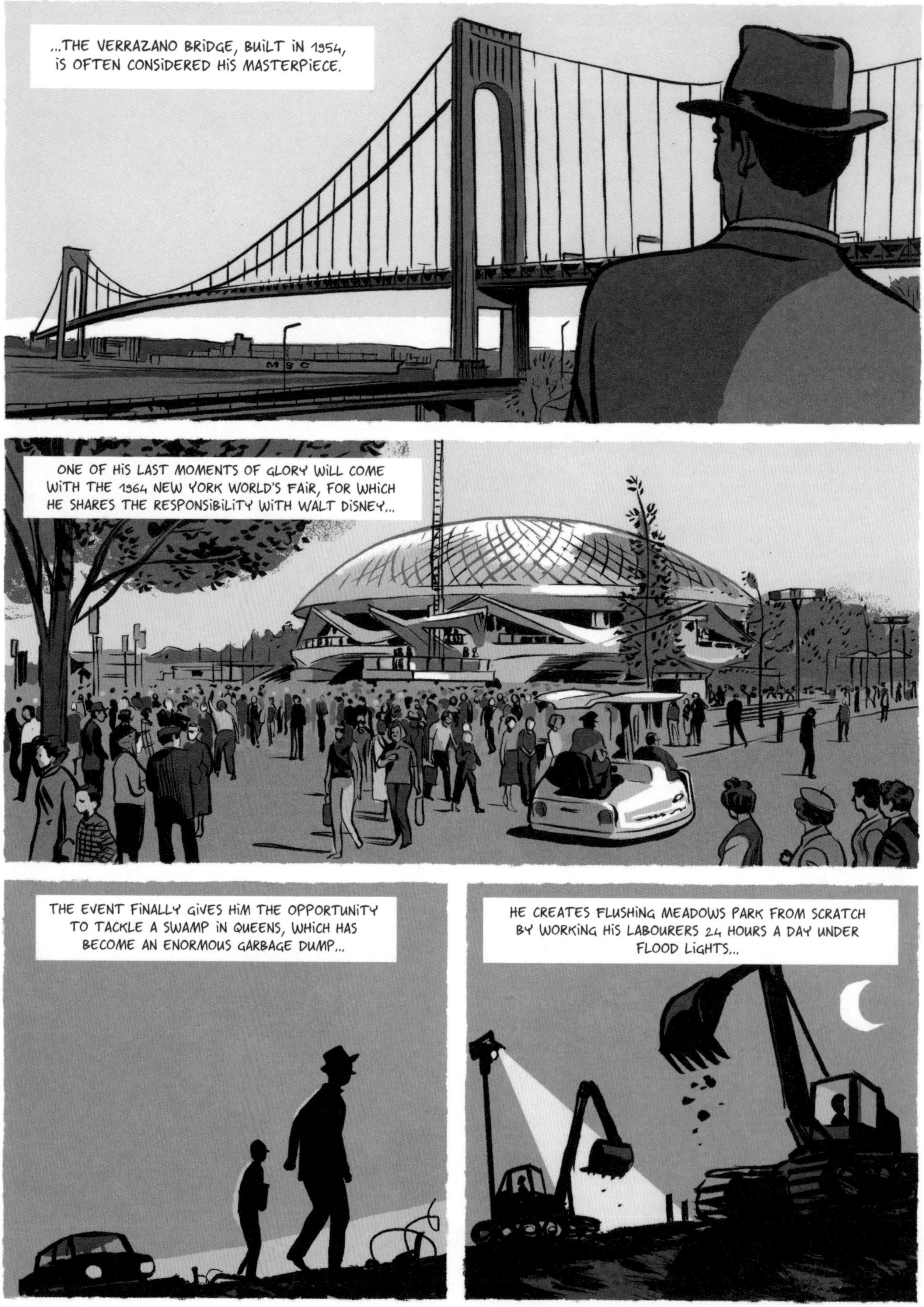
...THE VERRAZANO BRIDGE, BUILT IN 1954, IS OFTEN CONSIDERED HIS MASTERPIECE.
ONE OF HIS LAST MOMENTS OF GLORY WILL COME WITH THE 1964 NEW YORK WORLD'S FAIR, FOR WHICH HE SHARES THE RESPONSIBILITY WITH WALT DISNEY...
THE EVENT FINALLY GIVES HIM THE OPPORTUNITY TO TACKLE A SWAMP IN QUEENS, WHICH HAS BECOME AN ENORMOUS GARBAGE DUMP...
HE CREATES FLUSHING MEADOWS PARK FROM SCRATCH BY WORKING HIS LABOURERS 24 HOURS A DAY UNDER FLOOD LIGHTS...

THE THEME OF THE FAIR IS "THE WORLD OF TOMORROW" AND MOSES, AS USUAL, TAKES ADVANTAGE OF THE SITUATION TO GROOM HIS DEMIURGIC IMAGE.

IT REMAINS TODAY AS A HAGGARD MODERNIST SUBSIST, USED AS A BACKDROP FOR AN EXTRATERRESTRIAL SPACECRAFT LANDING IN THE FILM "MEN IN BLACK"...

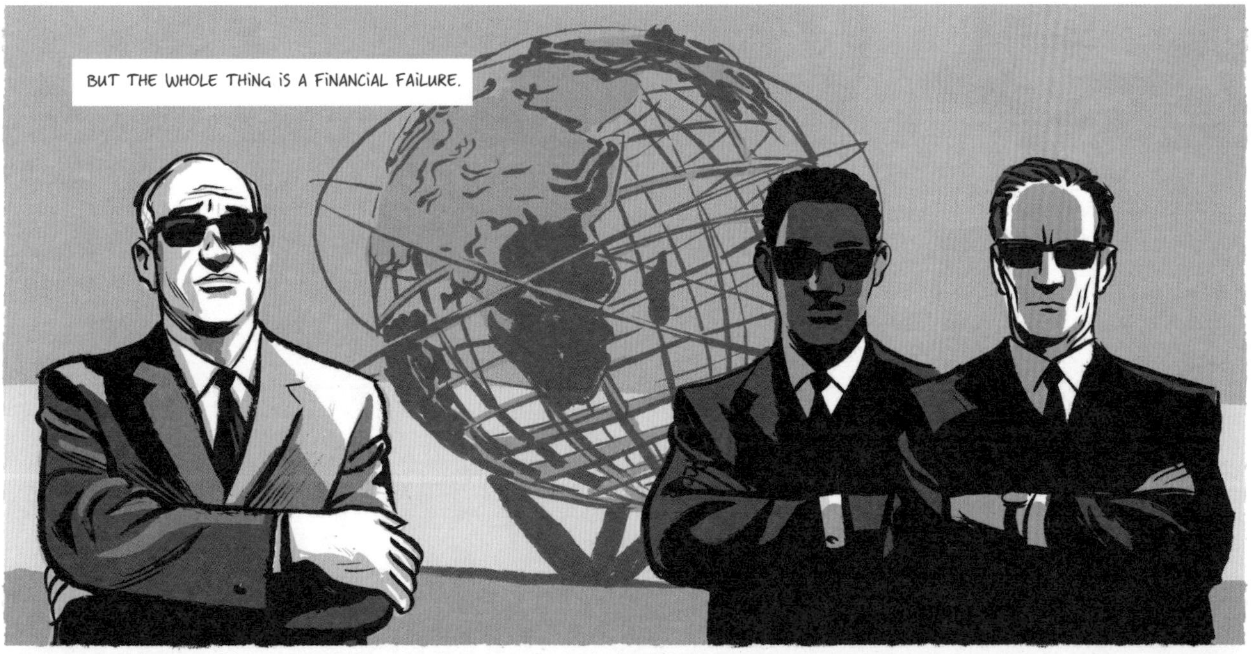
BUT THE WHOLE THING IS A FINANCIAL FAILURE.

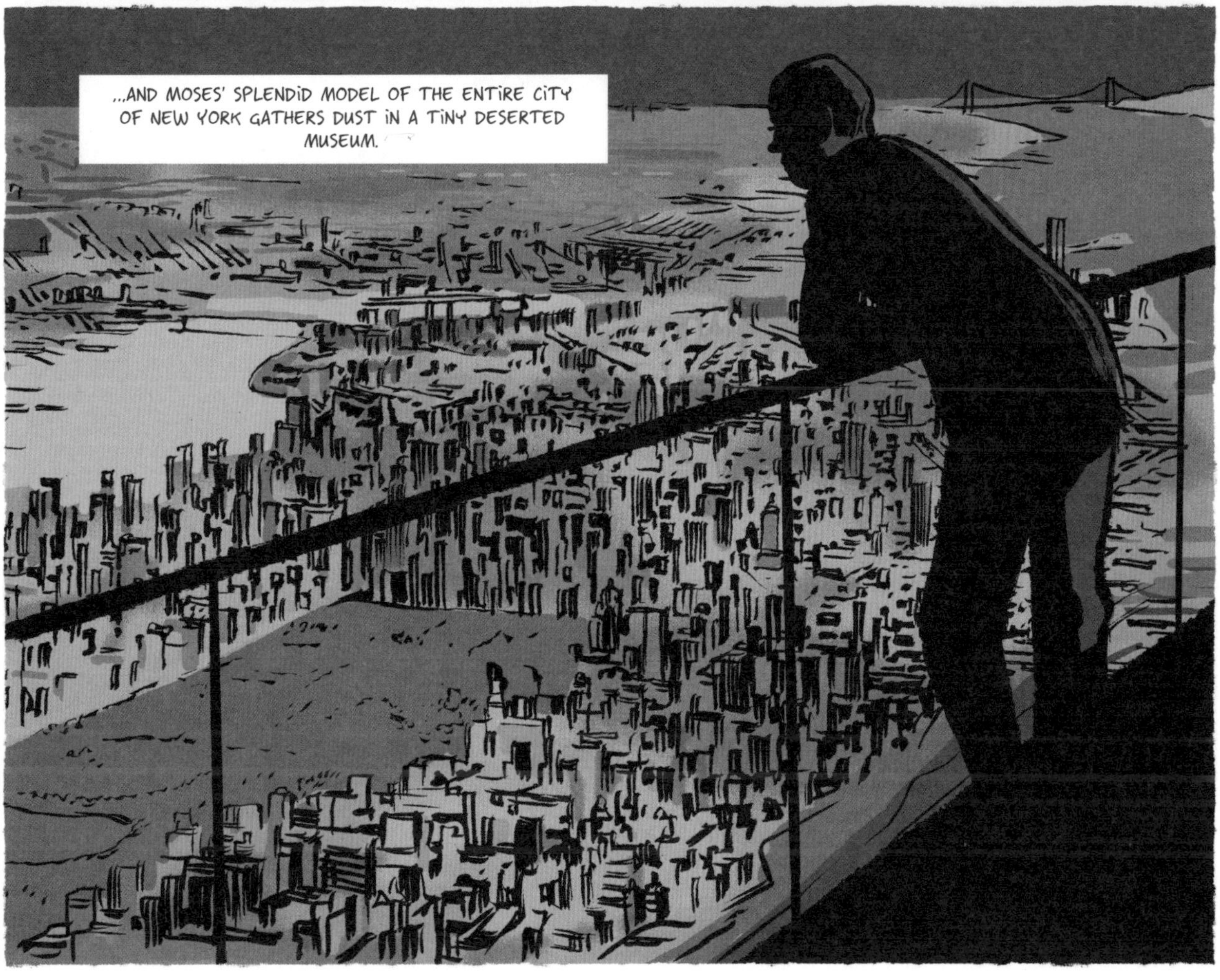
...AND MOSES' SPLENDID MODEL OF THE ENTIRE CITY OF NEW YORK GATHERS DUST IN A TINY DESERTED MUSEUM.

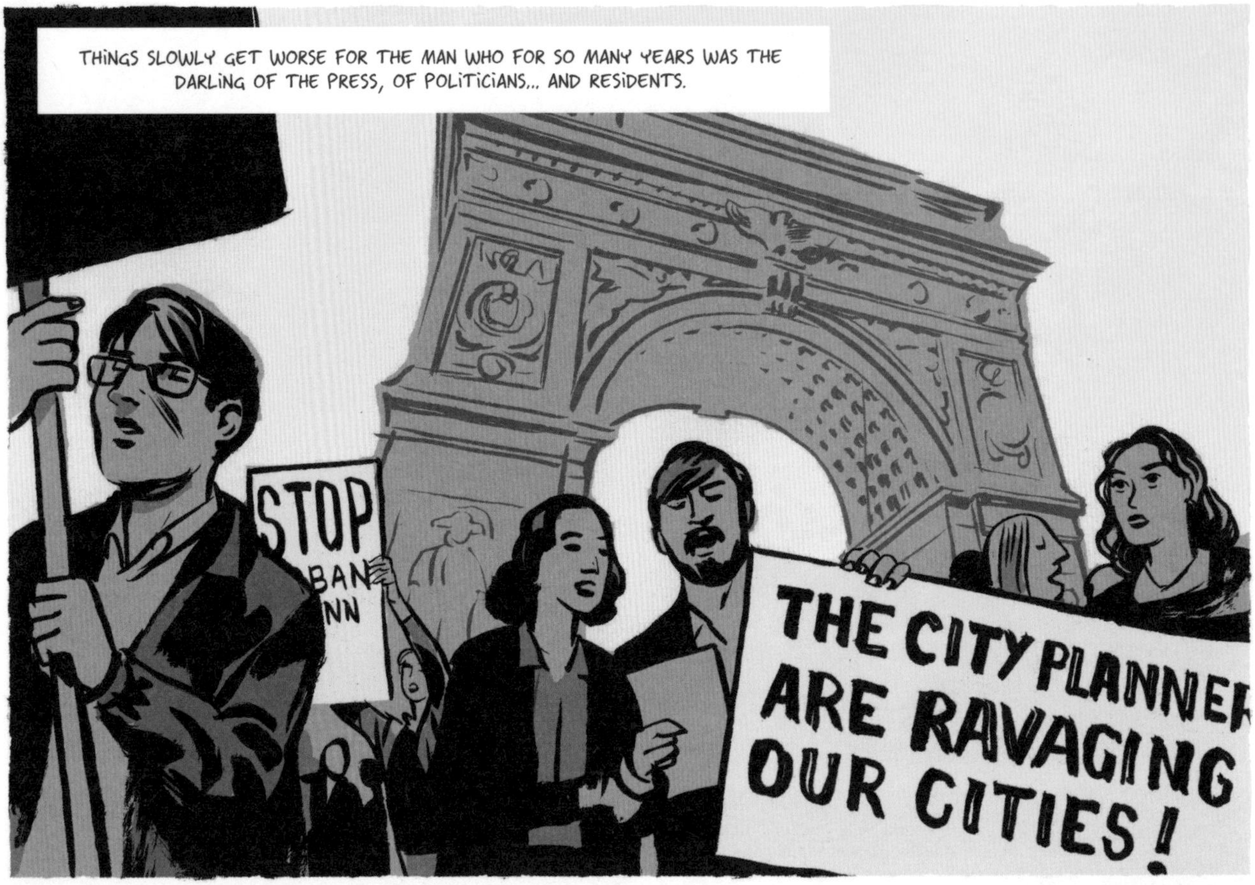
THINGS SLOWLY GET WORSE FOR THE MAN WHO FOR SO MANY YEARS WAS THE DARLING OF THE PRESS, OF POLITICIANS... AND RESIDENTS.
STOP
THE CITY PLANNER
ARE RAVAGING
OUR CITIES!

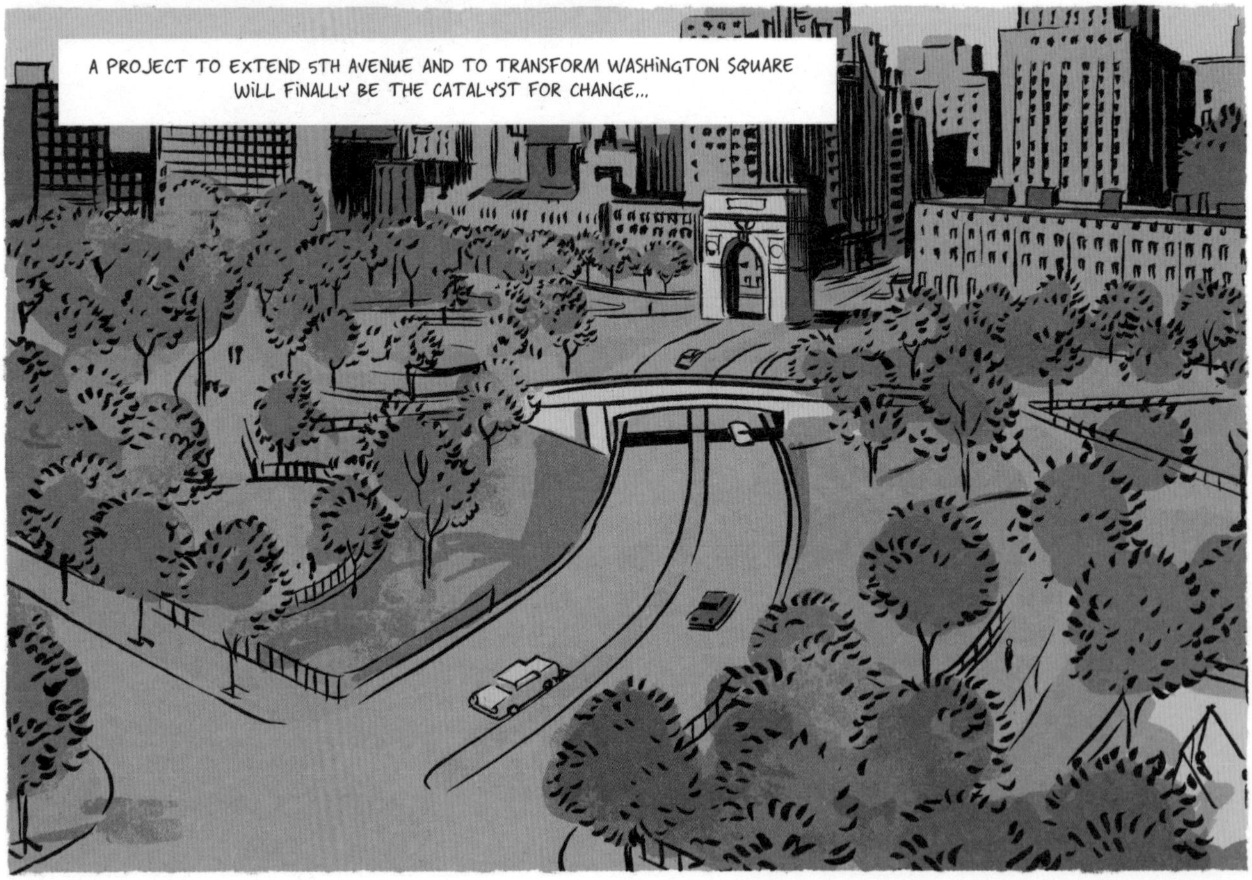
A PROJECT TO EXTEND 5TH AVENUE AND TO TRANSFORM WASHINGTON SQUARE WILL FINALLY BE THE CATALYST FOR CHANGE...

THIS INNER CITY OASIS CHERISHED FOR OVER A CENTURY BY WRITERS, PAINTERS, MUSICIANS AND EVERYDAY PEOPLE WILL FIND HISTORICAL DEFENDERS...

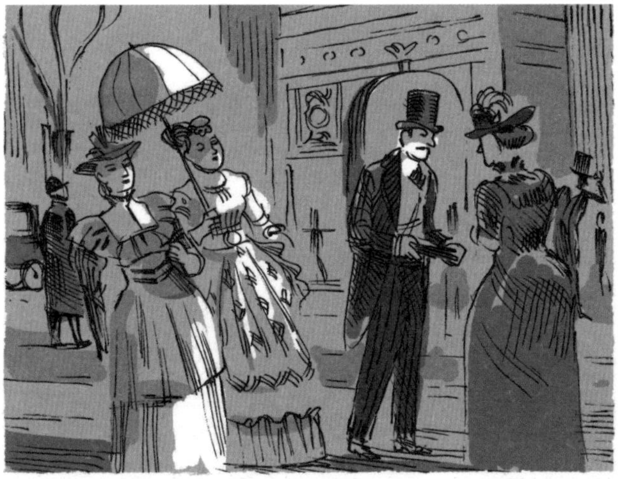

THE PROSPECT OF THIS SITE AND ITS SURROUNDINGS BEING DEVASTATED BY AN AUTOMOBILE INVASION OFFENDS A NEW SENSIBILITY TO THE OLD, PROVOKING RESISTANCE THAT IS AS STUBBORN AS IT IS SHREWD.

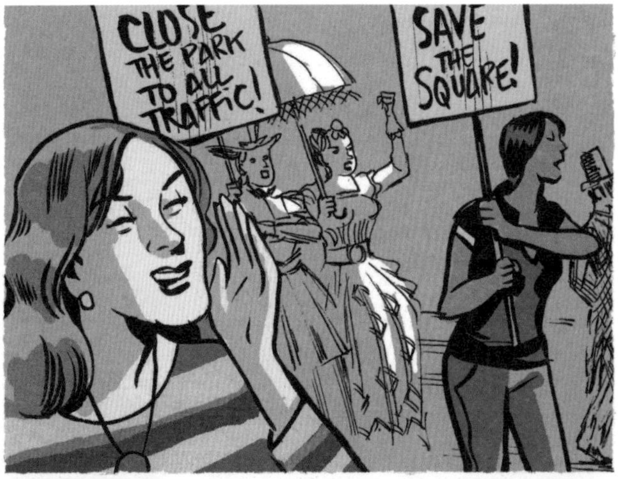
CLOSE THE PARK TO ALL TRAFFIC!
SAVE THE SQUARE!

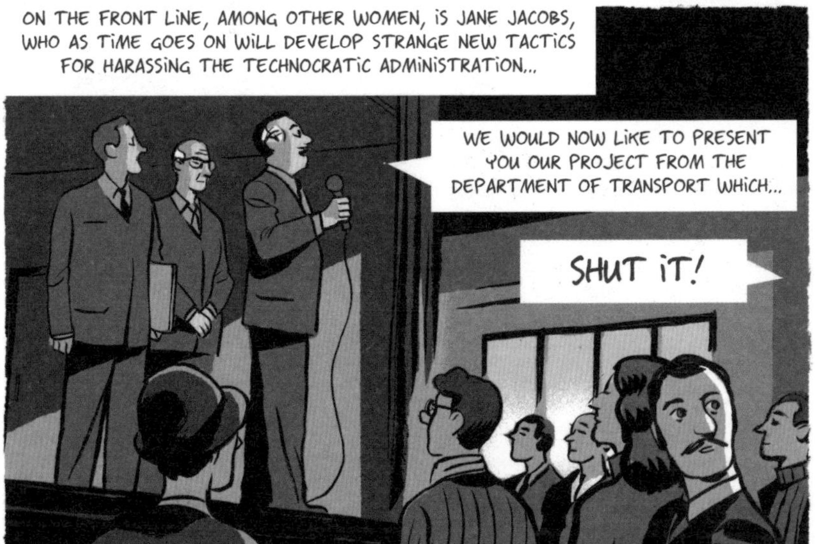
ON THE FRONT LINE, AMONG OTHER WOMEN, IS JANE JACOBS, WHO AS TIME GOES ON WILL DEVELOP STRANGE NEW TACTICS FOR HARASSING THE TECHNOCRATIC ADMINISTRATION...
WE WOULD NOW LIKE TO PRESENT YOU OUR PROJECT FROM THE DEPARTMENT OF TRANSPORT WHICH...
SHUT IT!

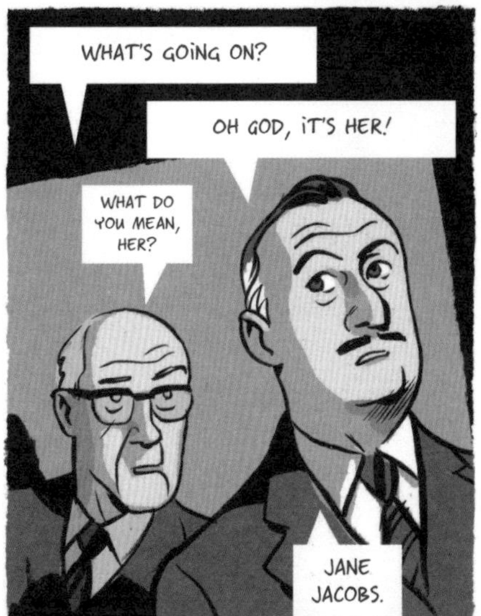
WHAT'S GOING ON?
OH GOD, IT'S HER!
WHAT DO YOU MEAN, HER?
JANE JACOBS.

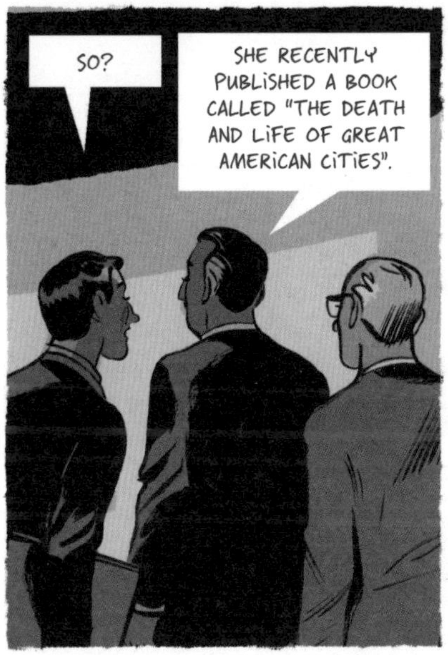
SO?
SHE RECENTLY PUBLISHED A BOOK CALLED "THE DEATH AND LIFE OF GREAT AMERICAN CITIES".

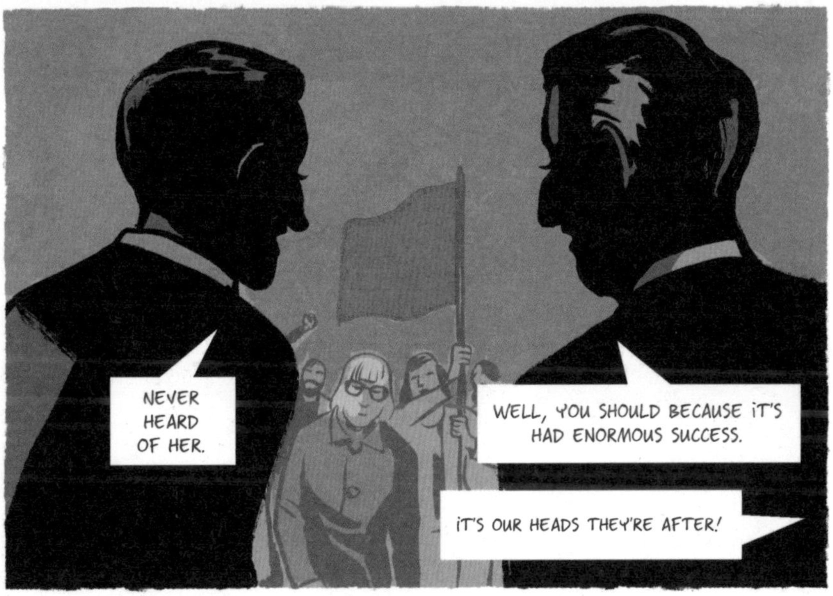
NEVER HEARD OF HER.
WELL, YOU SHOULD BECAUSE IT'S HAD ENORMOUS SUCCESS.
IT'S OUR HEADS THEY'RE AFTER!

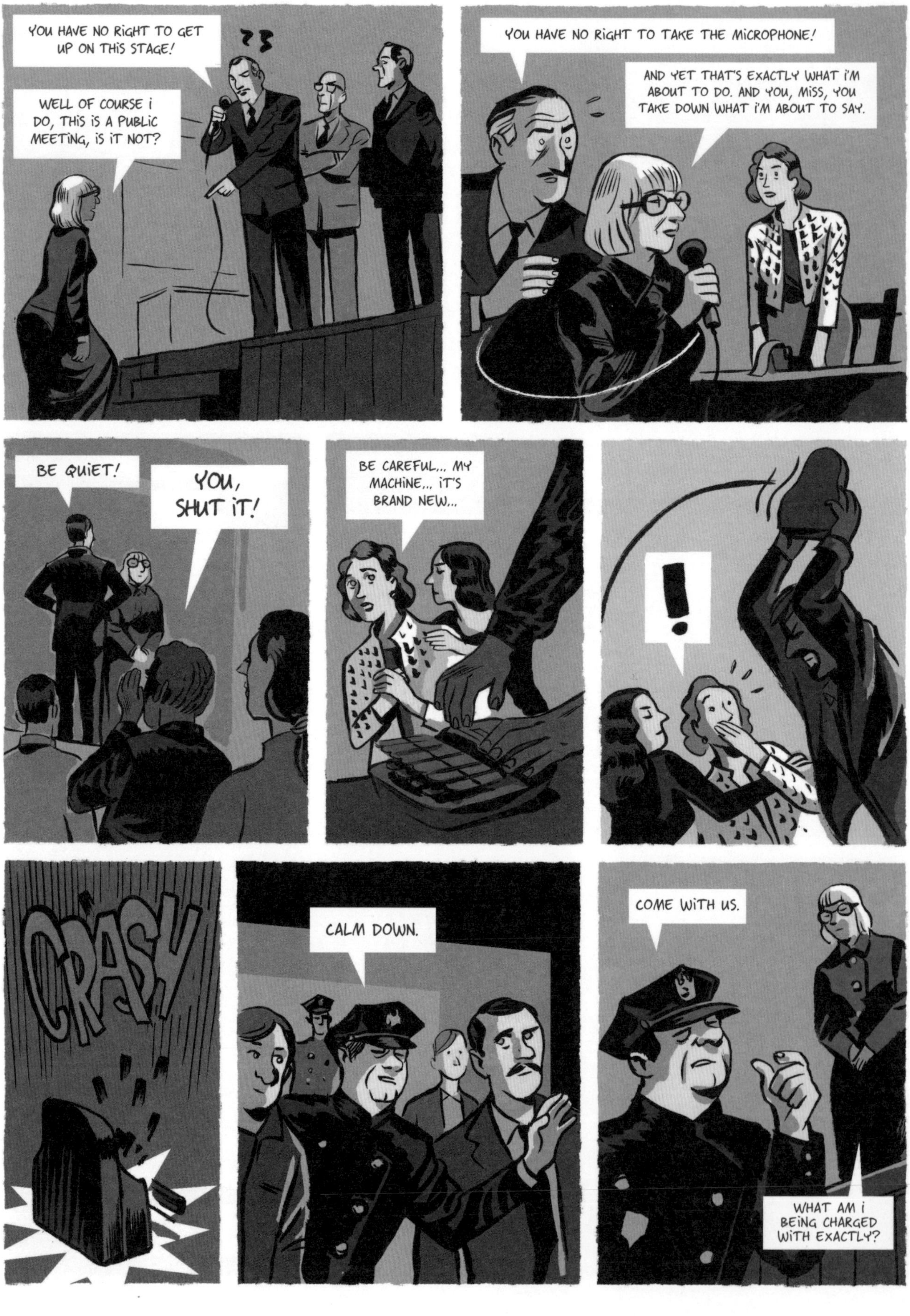
YOU HAVE NO RIGHT TO GET UP ON THIS STAGE!
WELL OF COURSE I DO, THIS IS A PUBLIC MEETING, IS IT NOT?
YOU HAVE NO RIGHT TO TAKE THE MICROPHONE!
AND YET THAT'S EXACTLY WHAT I'M ABOUT TO DO. AND YOU, MISS, YOU TAKE DOWN WHAT I'M ABOUT TO SAY.
BE QUIET!
YOU, SHUT IT!
BE CAREFUL... MY MACHINE... IT'S BRAND NEW...
!
CRASH
CALM DOWN.
COME WITH US.
WHAT AM I BEING CHARGED WITH EXACTLY?

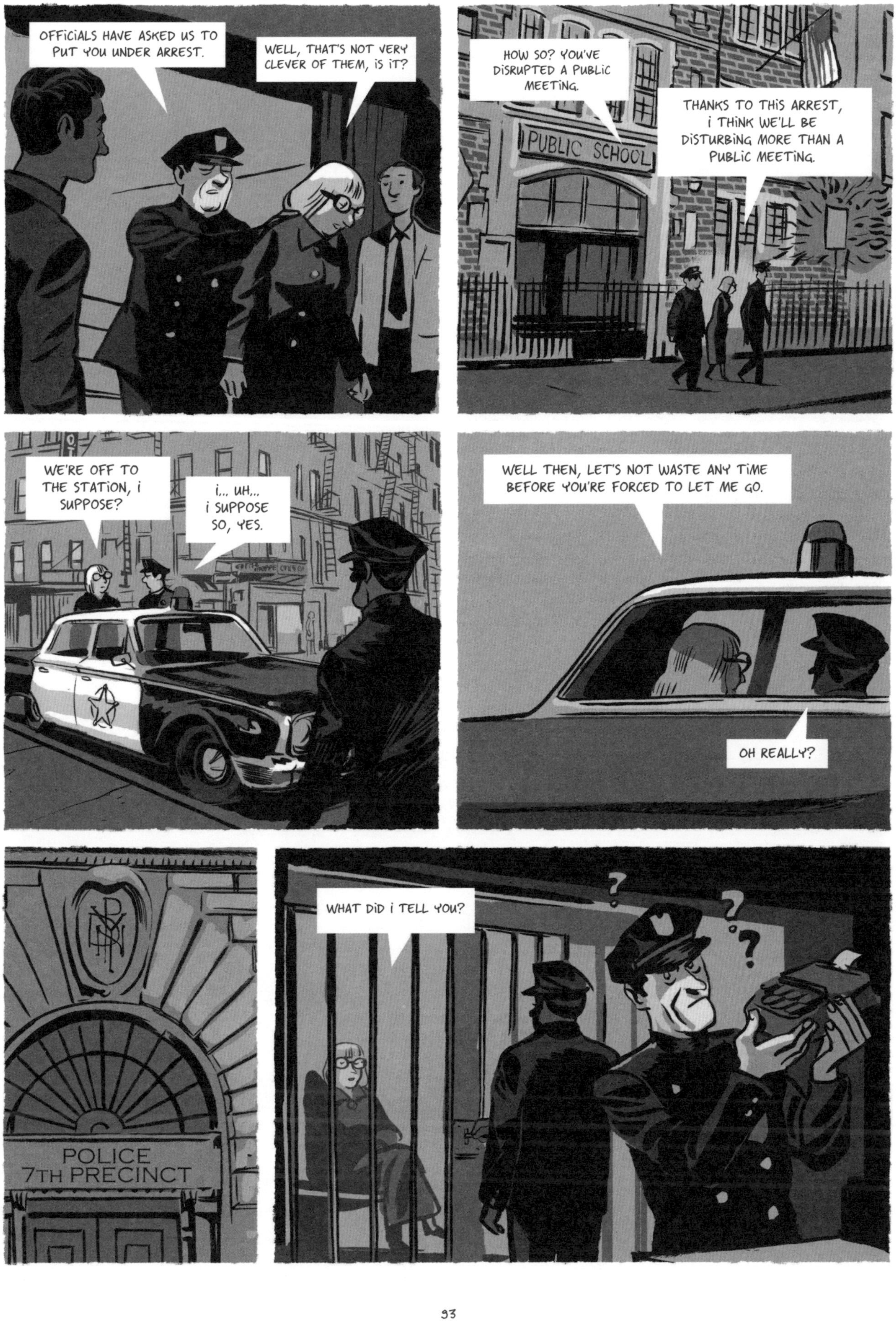
OFFICIALS HAVE ASKED US TO PUT YOU UNDER ARREST.
WELL, THAT'S NOT VERY CLEVER OF THEM, IS IT?
HOW SO? YOU'VE DISRUPTED A PUBLIC MEETING.
PUBLIC SCHOOL
THANKS TO THIS ARREST, I THINK WE'LL BE DISTURBING MORE THAN A PUBLIC MEETING.
WE'RE OFF TO THE STATION, I SUPPOSE?
I... UH... I SUPPOSE SO, YES.
WELL THEN, LET'S NOT WASTE ANY TIME BEFORE YOU'RE FORCED TO LET ME GO.
OH REALLY?
POLICE
7TH PRECINCT
WHAT DID I TELL YOU?
?
??

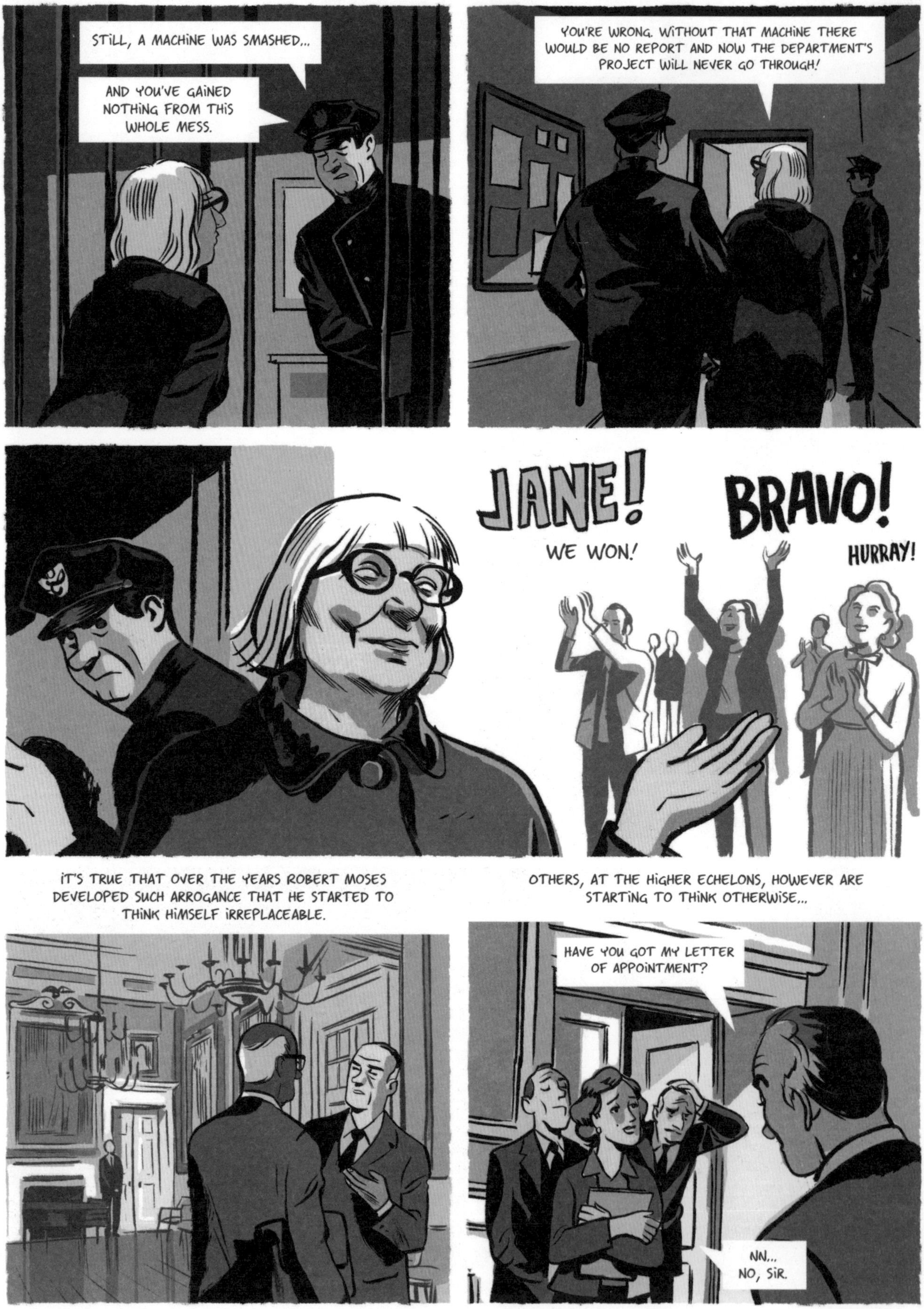
STILL, A MACHINE WAS SMASHED...
AND YOU'VE GAINED NOTHING FROM THIS WHOLE MESS.
YOU'RE WRONG. WITHOUT THAT MACHINE THERE WOULD BE NO REPORT AND NOW THE DEPARTMENT'S PROJECT WILL NEVER GO THROUGH!
JANE!
BRAVO!
WE WON!
HURRAY!
IT'S TRUE THAT OVER THE YEARS ROBERT MOSES DEVELOPED SUCH ARROGANCE THAT HE STARTED TO THINK HIMSELF IRREPLACEABLE.
OTHERS, AT THE HIGHER ECHELONS, HOWEVER ARE STARTING TO THINK OTHERWISE...
HAVE YOU GOT MY LETTER OF APPOINTMENT?
NN... NO, SIR.

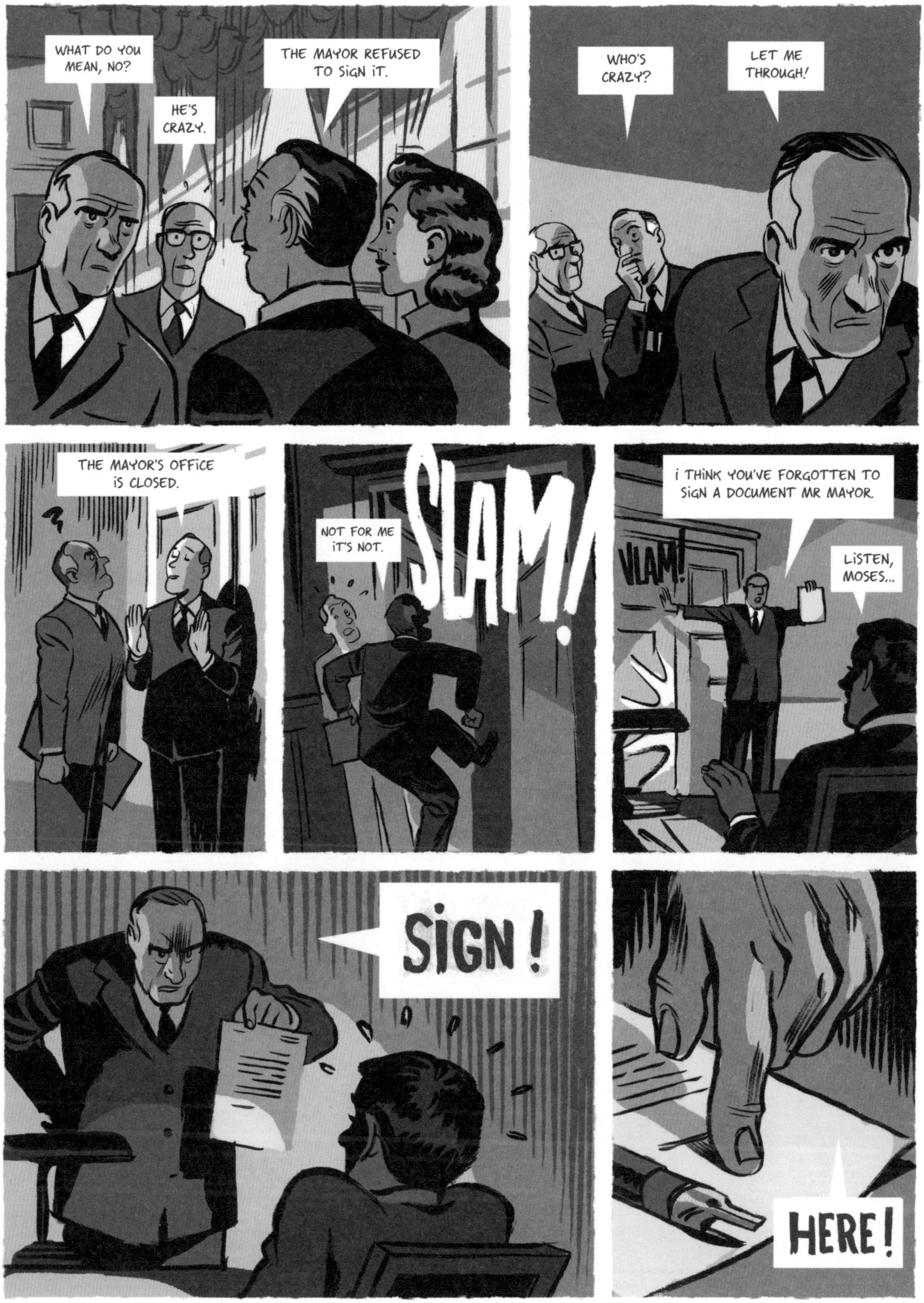
WHAT DO YOU MEAN, NO?
HE'S CRAZY.
THE MAYOR REFUSED TO SIGN IT.
WHO'S CRAZY?
LET ME THROUGH!
THE MAYOR'S OFFICE IS CLOSED.
NOT FOR ME IT'S NOT.
SLAM!
VLAM!
I THINK YOU'VE FORGOTTEN TO SIGN A DOCUMENT MR MAYOR.
LISTEN, MOSES...
SIGN!
HERE!

IT'S ALSO SAFE TO SAY THAT ROBERT MOSES IS ALWAYS DRIVEN BY A GLOBAL VISION OF THE CITY, A VISION HE IS NOT ABOUT TO ABANDON...

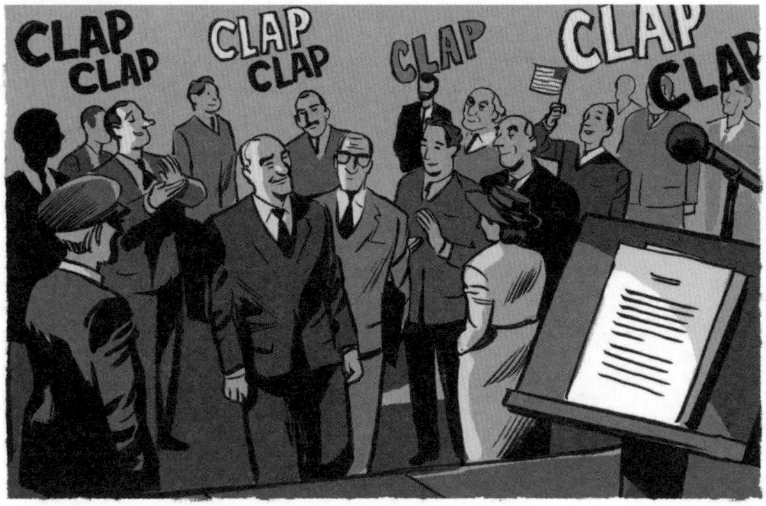
CLAP CLAP
CLAP CLAP
CLAP
CLAP CLAP

...AND MANY OTHERS ARE BEHIND HIM WHEN HE PRESENTS HIS IDEA OF THE FUTURE.

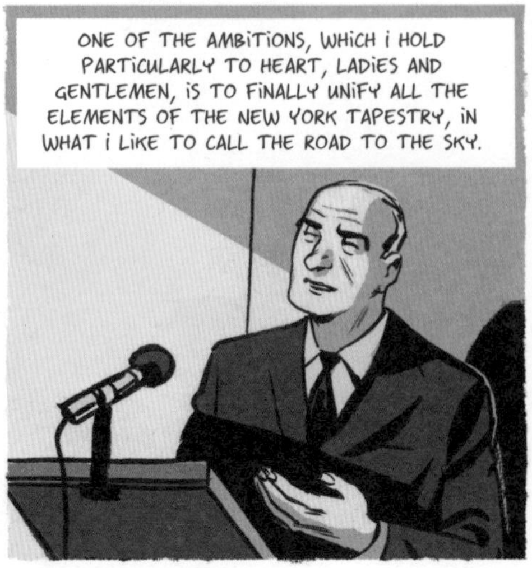
ONE OF THE AMBITIONS, WHICH I HOLD PARTICULARLY TO HEART, LADIES AND GENTLEMEN, IS TO FINALLY UNIFY ALL THE ELEMENTS OF THE NEW YORK TAPESTRY, IN WHAT I LIKE TO CALL THE ROAD TO THE SKY.

AMONG THESE COLOSSAL PROJECTS, IS THE MID-MANHATTAN EXPRESSWAY, AKA THE MME, INTENDED TO LINK THE LINCOLN AND QUEENS MIDTOWN TUNNELS...

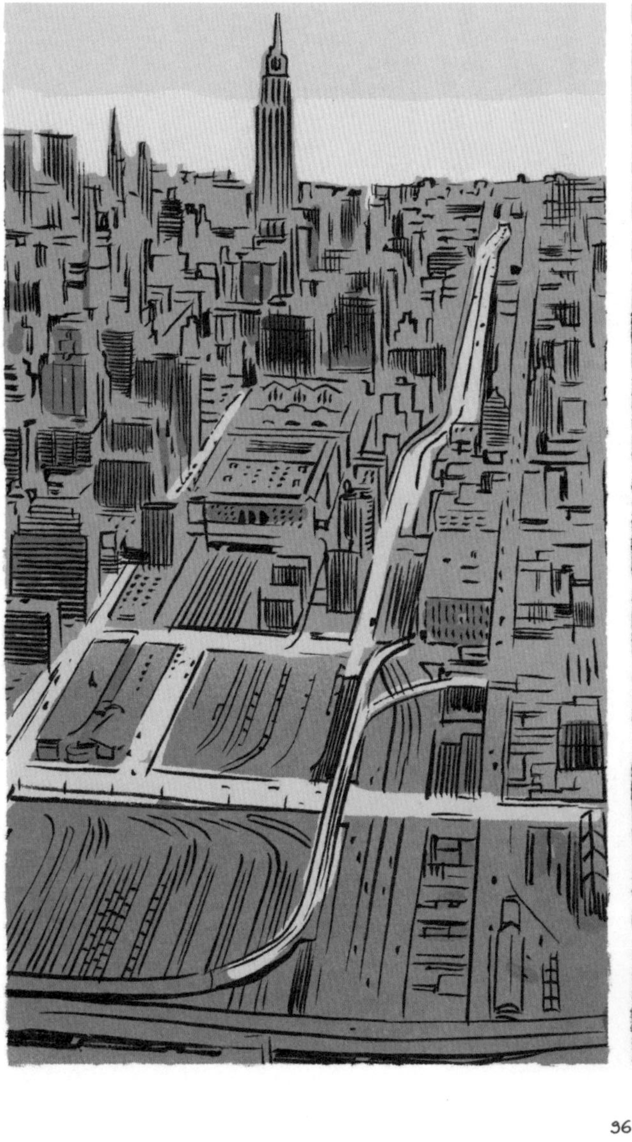

...AN ELEVATED URBAN HIGHWAY LEVEL WITH THE 8TH FLOOR OF THE EMPIRE STATE BUILDING, MOVING STRAIGHT THROUGH THE INTERIOR OF CERTAIN BUILDINGS AND CUTTING THE ISLAND IN HALF...

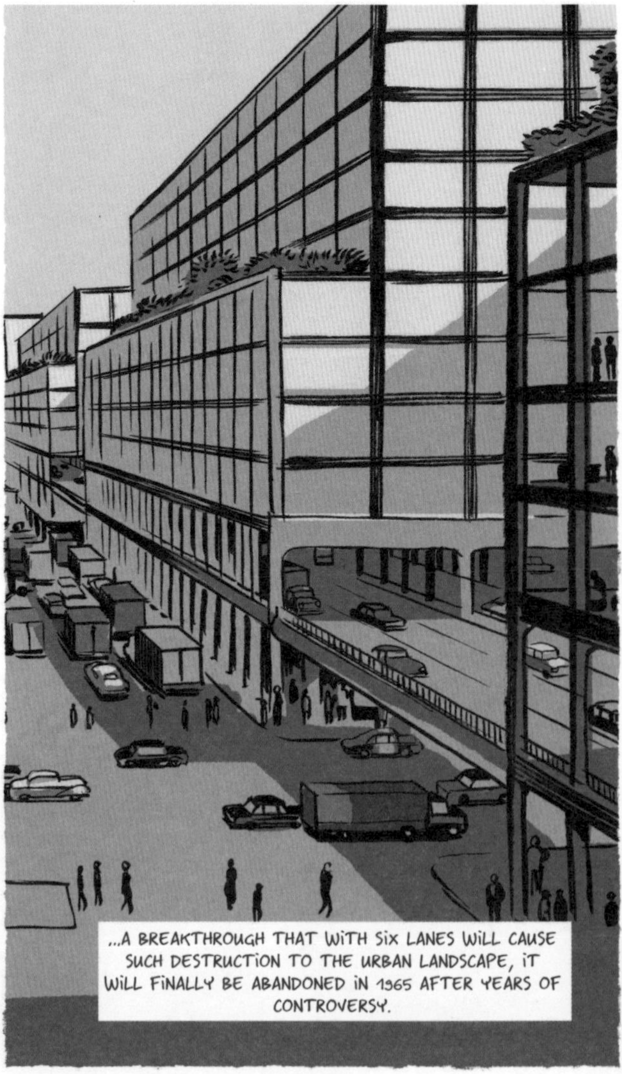
...A BREAKTHROUGH THAT WITH SIX LANES WILL CAUSE SUCH DESTRUCTION TO THE URBAN LANDSCAPE, IT WILL FINALLY BE ABANDONED IN 1965 AFTER YEARS OF CONTROVERSY.

BUT MOSES' FERTILE AND PERHAPS PERVERSE IMAGINATION HAS NO LIMITS AND A SECOND, EQUALLY GARGANTUAN PROJECT WILL BRING THE ANTAGONISM BETWEEN HIM AND JANE JACOBS TO A CLIMAX...

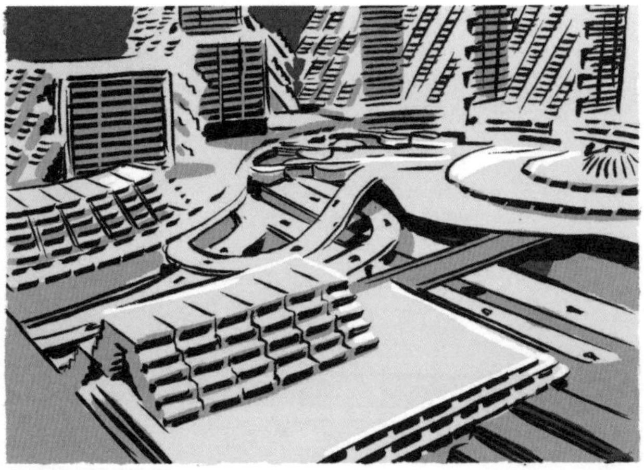

JANE HAS NO TROUBLE DENOUNCING THE MONSTROUS "SPAGHETTI BOWL" THAT WILL CONSTITUTE THE LOWER MANHATTAN EXPRESSWAY, SOON ALSO TO BE KNOWN AS THE LOMEX...

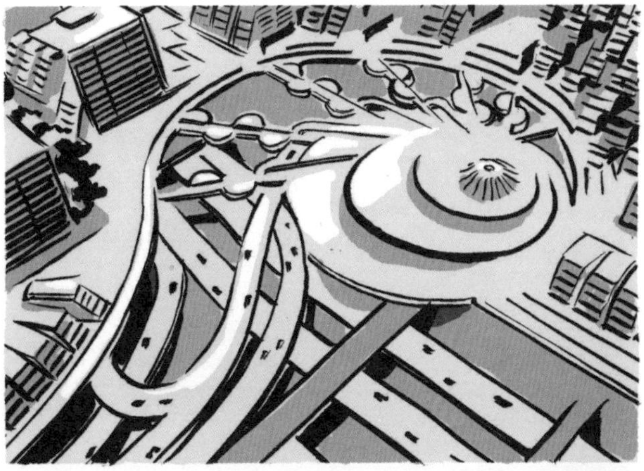

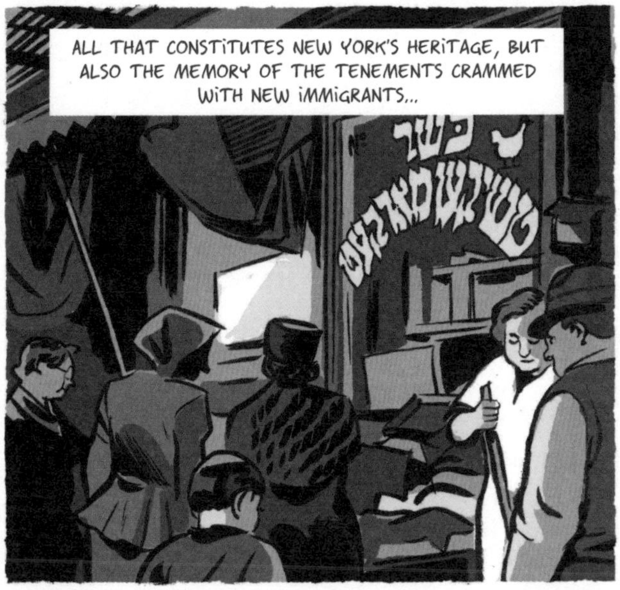
ALL THAT CONSTITUTES NEW YORK'S HERITAGE, BUT ALSO THE MEMORY OF THE TENEMENTS CRAMMED WITH NEW IMMIGRANTS...

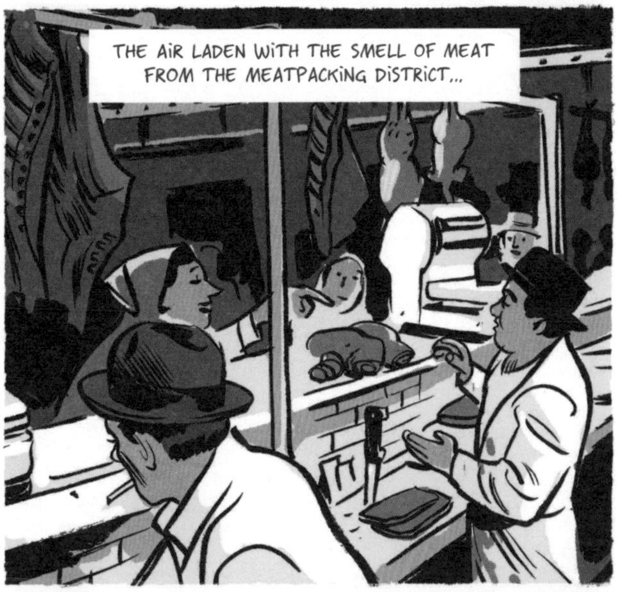
THE AIR LADEN WITH THE SMELL OF MEAT FROM THE MEATPACKING DISTRICT...

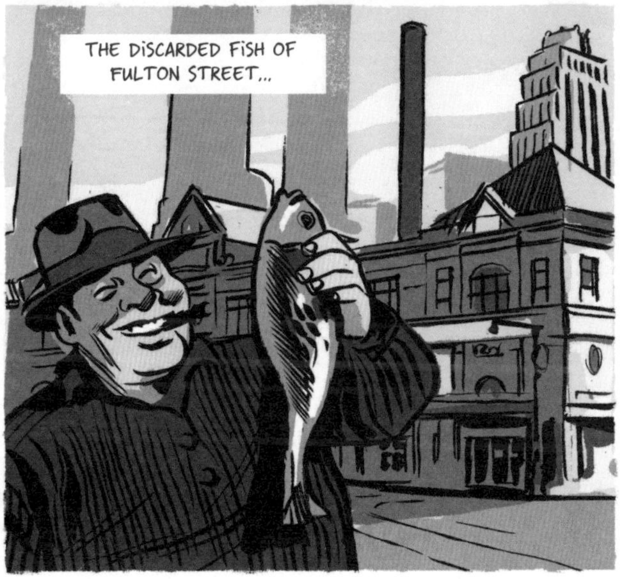
THE DISCARDED FISH OF FULTON STREET...

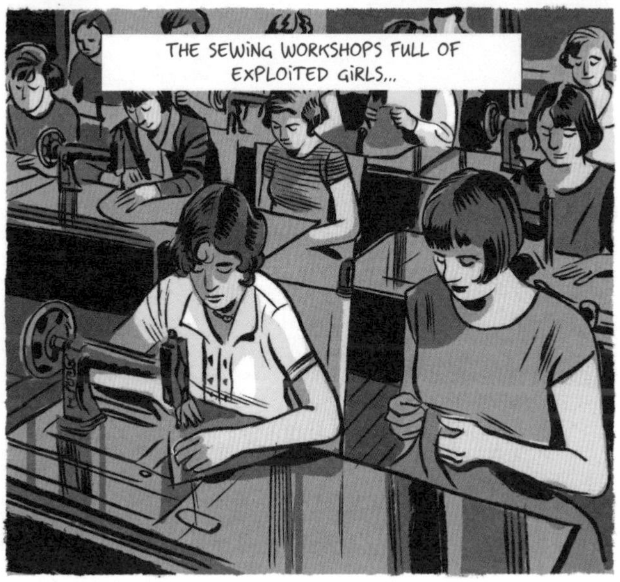
THE SEWING WORKSHOPS FULL OF EXPLOITED GIRLS...

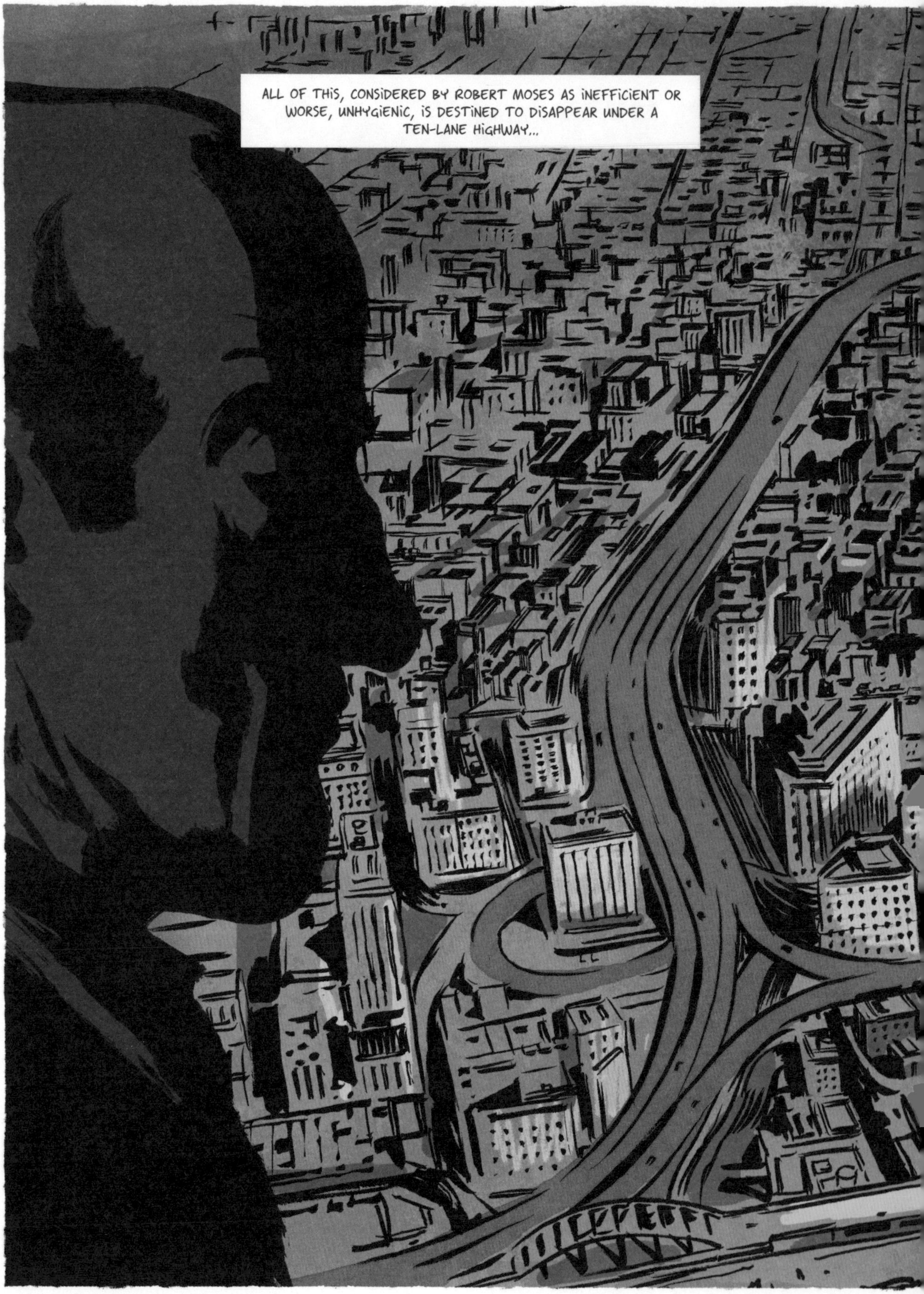
ALL OF THIS, CONSIDERED BY ROBERT MOSES AS INEFFICIENT OR WORSE, UNHYGIENIC, IS DESTINED TO DISAPPEAR UNDER A TEN-LANE HIGHWAY...

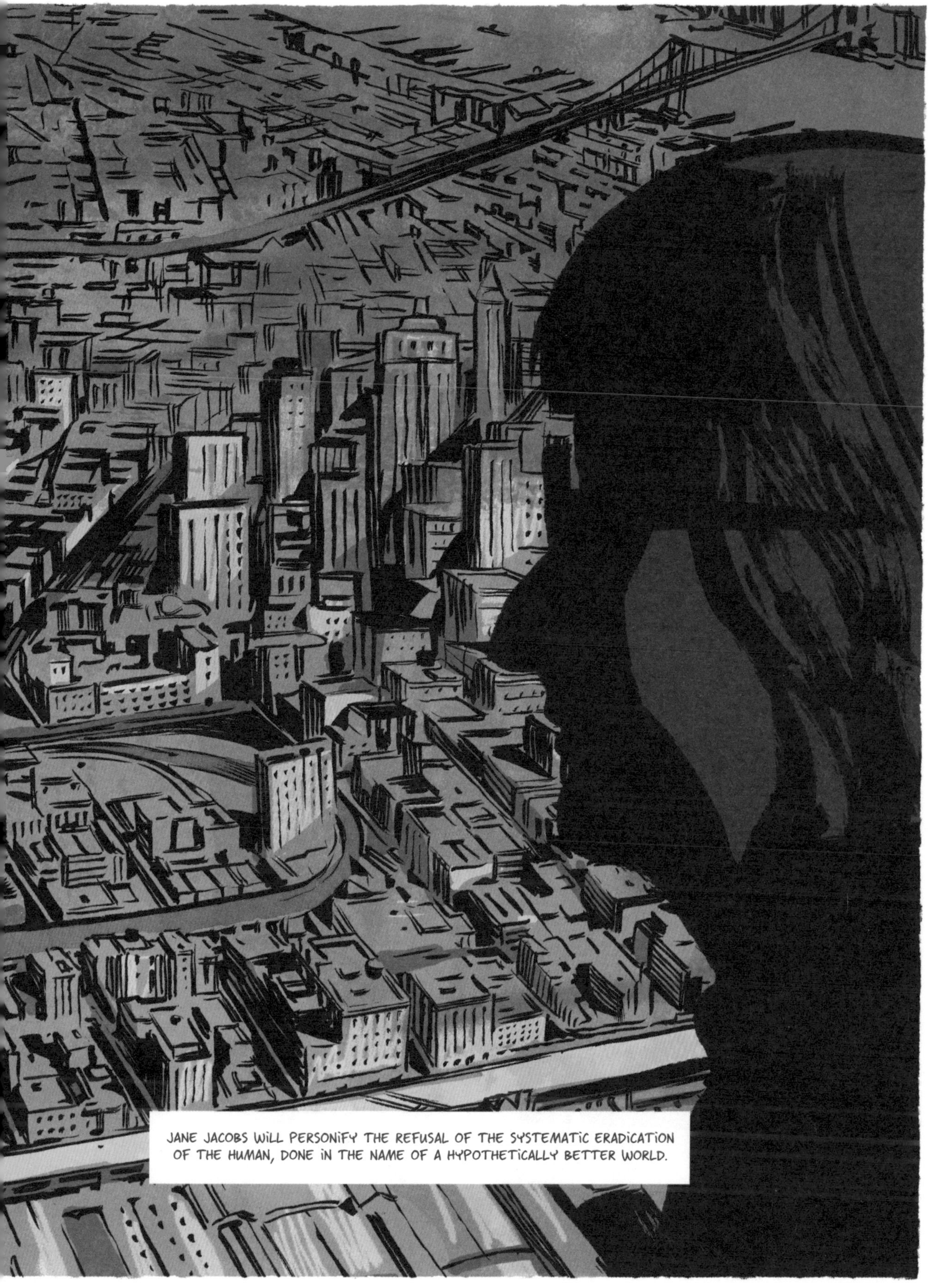
JANE JACOBS WILL PERSONIFY THE REFUSAL OF THE SYSTEMATIC ERADICATION OF THE HUMAN, DONE IN THE NAME OF A HYPOTHETICALLY BETTER WORLD.

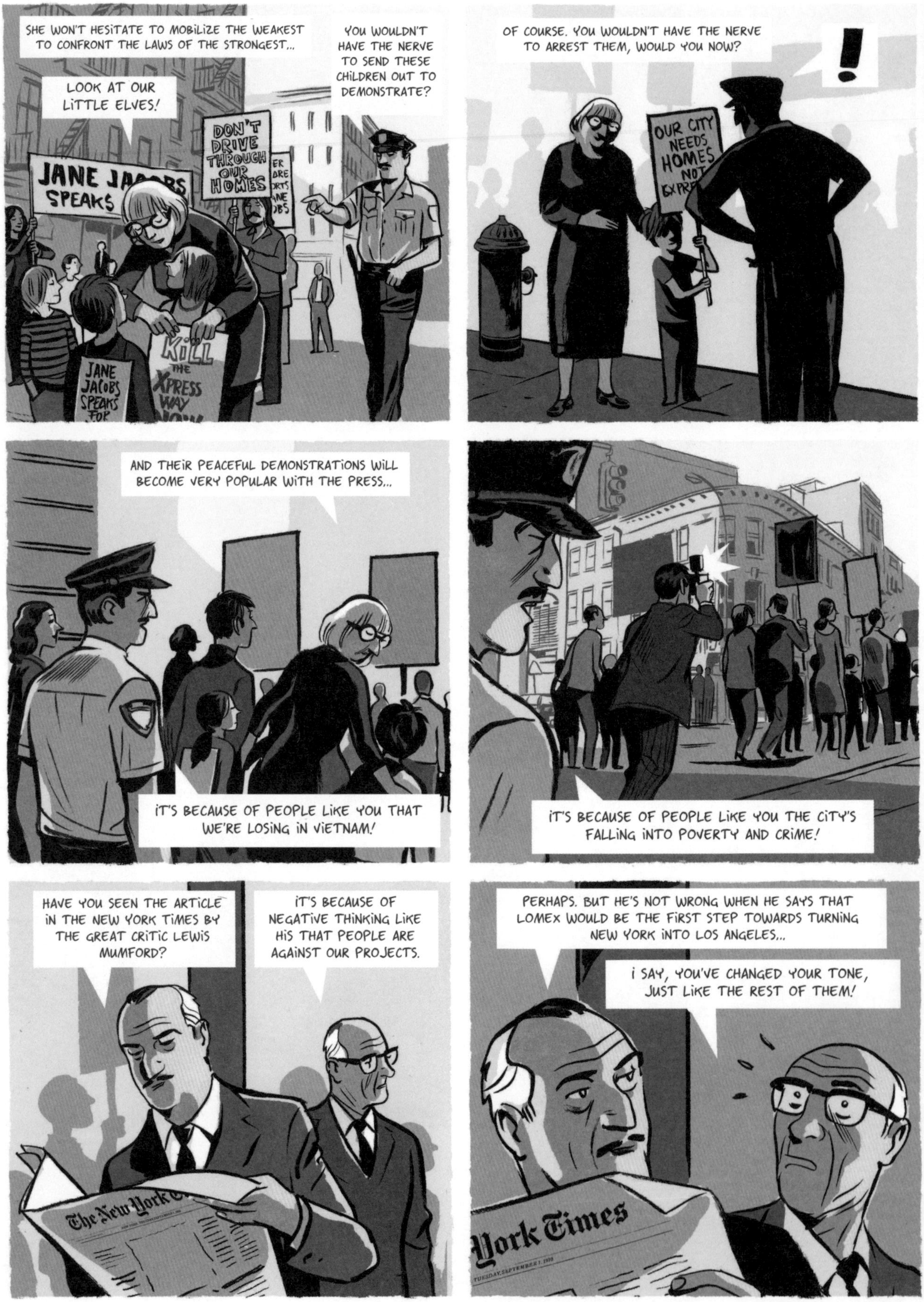
SHE WON'T HESITATE TO MOBILIZE THE WEAKEST TO CONFRONT THE LAWS OF THE STRONGEST...
LOOK AT OUR LITTLE ELVES!
YOU WOULDN'T HAVE THE NERVE TO SEND THESE CHILDREN OUT TO DEMONSTRATE?
DON'T DRIVE THROUGH OUR HOMES
SPEAKS
KILL THE XPRESS WAY
JANE JACOBS SPEAKS
OF COURSE. YOU WOULDN'T HAVE THE NERVE TO ARREST THEM, WOULD YOU NOW?
!
OUR CITY NEEDS HOMES
AND THEIR PEACEFUL DEMONSTRATIONS WILL BECOME VERY POPULAR WITH THE PRESS...
IT'S BECAUSE OF PEOPLE LIKE YOU THAT WE'RE LOSING IN VIETNAM!
IT'S BECAUSE OF PEOPLE LIKE YOU THE CITY'S FALLING INTO POVERTY AND CRIME!
HAVE YOU SEEN THE ARTICLE IN THE NEW YORK TIMES BY THE GREAT CRITIC LEWIS MUMFORD?
IT'S BECAUSE OF NEGATIVE THINKING LIKE HIS THAT PEOPLE ARE AGAINST OUR PROJECTS.
PERHAPS. BUT HE'S NOT WRONG WHEN HE SAYS THAT LOMEX WOULD BE THE FIRST STEP TOWARDS TURNING NEW YORK INTO LOS ANGELES...
I SAY, YOU'VE CHANGED YOUR TONE, JUST LIKE THE REST OF THEM!
York Times

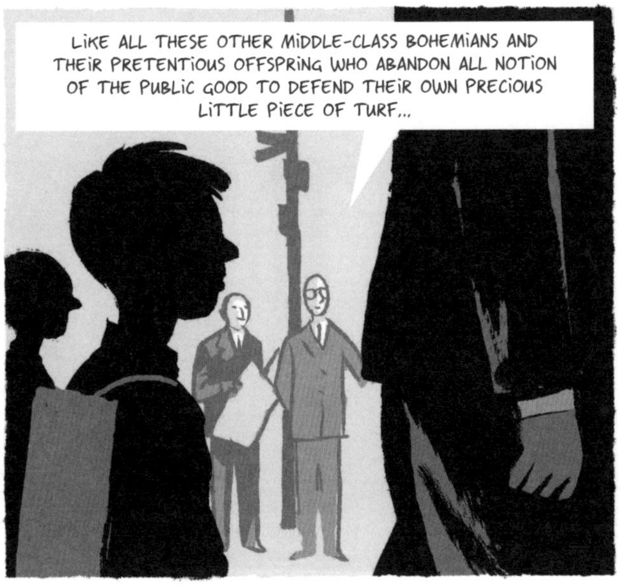
LIKE ALL THESE OTHER MIDDLE-CLASS BOHEMIANS AND THEIR PRETENTIOUS OFFSPRING WHO ABANDON ALL NOTION OF THE PUBLIC GOOD TO DEFEND THEIR OWN PRECIOUS LITTLE PIECE OF TURF...

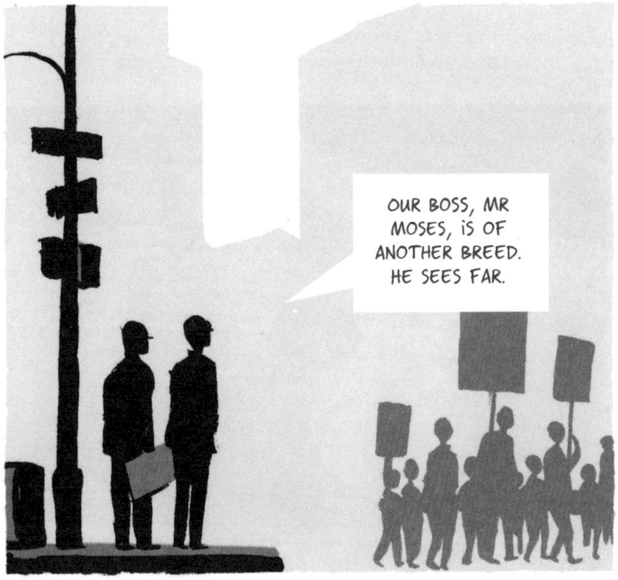
OUR BOSS, MR MOSES, IS OF ANOTHER BREED. HE SEES FAR.

IN THE END IT'S YET ANOTHER BIG FISH IN THE NEW YORK POND THAT WILL DECIDE THE FUTURE OF THE UNSINKABLE DOCTOR MOSES:

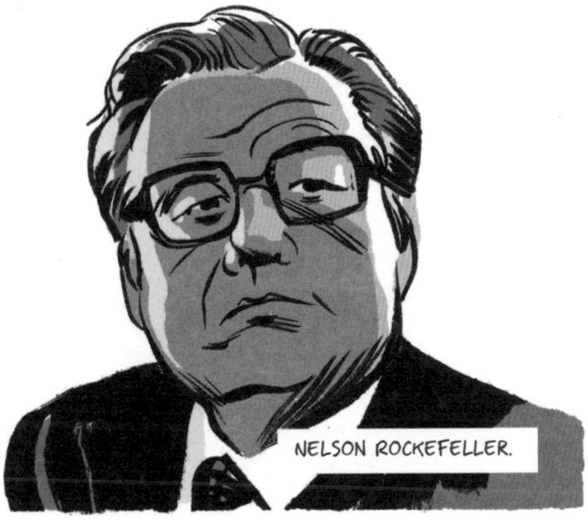
NELSON ROCKEFELLER.

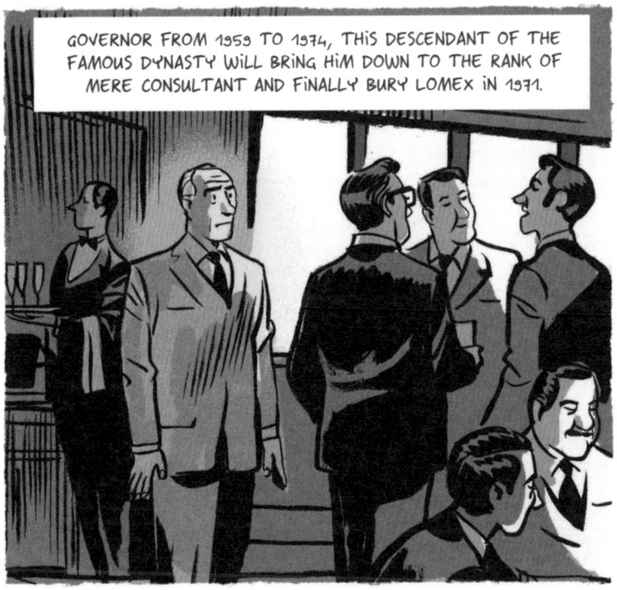
GOVERNOR FROM 1959 TO 1974, THIS DESCENDANT OF THE FAMOUS DYNASTY WILL BRING HIM DOWN TO THE RANK OF MERE CONSULTANT AND FINALLY BURY LOMEX IN 1971.

WHILE THE BRONX IS BURNING AND THE CITY IS SINKING IN BANKRUPTCY, SOME THINK THE WOUNDS INFLICTED ON THE CITY BY MOSES ARE TO BLAME FOR THE DISEASE.

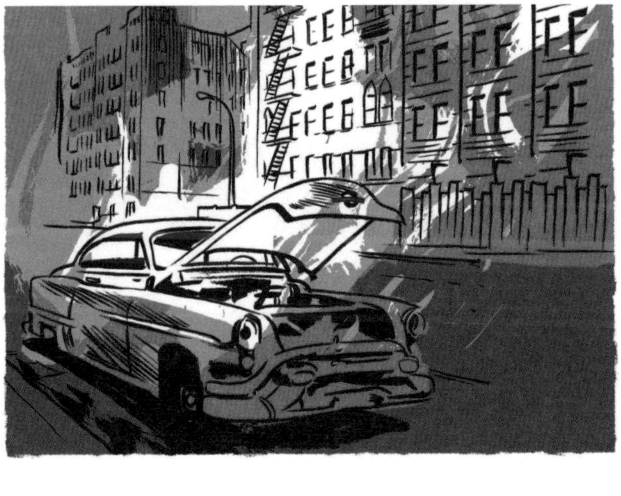

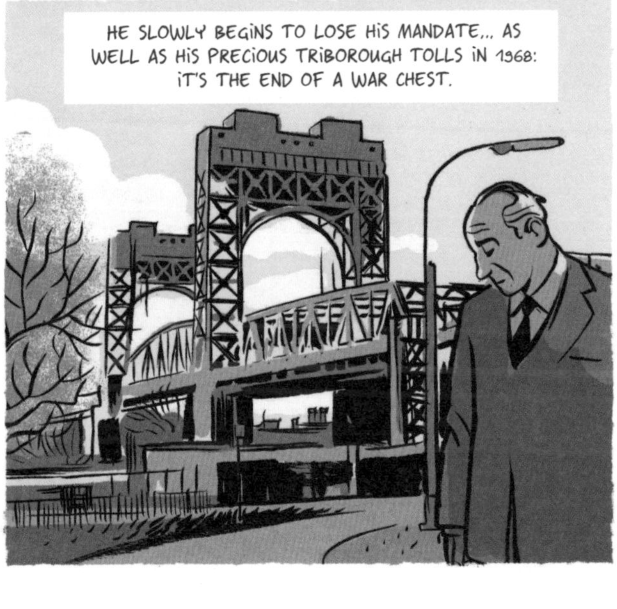
HE SLOWLY BEGINS TO LOSE HIS MANDATE... AS WELL AS HIS PRECIOUS TRIBOROUGH TOLLS IN 1968: IT'S THE END OF A WAR CHEST.

IN 1974, A DEVASTATING BIOGRAPHY BY ROBERT CARO PROPOSES "THE HISTORY OF NEW YORK AND THE STORY OF ROBERT MOSES ARE ONE AND THE SAME".

MOSES, WHO MARRIED HIS SECRETARY AFTER THE DEATH OF HIS WIFE, WILL END HIS DAYS IN HIS MODEST HOUSE ON GILGO BEACH WITH HIS LITTLE BOAT BOB...

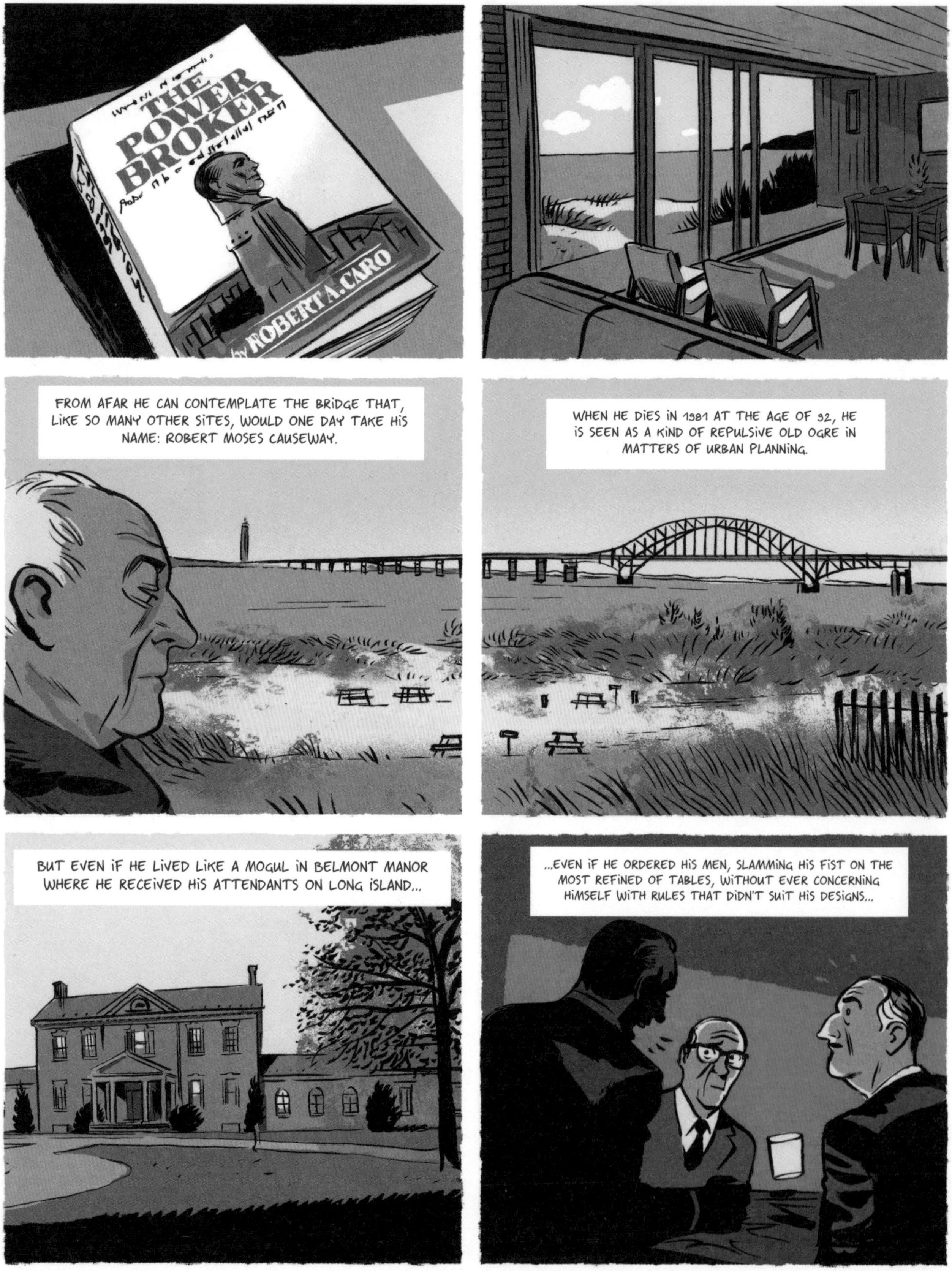
THE POWER BROKER
ROBERT A. CARO
by ROBERT A. CARO
FROM AFAR HE CAN CONTEMPLATE THE BRIDGE THAT, LIKE SO MANY OTHER SITES, WOULD ONE DAY TAKE HIS NAME: ROBERT MOSES CAUSEWAY.
WHEN HE DIES IN 1981 AT THE AGE OF 92, HE IS SEEN AS A KIND OF REPULSIVE OLD OGRE IN MATTERS OF URBAN PLANNING.
BUT EVEN IF HE LIVED LIKE A MOGUL IN BELMONT MANOR WHERE HE RECEIVED HIS ATTENDANTS ON LONG ISLAND...
...EVEN IF HE ORDERED HIS MEN, SLAMMING HIS FIST ON THE MOST REFINED OF TABLES, WITHOUT EVER CONCERNING HIMSELF WITH RULES THAT DIDN'T SUIT HIS DESIGNS...

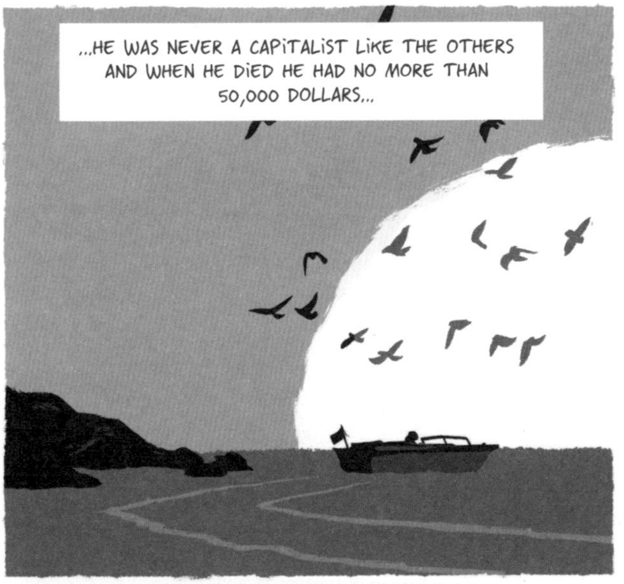
...HE WAS NEVER A CAPITALIST LIKE THE OTHERS AND WHEN HE DIED HE HAD NO MORE THAN 50,000 DOLLARS...

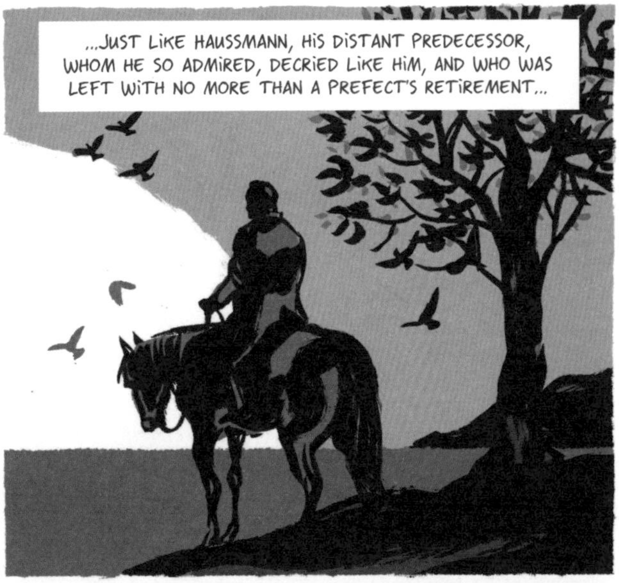
...JUST LIKE HAUSSMANN, HIS DISTANT PREDECESSOR, WHOM HE SO ADMIRED, DECRIED LIKE HIM, AND WHO WAS LEFT WITH NO MORE THAN A PREFECT'S RETIREMENT...

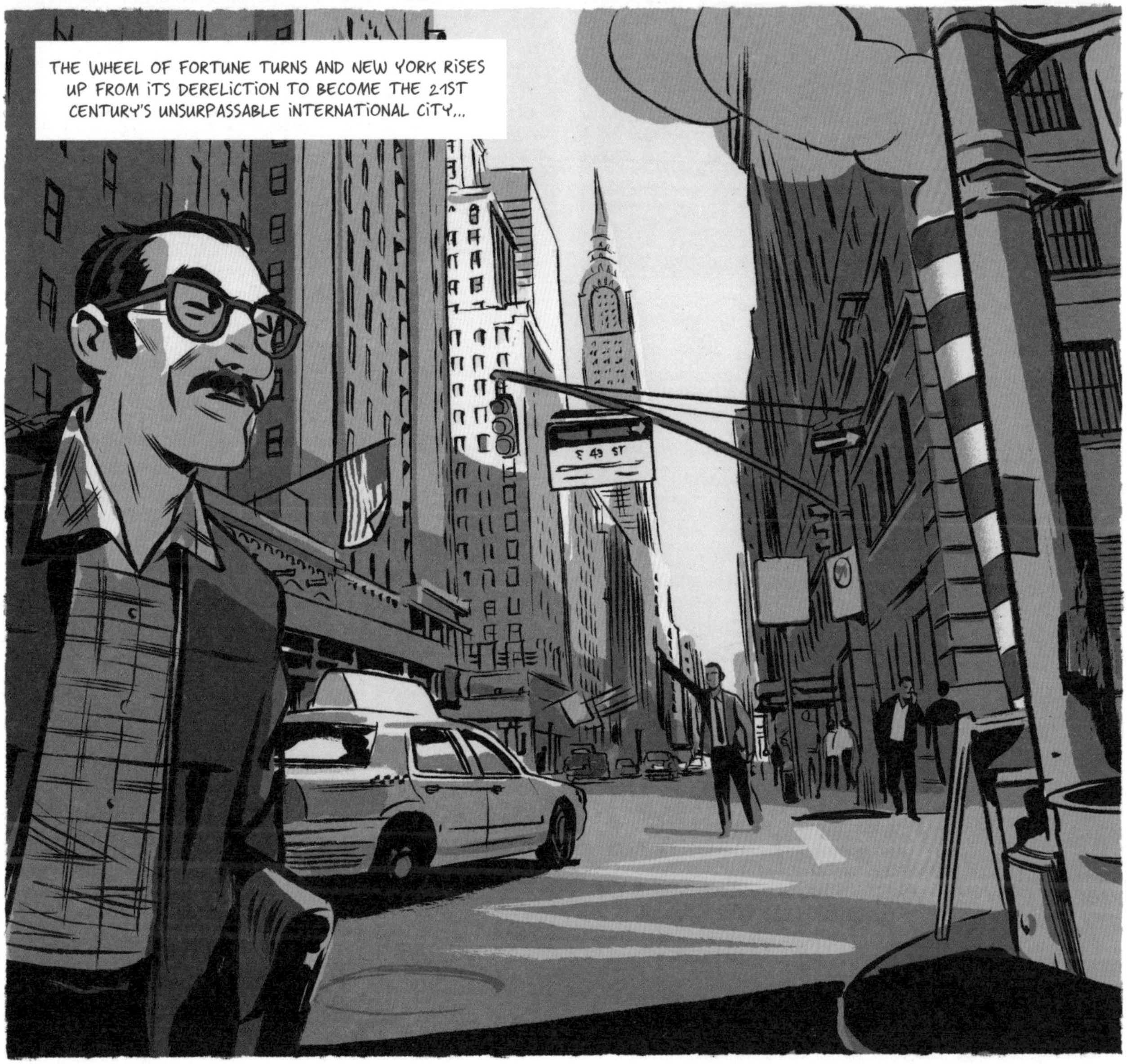
THE WHEEL OF FORTUNE TURNS AND NEW YORK RISES UP FROM ITS DERELICTION TO BECOME THE 21ST CENTURY'S UNSURPASSABLE INTERNATIONAL CITY...
E 49 ST

AT A TIME WHEN TAX EVASION IMPEDES ANY REAL FORM OF PUBLIC INITIATIVE, PEOPLE ARE REDISCOVERING THE GREAT BUILDER, ROBERT MOSES, WHOSE LEGACY HAS ALLOWED THE CITY TO ENDURE...

BUT IT IS JANE JACOBS, VICTORIOUS OVER LOMEX, WHO HAS BECOME THE URBAN HERO, WHO EVERY 28TH OF JUNE HAS A DAY OF COMMEMORATION IN HER HONOUR...

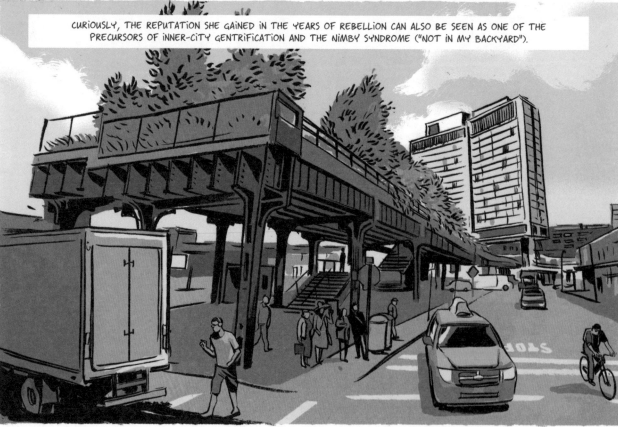

CURIOUSLY, THE REPUTATION SHE GAINED IN THE YEARS OF REBELLION CAN ALSO BE SEEN AS ONE OF THE PRECURSORS OF INNER-CITY GENTRIFICATION AND THE NIMBY SYNDROME ("NOT IN MY BACKYARD").

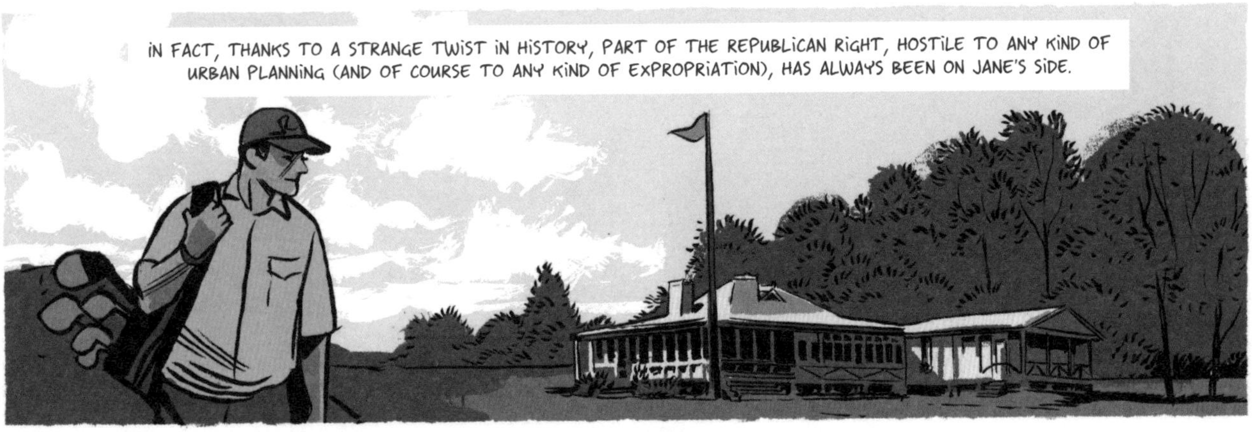
IN FACT, THANKS TO A STRANGE TWIST IN HISTORY, PART OF THE REPUBLICAN RIGHT, HOSTILE TO ANY KIND OF URBAN PLANNING (AND OF COURSE TO ANY KIND OF EXPROPRIATION), HAS ALWAYS BEEN ON JANE'S SIDE.

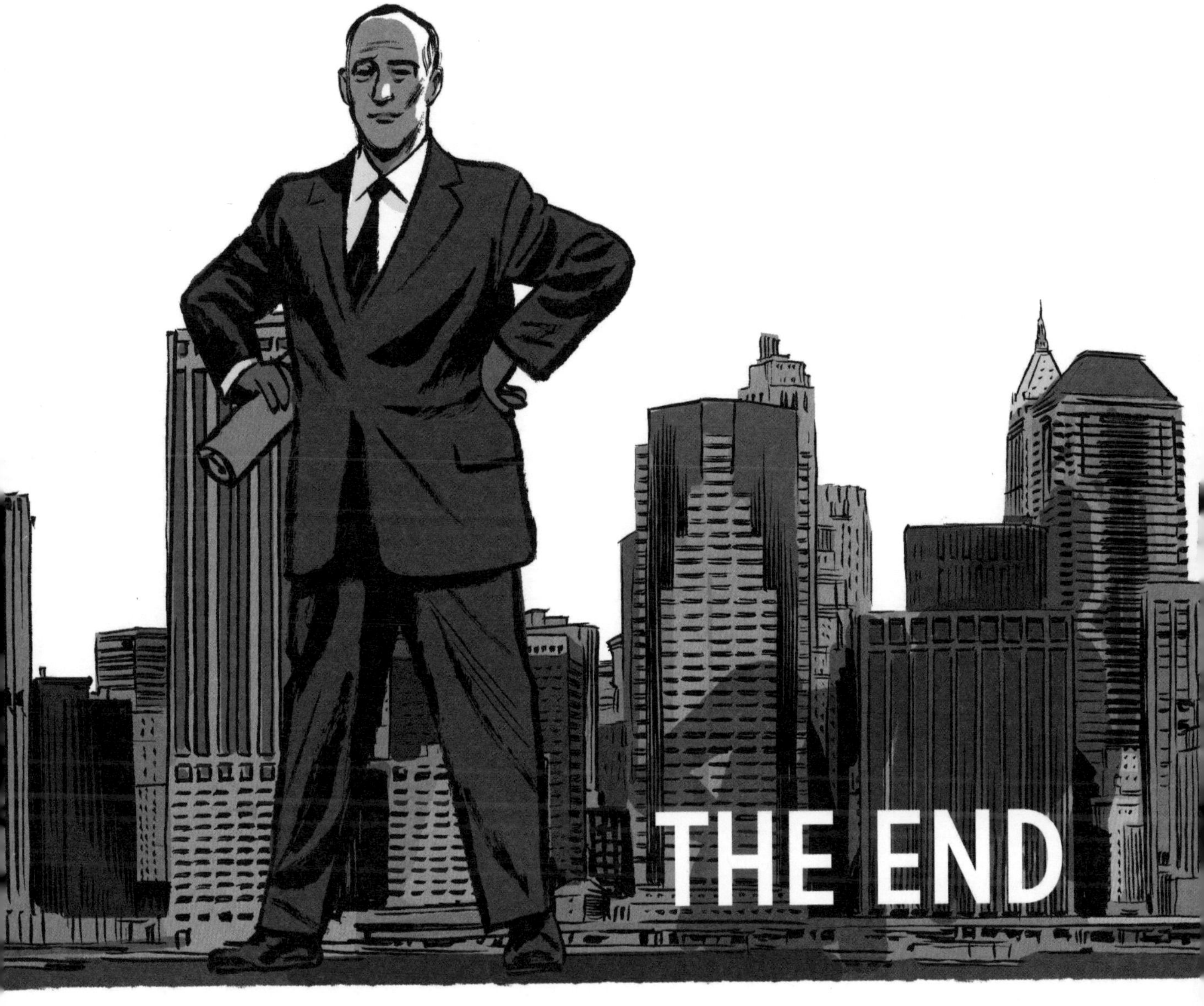
AND YET, THOUGH THE NAME REMAINS OBSCURE TO MANY OF ITS INHABITANTS, IT IS STILL THE SHADOW OF MOSES THAT DOMINATES NEW YORK'S SKYLINE THAT, FOR BETTER OR FOR WORSE, HE SHAPED.
THE END

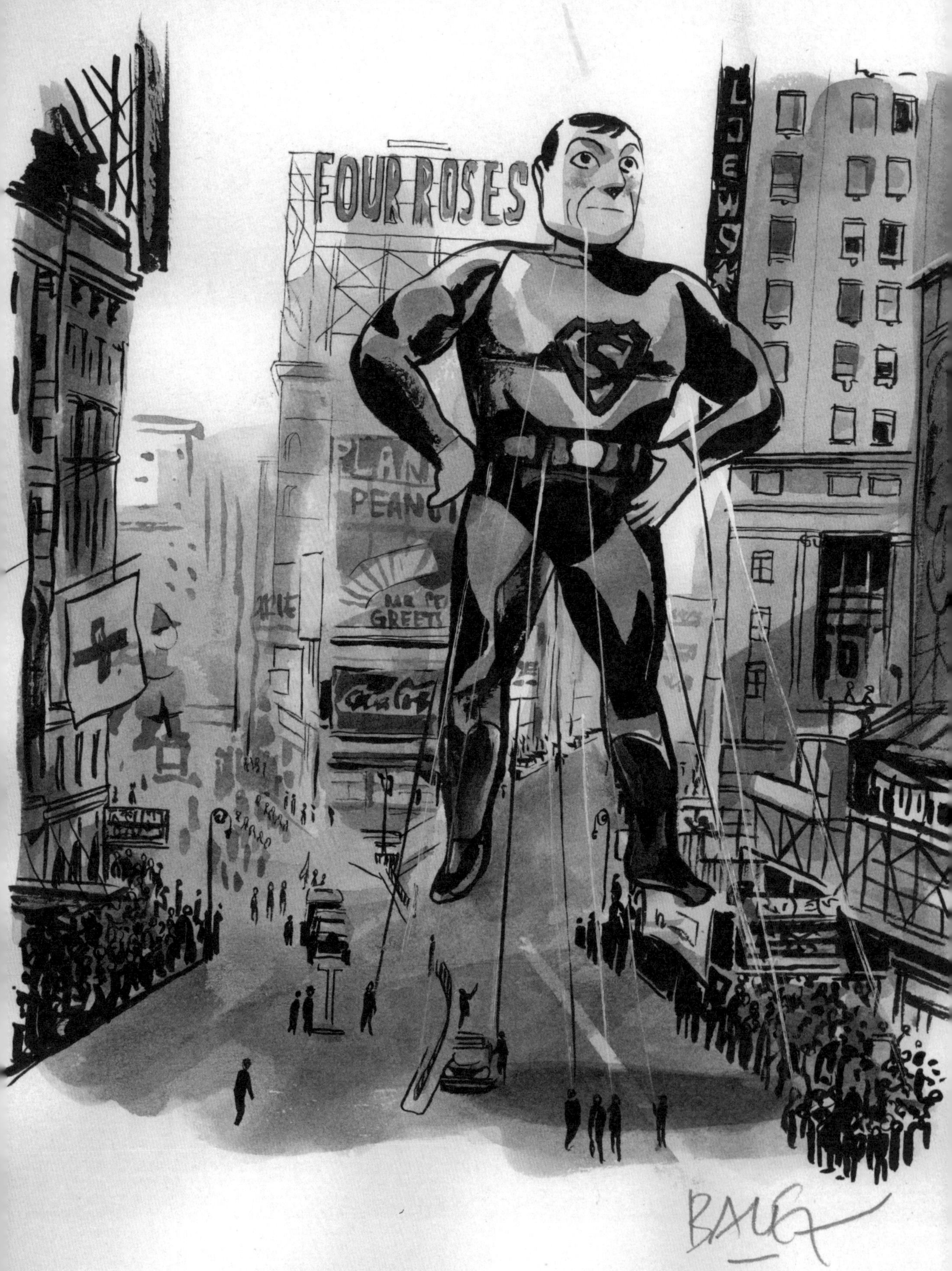
FOUR ROSES
GREETS

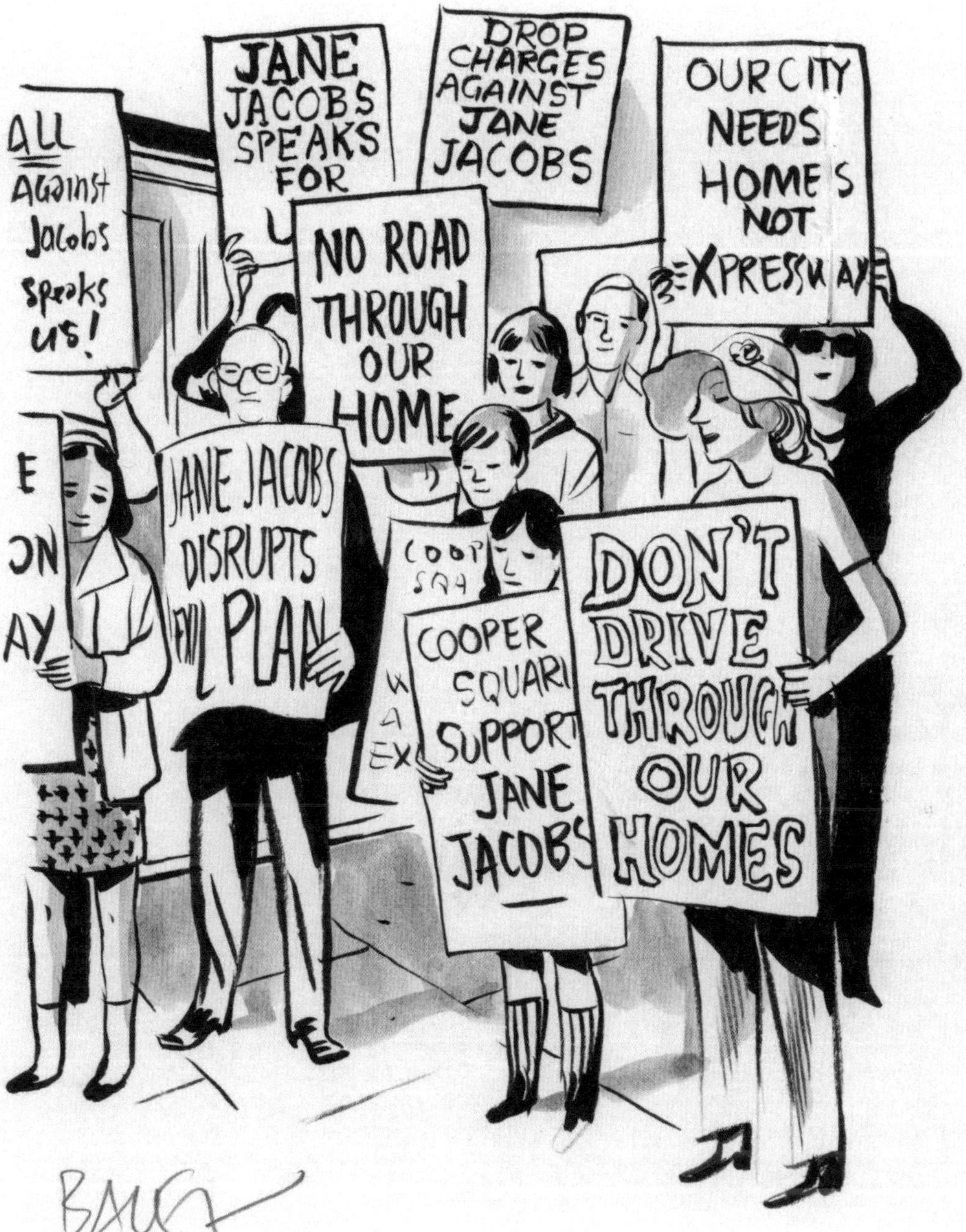
ALL Against Jacobs speaks us!
JANE JACOBS SPEAKS FOR
DROP CHARGES AGAINST JANE JACOBS
OUR CITY NEEDS HOMES NOT EXPRESSWAY
NO ROAD THROUGH OUR HOME
JANE JACOBS DISRUPTS EVIL PLAN
COOPER SQUARE SUPPORTS JANE JACOBS
DON'T DRIVE THROUGH OUR HOMES

**Further Reading**

Many books about Moses have been published, including the Pulitzer Prize-winning biography (even if some of its findings are now questioned): *The Power Broker: Robert Moses and the Fall of New York*, Robert Caro, Vintage Books, Random House, New York, 1975.

A beautifully illustrated book: *Robert Moses and the Modern City, the Transformation of New York*, Hilary Balion and Kenneth T. Jackson, The Queens Museum of Art, 2007.

On Jane Jacobs: *Wrestling with Moses, How Jane Jacobs took on New York's master builder and transformed the American City*, Anthony Flint, Random House, New York, 2009.

Of Jane Jacobs: *The Death and Life of Great American Cities*, Random House, New York, 1961.

**Bibliography**

*Lost New York* (Marcia Reiss); *Long Island's Gold Coast* (Paul J. Mateyunas); *Greenwich Village* (Anita Dickhuth); *The 1964-65 New York's World Fair* (Bill Cotter and Bill Young); *New York* (Reuel Golden) as well as articles in the New Yorker, the New York Times, etc.

In French: *Les Faiseurs de villes: 1850-1950*, Thierry Paquot, Infolio, 2010.

Thanks go to the Museum of the City of New York and the Queens Museum of Art (Corona Park, Flushing Meadows).

Thank you to Angèle Christin and Andrei Pesic, who guided and accompanied Pierre Christin in the footsteps of Robert Moses around New York and Long Island.